IMAGES
of America

LURAY and PAGE COUNTY Revisited

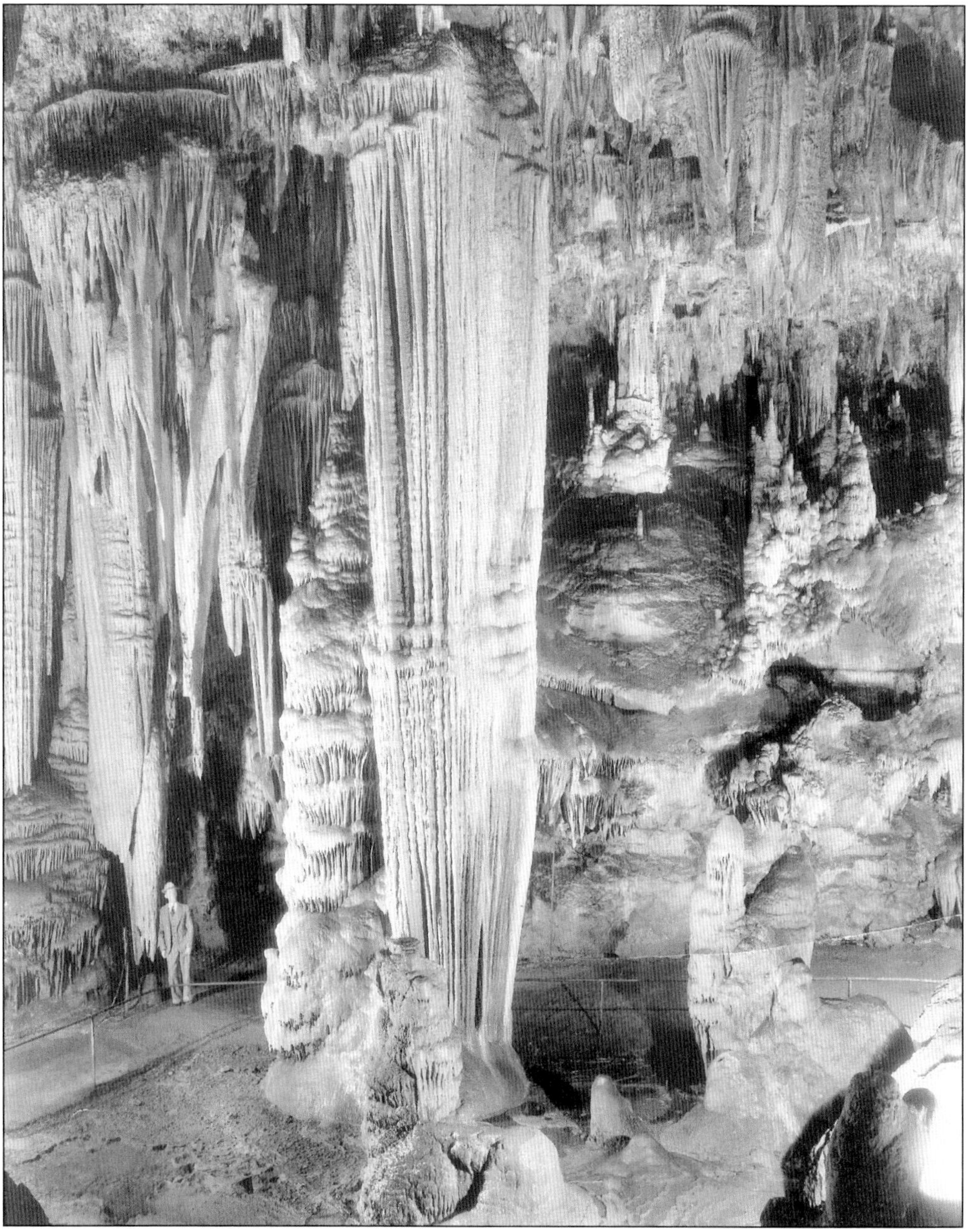

A major exploration of Luray Caverns took place in May 1906, when the cave was examined by over 700 members of the National Geographic Society. *The National Republic* gave its praise when stating, "Exaggeration seems impossible." The largest excursion ever was on October 27, 1921, when 13 trainloads brought 9,470 tourists to see the "Underground Wonder." (*Page News and Courier.*)

ON THE COVER: Proprietor John A. Roller, of the Roller Company, poses in 1912 in his B. F. Board delivery truck. Opening on May 27, 1905, in the old YMCA on East Main Street, the establishment offered free ice water and Edison talking machine music and was advertised as Luray's greatest store. (Marleen Hansen.)

IMAGES
of America

LURAY *and* PAGE COUNTY *Revisited*

Dan Vaughn

ARCADIA
PUBLISHING

ISBN 978-0-7385-4417-5

Published by Arcadia Publishing
Charleston, South Carolina

Printed in the United States of America

Library of Congress Catalog Card Number: 2006938391

For all general information contact Arcadia Publishing at:
Telephone 843-853-2070
Fax 843-853-0044
E-mail sales@arcadiapublishing.com
For customer service and orders:
Toll-Free 1-888-313-2665

Visit us on the Internet at www.arcadiapublishing.com

This book is in memory of my brother, John Garfield "Johnny" Vaughn, 1956–1969.

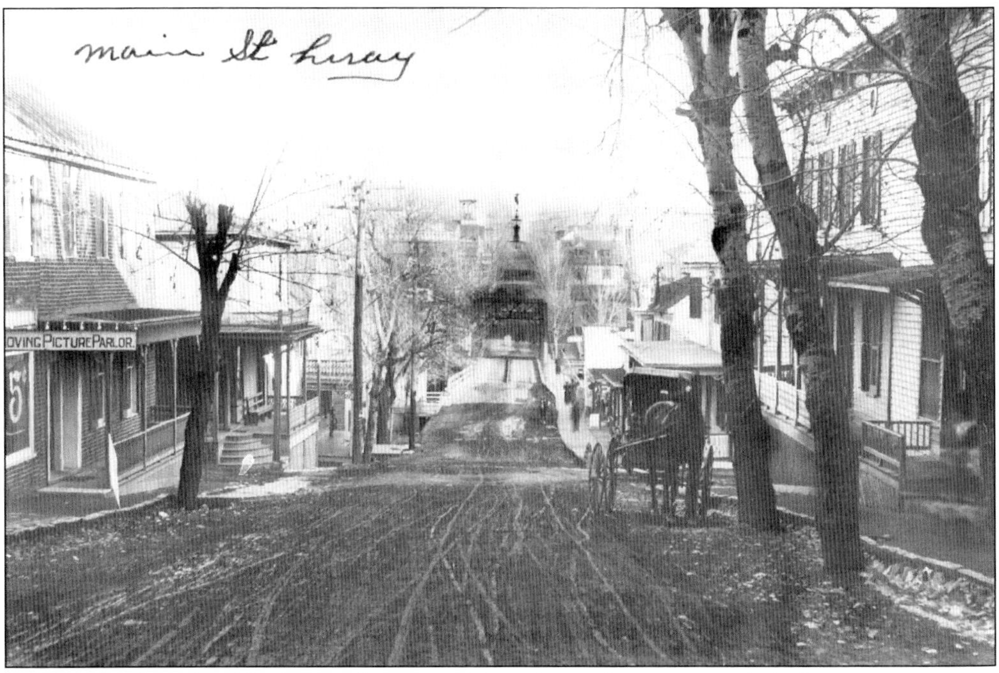

Wagon wheel tracks tell of a simpler time. A less-than-adequate streetlight hangs at center in this c. 1910s image, while pedestrians traverse the newly laid boardwalk paralleling Luray's West Main Street. A lone horse and carriage wait patiently outside the Amiss Building, and in the old 1880s Luray Post Office, a newfangled item, a motion picture parlor (at left in the Rosser Building), advertises shows for 5¢. (Lillian Coleman.)

Contents

ACKNOWLEDGMENTS

This project only materialized by the mutual relationship that was formed by the author and those willing to share in the desire to preserve our local heritage. The work was nothing less than a joint accomplishment. A broad thank-you is given to all who encouraged the two-volume, four-year venture. A very special thank-you goes to the entire *Page News and Courier* (*PN&C*) staff, especially editor Randy Arrington—who allowed me free reign of its archive—and both Deloris Judy and Bonnie Ellis, whose compilations of the paper's "Yesteryears" column, again, were of major importance. Without this organization's preserved historical records and its open-door policy, this pictorial, nor the author's first work, would have been possible. The most special thank-you goes to my wife, Alesa, who endured much. Thanks also to David Breneman, Carolyn Palmer, and Joshua Vaughn for their continued generosity of editing. Ann Vaughn and Pam Furman helped greatly in the project's layout. Gleanings of Page County historical reference material by local historians Debbie Owens and Judy Campbell were very helpful. It is my pleasure to recognize the following individuals who contributed as well, and I am indebted to their willingness to share: Howard W. Ameling, Casey Billhimer, Jennifer Bodine, Mildred Stirewalt Coleman, Bob Graves, Rod Graves, Marleen Hansen, Curtis Harrell, Philip and Isabel Harrell, Arcadia's Brooksi Hudson, Lloyd Kibler, Jean Kite, Walter and Sharon Lucas, Debbie McDonough, Jeppy McDowell, William and Frances Menefee, J. R. Mims Jr., Kim Parker, Nancy Racer, Ruth Reid, Allan Rinaca, Nancy Lee Shifflett, Billy Stacey, Bob Stacey, Charles Stevens, Brandon Vaughn, Graham Vaughn, Joshua Vaughn, Jordan Vaughn, Gaylon Waters, and Kenneth Weakley. I also want to thank the following institutions for their generosity in permitting the use of archival material: Virginia Historical Society, Library of Virginia, Virginia Tech Special Collections, Page Public Library, Page County Genealogy Society, Town of Stanley, Luray Caverns Corporation, University of Virginia, National Archives, *Richmond Times-Dispatch*, A. Aubrey Bodine Collection, George Eastman House, Library of Congress, Norfolk Southern Corporation, Norfolk and Western Historical Society, and O. Winston Link Museum.

INTRODUCTION

One can only imagine the past in the mind's eye, apart from some form of historic documentation. With the invention of the *camera obscura* came the primitive beginnings that would speak volumes of lasting proof. French inventor Nicéphore Niépce would produce the world's first permanent photograph in 1826. The daguerreotype process and wet-plate collodion process—which included the ambrotype (glass-plate positives), tintype (tin-plate positives), and albumens (positive prints)—recorded images throughout the mid- to later 1800s. But it was George Eastman's invention of gelatin roll film, as opposed to plates, in 1885, and his Brownie camera, introduced in 1900 with millions selling into the 1960s, that introduced photography to the multitudes. His company name of Kodak had no specific meaning, other than it became synonymous with picture taking and photographic prints.

Arising during the Reconstruction era in Page, as in many communities, were a multitude of local photographers. Documenting history throughout the Gilded Age and into the 20th century, they inadvertently preserved our past in print for a nominal fee. Very little is known of these early image makers themselves, as they generally were on the opposite side of the camera lens. James H. Bushong and William Campbell produced early pictures during Luray Caverns' pre-discovery years, but it was C. H. James and later Joseph D. Strickler that the caverns employed to document the underground formations. Newspaper publisher turned photographer Benton Pixley Stebbins would codiscover Luray Caverns shortly after his arrival in Luray, all the while continuing his newly established occupation. Two worlds met when the Shenandoah Valley Railroad reached Page in 1881. The railroad, in hiring William Rau to document the line, recorded grandeur images of the Queen Anne–style Luray Inn. Popular Luray photographer Silas K. Wright would partner as Wright and Crabill, but he is most known for his independent work at his 4 South Broad Street location in Luray. Operating under both Sunbeam Galleries and the Excelsior Studios, his cabinet card work was widely regarded. His image of the Luray Inn burning is possibly his most recognizable. East Main's Daniel Holmes and West Main's Max Frensley, along with the League Studio, all in Luray, were kept busy with the growing popularity of their trade and the continual flow of caverns' excursionists. Early Shenandoah photographers included the Star Studio, Gem Studio, F. P. Hammers, and the partnership of Rippel and Israel on the town's First Street. Federal Trade Commission photographer Wallace K. Rhodes, operating out of the Mason Building, would document many structures and events throughout the first half of the 1900s. The Pinkerton Studios and freelancer Michael Lackovitch were some of the last of the local photographers, with both operating throughout the 1950s and 1960s. These—along with others such as J. S. Strole, Bobby Frazier, William A. Johnston, partners Darnell and Foltz, and J. A. Melton of Water (present-day Hawksbill) Street in Luray, and Elmer L. Rickard and Rumsey N. Heiston of Kimball—were the recorders of early imagery in Page.

A very different world existed in this bygone time. Changes happened quickly, for security was not a way of life for most. The structural landscape was constantly changing, not only by wind, fire, and flood, but also by economics. With events like the Panic of 1893 and the Great Depression of the 1930s came an unsettledness that affected the entire country. Only half the story can be told through the photographers' works though. Without information to accompany the images, the story is incomplete, as is the case, unfortunately, with all too many vintage pictures.

No less a treasure are the writings of the early newspaper journalists in Page County as they recorded the daily events that have become the basis of our local history. When James H. Larkins and Harrisonburg businessman Samuel J. Price, editors of Page County's first newspaper, printed their inaugural four-page edition of the *Page Valley Courier* by kerosene lamp on March 15, 1867, a rapport was forged with the citizens. The paper's March 8 edition was delayed because of a supplier's late delivery of the press to their first location in the Depot Building (the pre–Luray Graded School structure) on South Court Street near the Page County Courthouse. With G. T. Jones as its first subscriber, the paper would have multiple publishers and editors over the next decade. Its popularity, though, caused an eruption of competitors. The first edition of the *Luray Advance*, the town's second publication, was printed on December 1, 1880. The following year, the paper was bought by brothers Charles H. and Dr. Frank W. Grove and renamed the *Page News*, the *Courier*'s ultimate rival. The quaint *Luray Breezes*, printed by New Market's Henkel Press with Nena Barbee as editress, was popular in the 1880s. Luray's *Weekly Union* and the *Stanley Herald*, the lone newspaper of that town, had parallel successes when they began their boom era, reporting in 1890 and 1891 respectively, but both were finished by the late 1890s, victims of the mid-decade depression. Interestingly, Luray would have three weeklies printing simultaneously by 1895. With a generous hand of community spirit, in August 1887, the *Courier* actually helped print the *Page News* when its editor had to suspend the paper for a brief period because of illness. Thereafter, the *Page Courier* reluctantly succumbed to a buyout-merger forming the present-day *Page News and Courier* in 1911. This initiated the alternative *Page Valley Record* from 1912 to 1914. The short-lived *Commonwealth Review* and its successor the *Sun*, both printed on Luray's South Court Street beginning in the mid-1940s, had political connotations. Shenandoah was also home to a number of newspapers as well, including the *Shenandoah Advance*, *Shenandoah Argus*, *Herald of Progress*, and *Shenandoah Tribune*. The earlier *Milnes Weekly*, titled after a former name for the town, and the *Riverside* and the *Rockdale Enterprise*, company newspapers that had originated in the previous Shenandoah Iron Works, were all printed in Shenandoah in the 1880s. Two lesser-known sources, the *Luray Gazette* and the *Court Street Dispatch*, were also just a part of the news tapestry that helped to preserve our historic past. Sources of communication were limited during earlier times, and readers, anticipating the next issue, pored over the news as the papers came, monthly, weekly, semi-weekly, and, in the case of the *Luray Times*, daily for a brief period. This very informative local was printed in the basement of the Excursion House Restaurant by the Valley Land and Improvement Company in the early 1890s. When the land company failed, the paper reverted to its original name of the *Page News*. From the *Page Courier*'s kerosene lamplight, to the first application of electricity in Luray to operate machinery in March 1905, to the final edition printed in-house on June 24, 1970, the current-day reporting of the *Page News and Courier* has continued to provide anticipation for the local news.

Time does not stand still, but within these pages, the early photographers achieve this improbable feat. This pictorial vestige of Page County, beginning more than a century ago, records the events, the architecture, the daily life, and more importantly a simpler time that beckons to rescue us from today's busyness, hopefully causing us to consider life's most important lesson. Enjoy—again.

—Dan Vaughn
Luray, Virginia

One

The Early Years

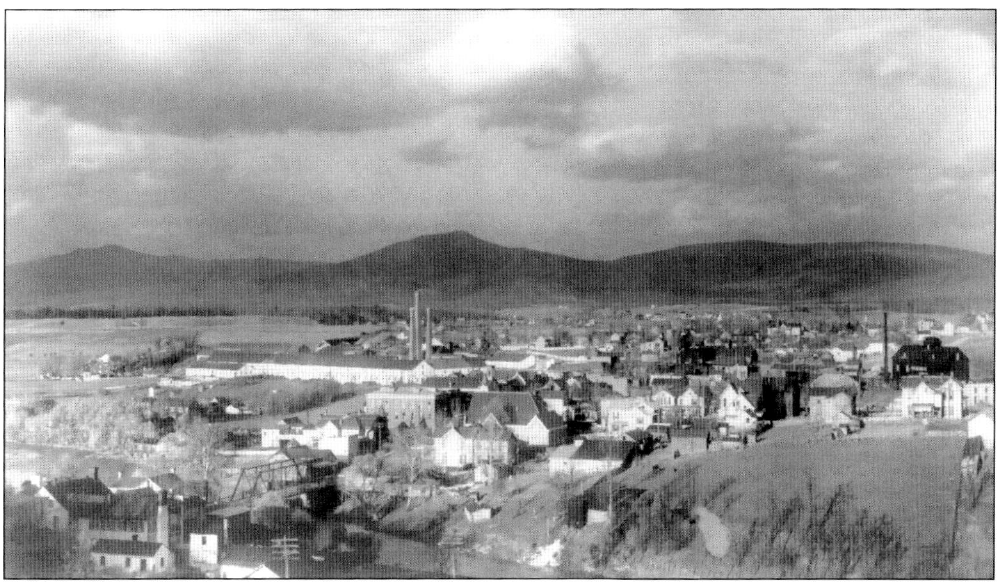

Luray wasn't quite a century old when this c. 1910 photograph was taken. Nestled between the Blue Ridge and Massanutten Mountain ranges, the quaint town was established on August 21, 1812, only after a prerequisite within an act of the Virginia General Assembly was fulfilled to first "survey off the town lots" before it could be deemed official. (Library of Congress.)

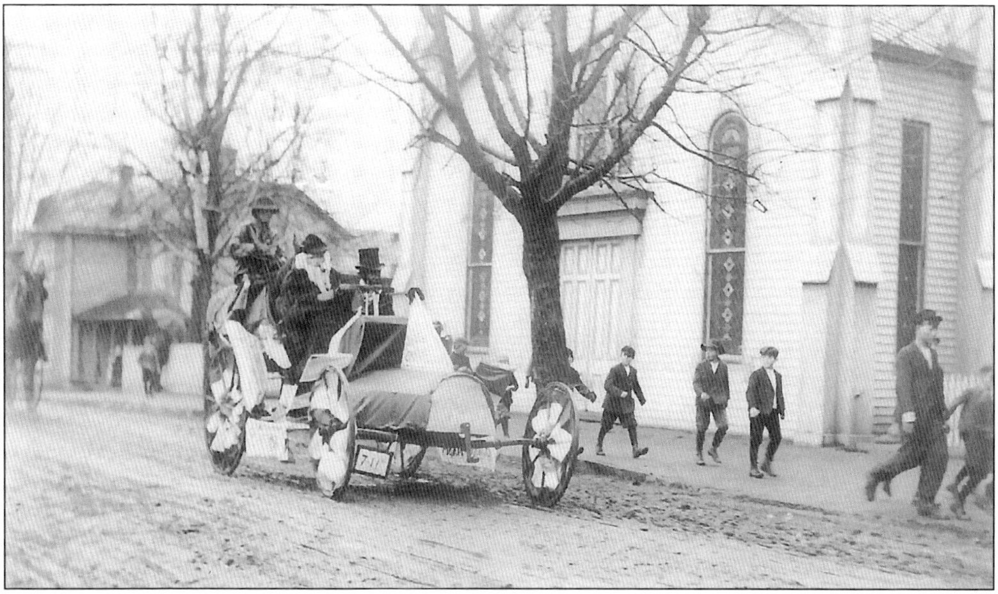

The children alongside this 1910 Luray Christmas Parade were captivated by the mystique of Santa Claus, portrayed by John P. Jobe, at left with beard. An old buggy representing an automobile was actually propelled by the horse immediately following as it passes St. Mark's Lutheran Church. Jobe was advertising his restaurant, complete with "Oysters, Any Style," located on West Main Street at the bridge. (Warren Settle Frank.)

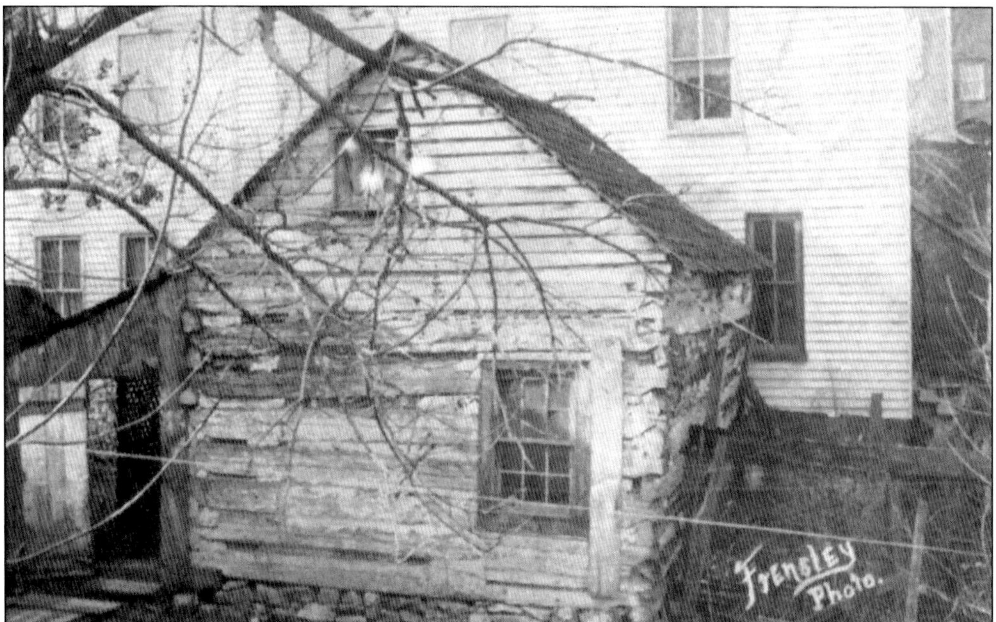

Max Frensley documented one of his most underestimated Luray images when he photographed this humble log cabin around 1910. An 1876 *Page Courier* article reminisced, "The first building being erected . . . a small log hut." Casper Bradley would later use the primitive structure, built in 1812 between Hawksbill and Bank Streets, as his office. Approaching 150 years old, it still stood as of 1959, but progress took precedence. (Bobby and Tammy Painter.)

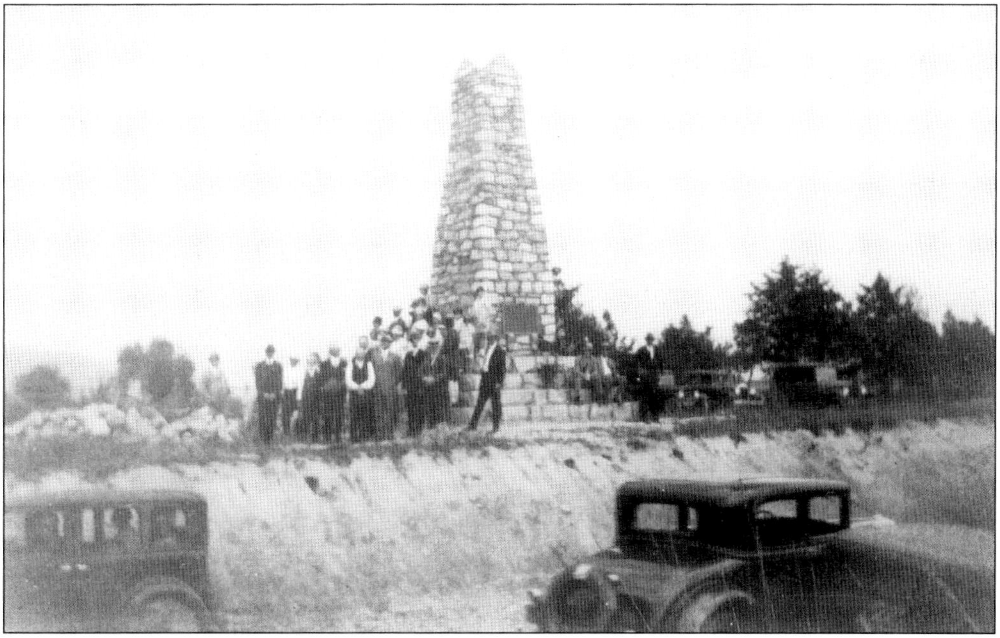

In 1929, the Massanutten Society held ceremonies in honor of the 200th anniversary of the first settlement west of the Blue Ridge. Among attendees were John Wayland, P. M. Kauffman, P. S. Rhodes, Willie Burner, and, at left, Arthur Grove amid excess monument stone. Jacob Stover, obliged to list the settlers to obtain a land patent, bypassed Virginia's governor and persuaded the King of England to grant the 5,000-acre patent, interestingly enough, by giving his farm animals human names. (University of Virginia.)

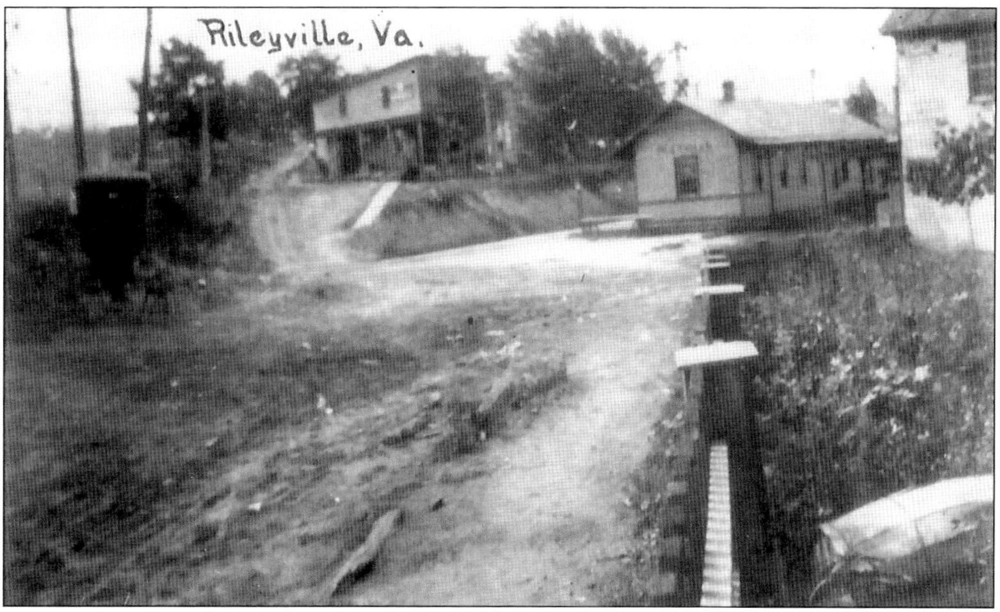

In this 1914 view are, from left to right, J. W. Huffman Store, Rileyville Depot, and Hugh Wood's General Merchandise. One could only suppose that the lone carriage at left belongs to the photographer. With the carriage being outmoded, the redirected road macadamized, the two stores closed, and the depot torn down, much has changed in Rileyville. (Dan Vaughn.)

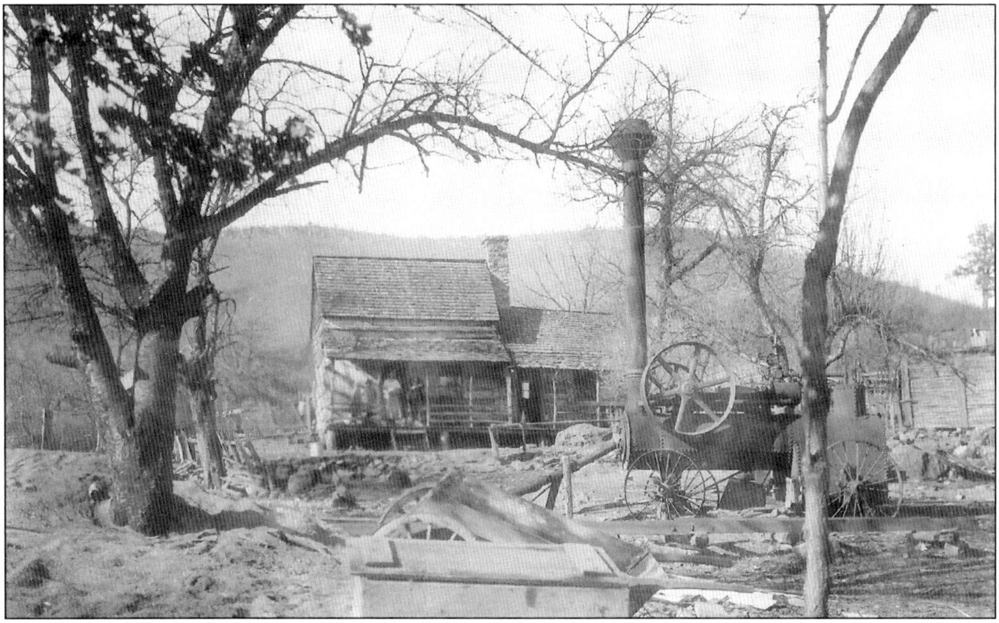

This 1927 image of a wooden-shingled log cabin steps back in time in the Tanner's Ridge section of Page County. A wooden wheelbarrow, feed box, and a steam engine litter its front lawn. The yard is rather lacking, thanks to probable overgrazing and the fact that survival priorities outweighed frivolity during this time. (St. George's Episcopal.)

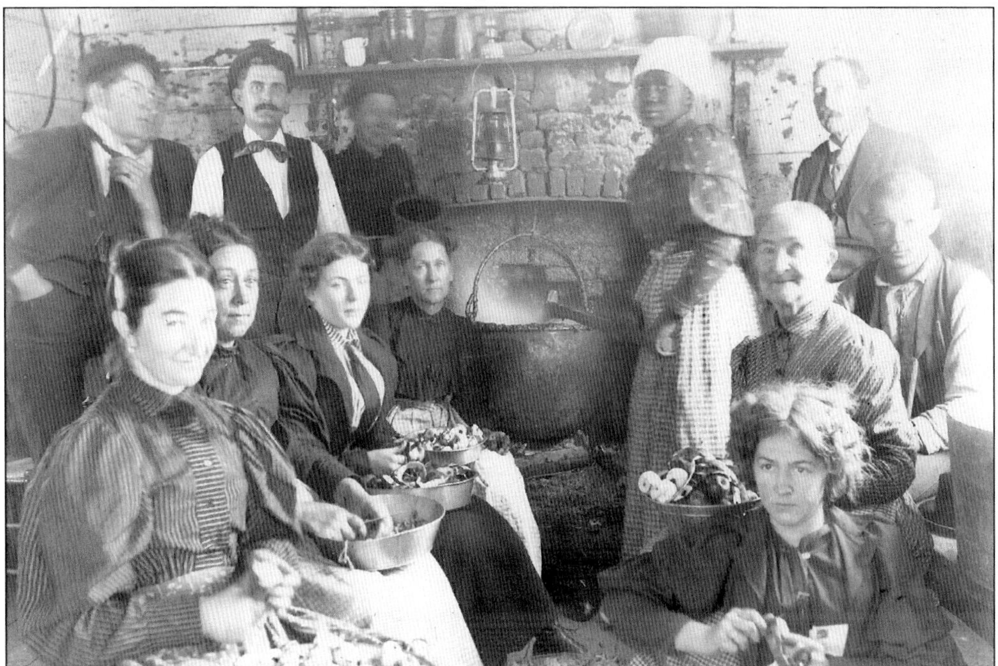

This simplistic image of apple butter making is representative of a bygone Page County. Bitter cold had possibly forced the otherwise outdoor activity into the cramped quarters. Among the cooperative effort is Fred T. Amiss, at left facing the photographer, in this *c.* 1905 photograph. (William and Frances Menefee.)

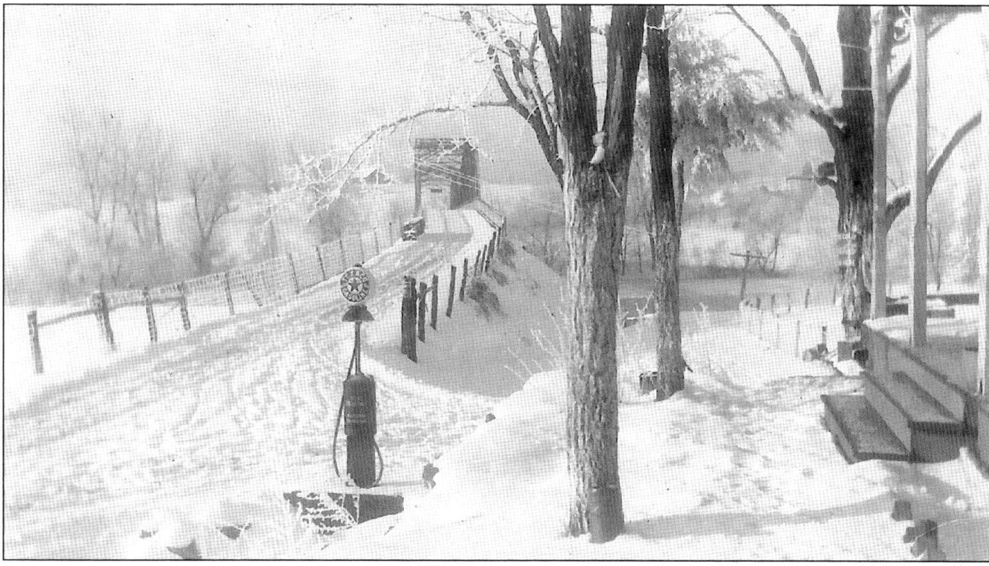

This 1920s wintry view shows the fourth bridge at White House Crossing. Funneling here to cross, travelers stopped at Lester and Annie Ruffner's store, at right. Built shortly after the 1870 flood and torn down in February 1946, it originated as the first location of the mercantile firm Grove and Brother. (Nancy Lee Shifflett.)

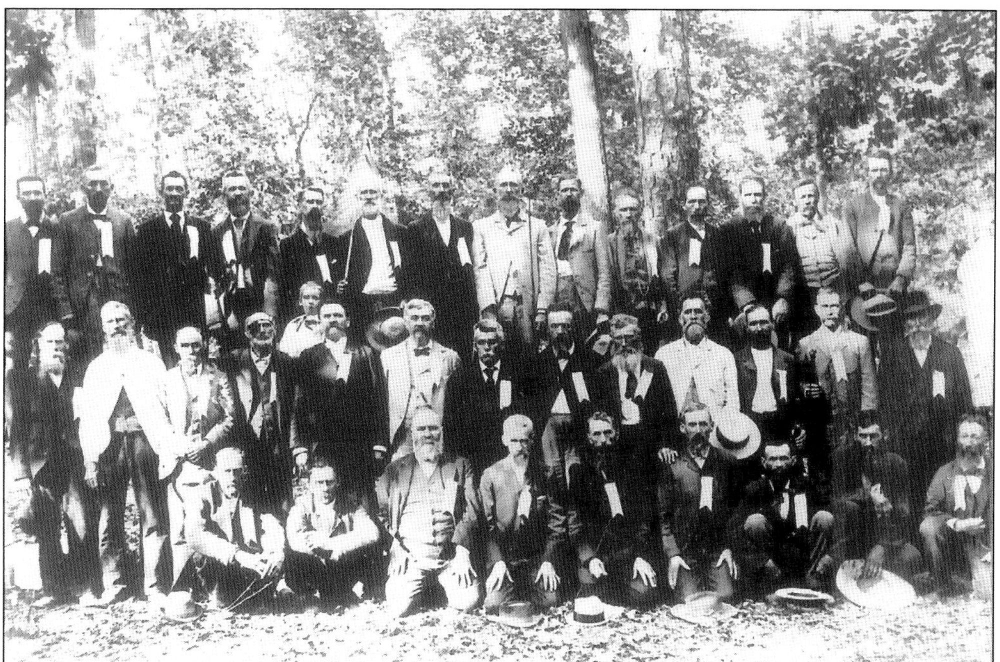

This reunion of Confederate soldiers from the Civil War, survivors of Col. Elijah Viers White's Battalion of the Virginia Volunteer Cavalry, along with Company E, was held in Luray on August 2–3, 1894. Photographer Silas Wright documented the gathering of those referred to as "White's Comanches," the first since that great tragedy. Peter Keyser of Rileyville, Page County's last remaining veteran of the war, passed away on January 4, 1939, at age 91. (Dan Vaughn.)

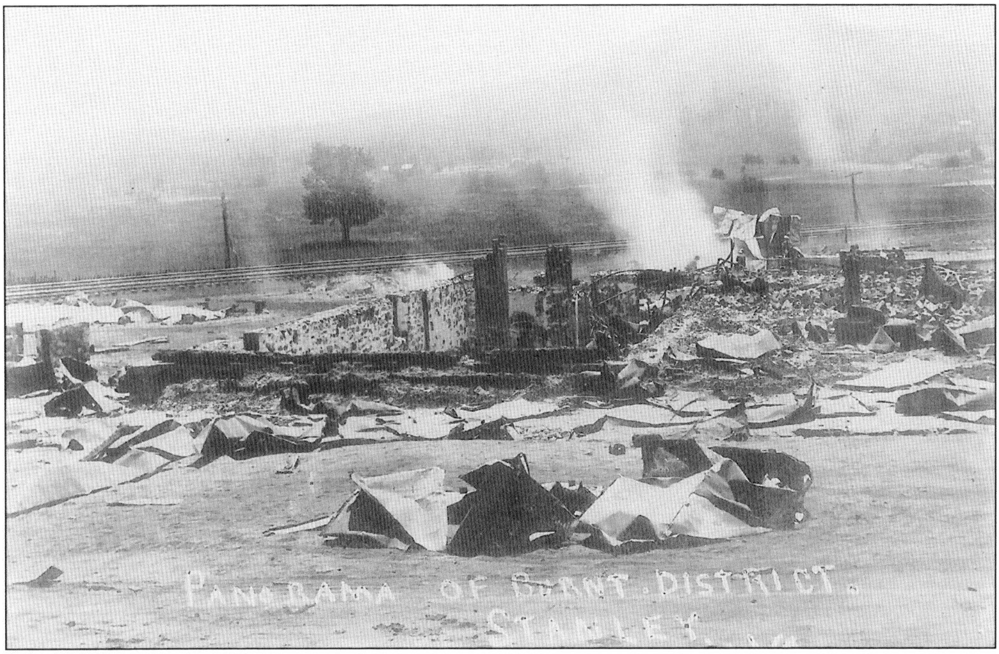

Rising beyond the ashes of Stanley's "Great Fire" is their landmark Roundhead Mountain. The Bible says in Psalms, "Our days are consumed like smoke, but God's strength sets fast the mountains." This truth came to a head on May 4, 1909, when the town's main business district was reduced to mere rubble as a result of the tragic event. A quarter-century's worth of commerce was gone in an instant. (Town of Stanley.)

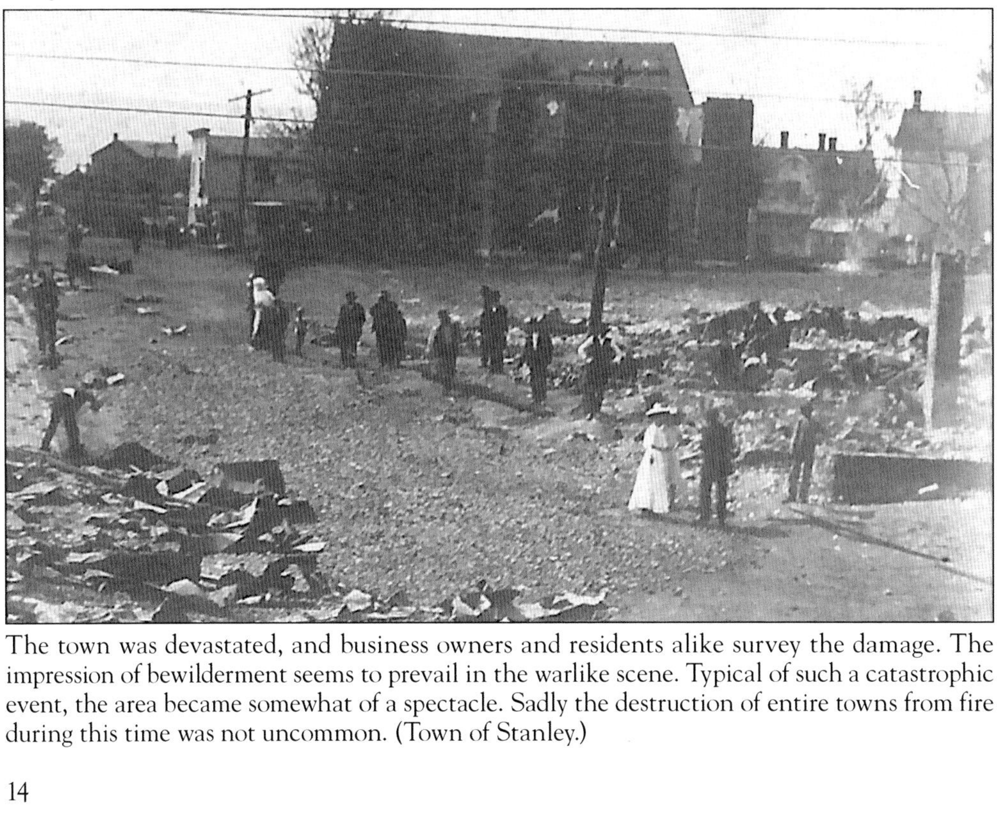

The town was devastated, and business owners and residents alike survey the damage. The impression of bewilderment seems to prevail in the warlike scene. Typical of such a catastrophic event, the area became somewhat of a spectacle. Sadly the destruction of entire towns from fire during this time was not uncommon. (Town of Stanley.)

This surreal image of the old Karl Jenkins house on Stanley's Main Street includes a stone carriage boarding block. Renowned architect Stanford White had designed the three-story, multifaceted structure in 1890 for Thomas MacSpeiden of the Stanley Furnace and Land Company. A 1909 Stanley fire survivor, the ornate charm was lost when, in 1971, it was torn down to build another bank. (Doug Gochenour.)

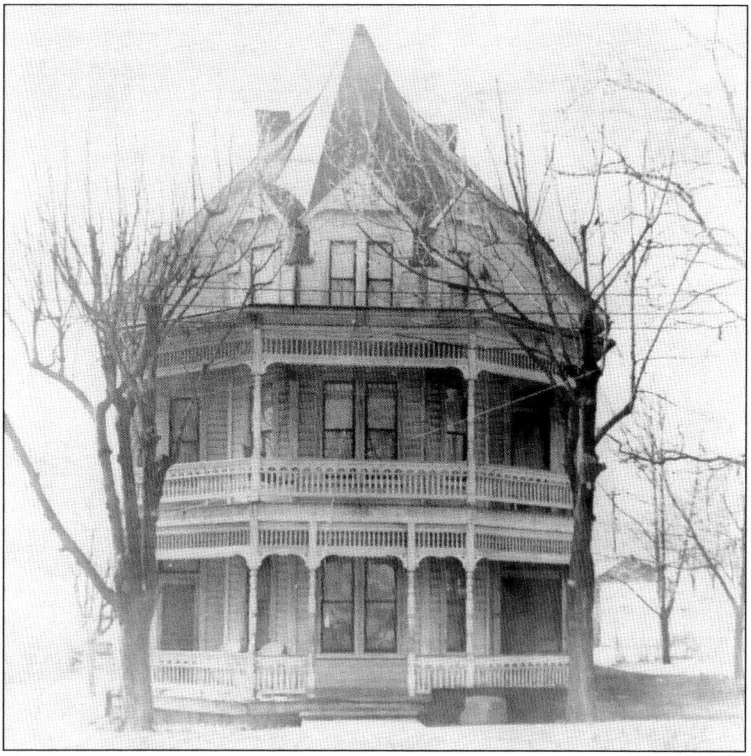

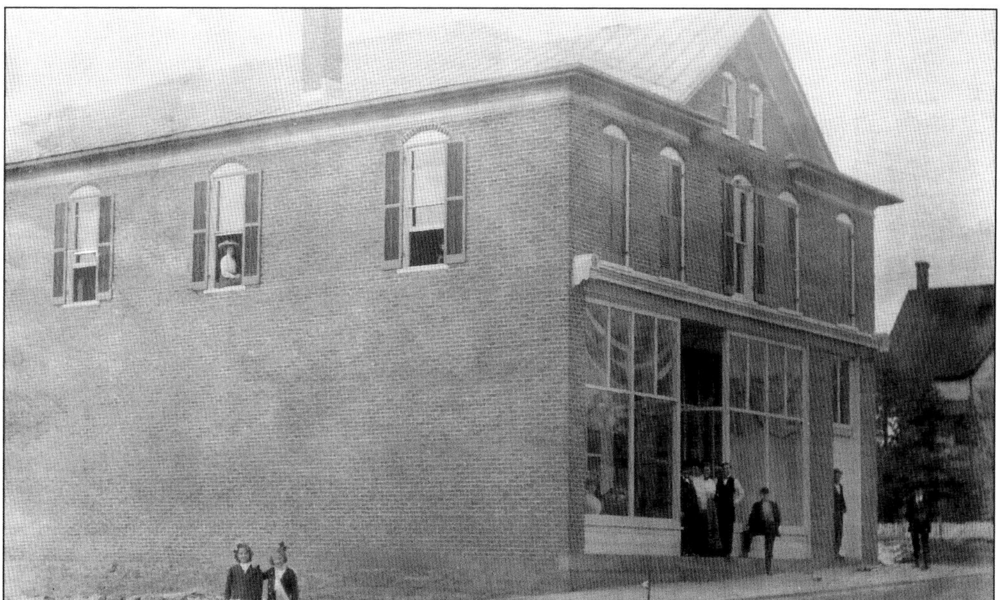

In this building, constructed around 1910, William Robinson opened Robinson's Friendly Store in 1919. In 1933, classes were held here, and at other Stanley locations, because the new school was not completed. Lee Louderback purchased the structure in the late 1950s, and the Stanley Food Market (later IGA) moved here in 1961. The near century-old building still stands on Main Street. (Town of Stanley.)

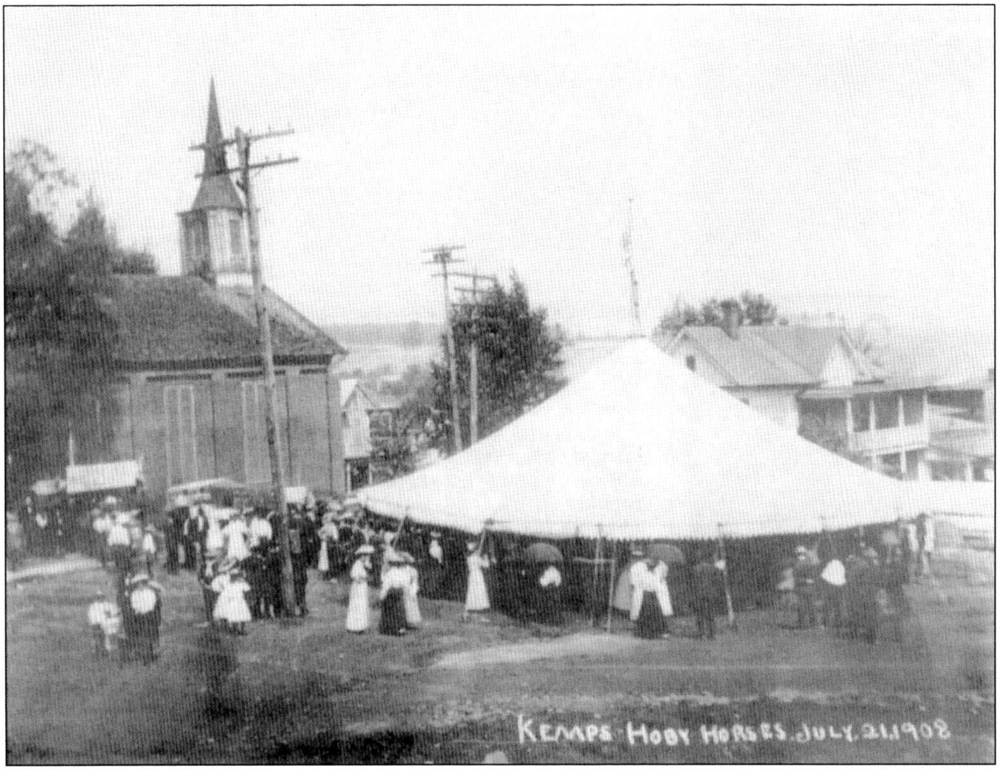

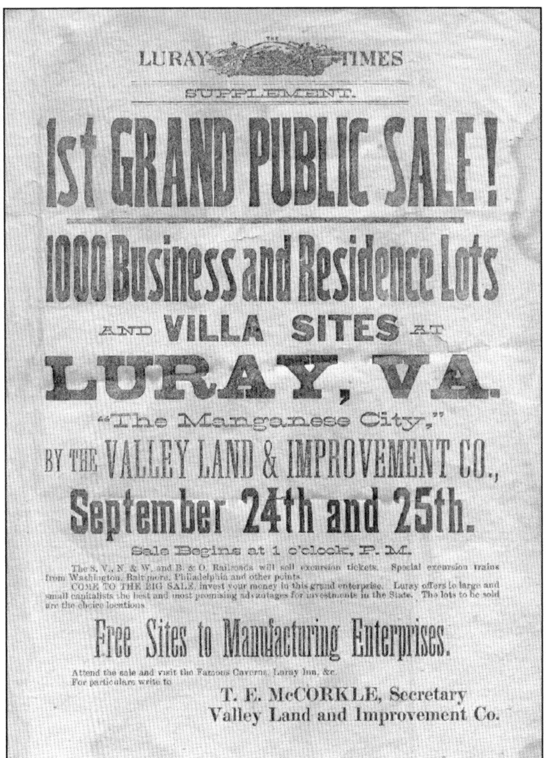
LURAY TIMES

SUPPLEMENT.

1st GRAND PUBLIC SALE!

1000 Business and Residence Lots

AND VILLA SITES AT

LURAY, VA.

"The Manganese City,"

BY THE VALLEY LAND & IMPROVEMENT CO.,

September 24th and 25th.

Sale Begins at 1 o'clock, P. M.

The S. V., N. & W. and B. & O. Railroads will sell excursion tickets. Special excursion trains from Washington, Baltimore, Philadelphia and other points.

COME TO THE BIG SALE, invest your money in this grand enterprise. Luray offers to large and small capitalists the best and most promising advantages for investments in the State. The lots to be sold are the choice locations.

Free Sites to Manufacturing Enterprises.

Attend the sale and visit the Famous Caverns, Luray Inn, &c.
For particulars write to

T. E. McCORKLE, Secretary
Valley Land and Improvement Co.

Wallace Rhodes captured this image of the circus in Luray. Frank Robinson's Circus had come as early as 1886. A 1905 *Page Courier* article stated, "The circus had more fakers and gamblers than any that had visited the town for a long time, and the crop of 'suckers' in Page seemed to have been unusually large." At left is Broad Street's Mount Carmel Baptist Church. (Dan Vaughn.)

When this Valley Land and Improvement Company broadside ran in the *Luray Times* in 1890, D. F. Kagey was not only company president, but also operated Page County's only bank. To promote industry, "free" sites were offered to manufacturers willing to locate here. But with a brewing economic collapse, the sale of the 1,000 lots did not materialize as anticipated, considering J. P. Grove of Luray purchased two lots for a mere $1. Luray's "boom" field remains today as a partially undeveloped remnant of the venture. (Ronnie Kauffman.)

In October 1931, road contractors would begin construction on a new north-south highway in Page County—State Route 340 (renamed SR 12 and finally U.S. Route 340). At Luray's southern town limits is Thelma Emerson Nevitt. With billboards already lining these primitive beginnings, the wooden barn (at left) advertising Brown's Restaurant would become a Luray landmark. (Rod Graves.)

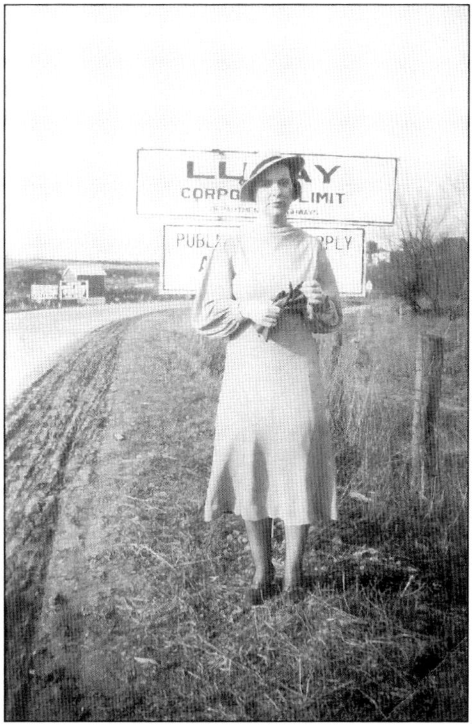

These Luray citizens pose in front of the middle limestone pier at Norfolk and Western (N&W) Railroad's Hawksbill Crossing in 1925. The pier's replacement by concrete coincided with the 1930s Virginia Avenue Bridge erection. This main support, originally constructed of timber, had stood since 1881. Located across the creek, at left, is the steam-era Luray water tank pump house. (Jean Kite.)

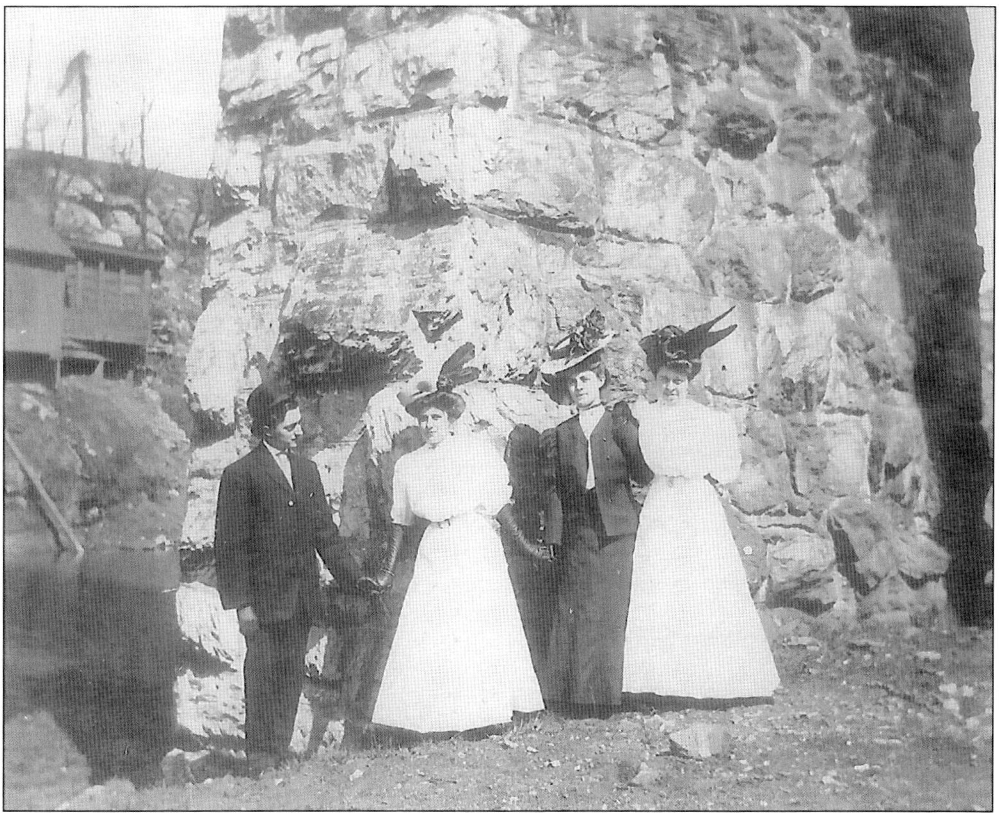

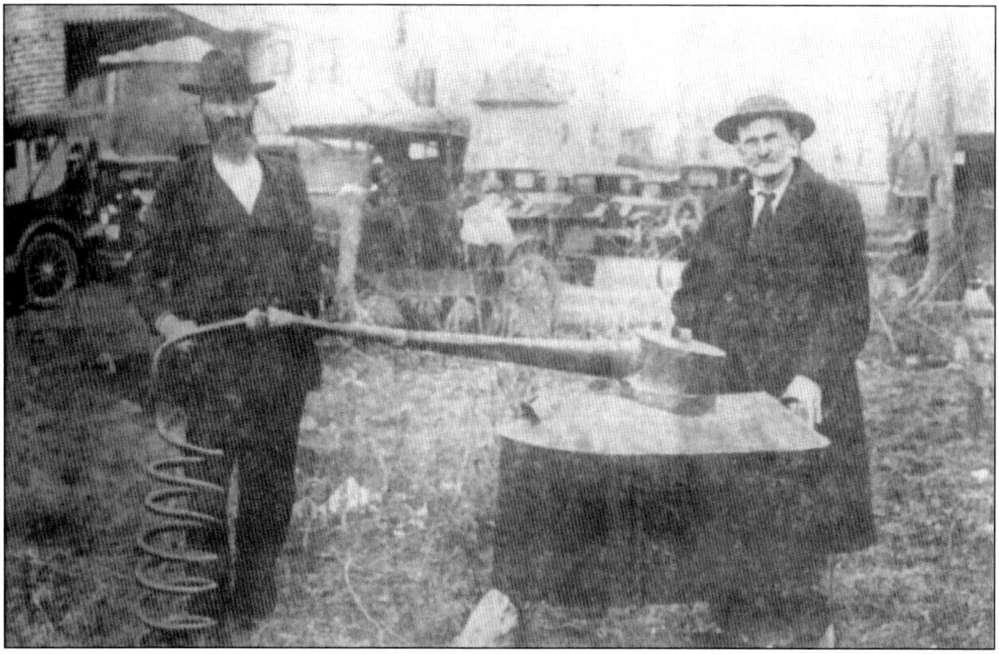

Distillery licenses were granted by the state. In 1886, there were 42 distilleries in Page County, but this homemade still was captured shortly after World War I, during Prohibition (1920–1933). At left is J. D. Frazier, Page County justice of the peace, with Deputy J. D. Tate of the ABC Board. Tate had a reputation for confiscating the "stagger juice" apparatuses. (*PN&C.*)

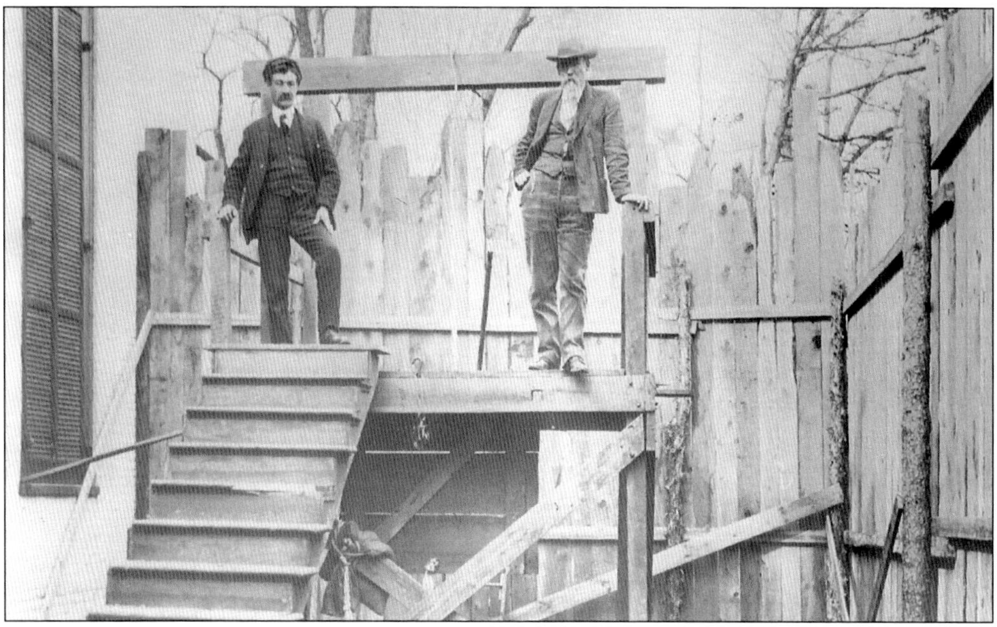

The last legal hanging in Virginia took place on South Court Street in Luray when Peter Good, convicted of killing his sweetheart, Fannie Stroup, was hanged on Friday, March 22, 1907. Shown pictured on the gallows are, Deputy J. Vic Renalds (left) along with Page County sheriff Nathan Sedwick. Though the enclosed fencing was erected for privacy, as many as 150 spectators witnessed the event. (*PN&C.*)

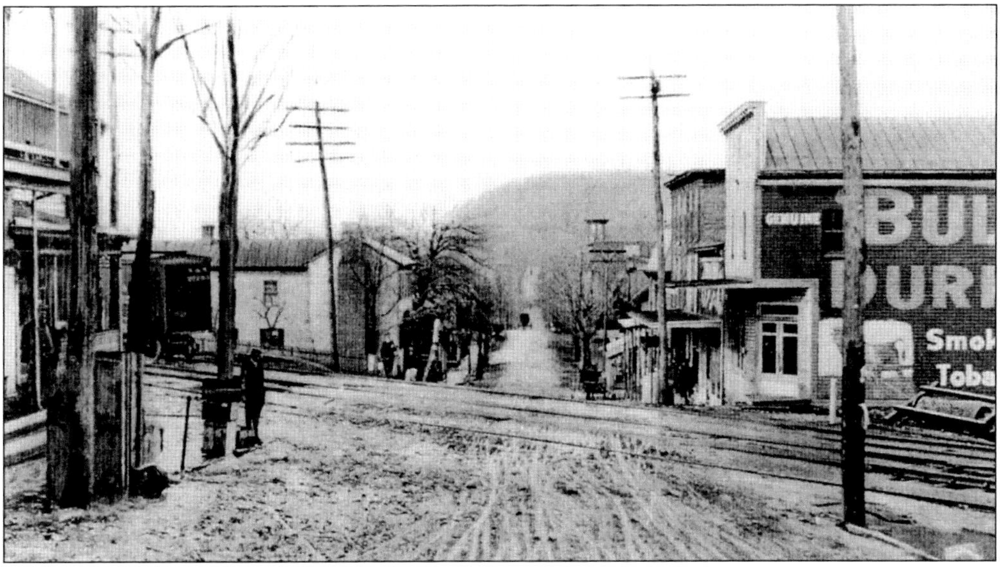

A young man at left poses unintentionally in this 1910s view. Luray's Main Street remained dirt for another quarter-century until it was paved in 1937. On the W. G. Fitch Store at right, Bull Durham Smoking Tobacco is prominently advertised for both road and rail traffic. Thomas Bradley built the structure, which would be destroyed by fire on March 7, 1949. (Dan Vaughn.)

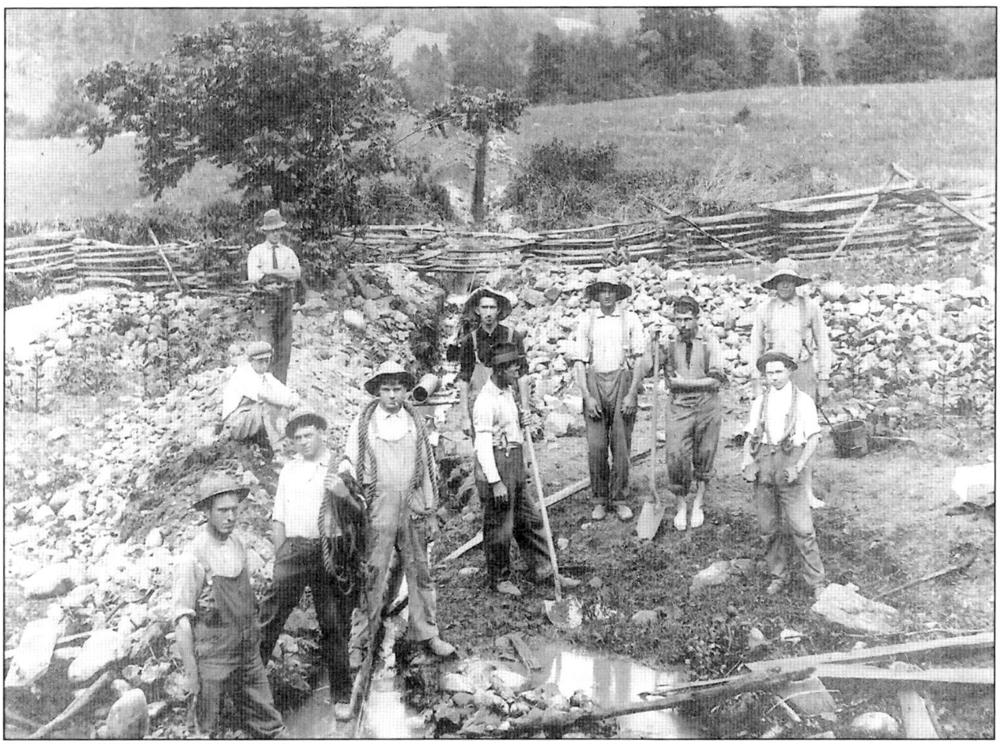

This work crew from J. T. Campbell Plumbing is obliged to pause for the photographer during this project. Campbell, second from front, ran this water line from Luray's reservoir to Pass Run, increasing the supply to the town. The Blue Ridge is just beyond them in this July 1912 image. (Tim and Clarice Rickard.)

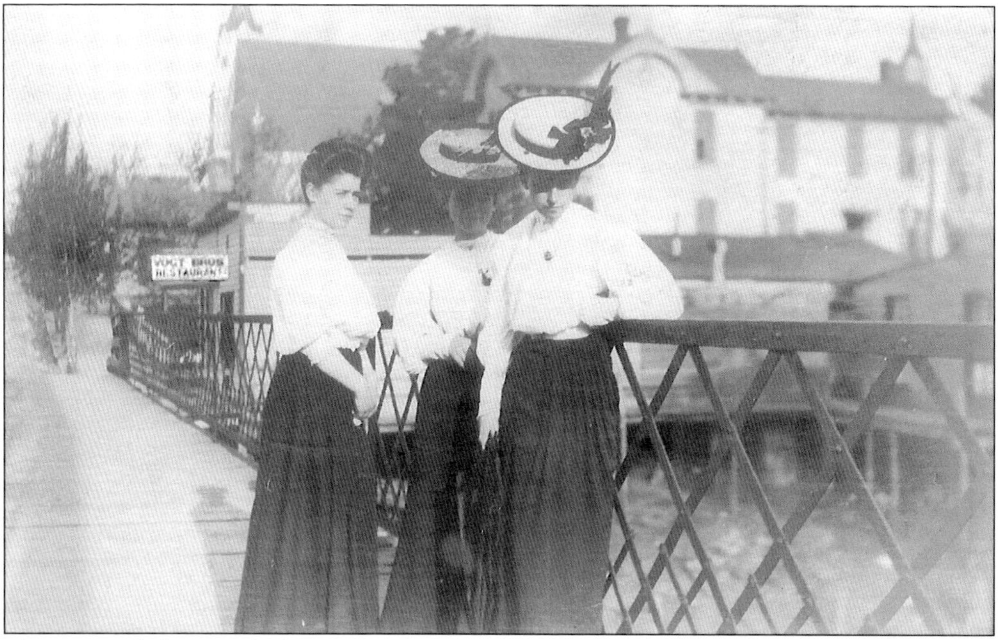

These Luray ladies posed reluctantly on Hawksbill Creek's walk bridge in 1927. The townspeople had sought the auxiliary bridge for years because of the dangers pedestrians had crossing with traffic. The old Wade Bohannon house stands at right, removed for a Page Valley National Bank relocation the following year. Purchasing the Singer's Restaurant, George Vogt Jr. and brother William opened Vogt Brothers Restaurant (behind the ladies) in 1906. (Jean Kite.)

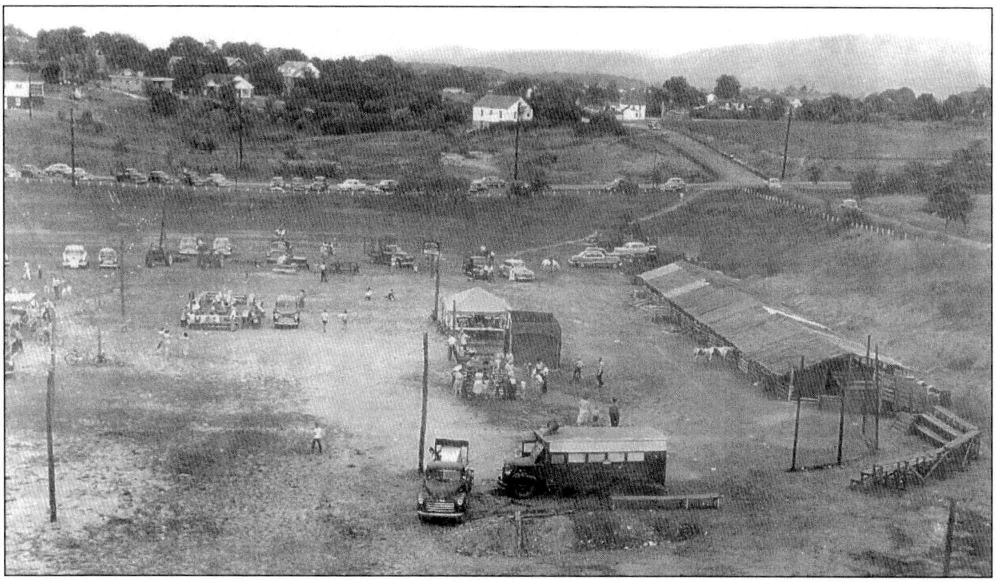

An agricultural fair at Massanutten Heights operated in the 1930s, and Frank Rosser's Page County Fair on North Hawksbill Street ran from 1934 to 1966. Here the first Page Valley Agricultural and Industrial Fair was held August 7–8, 1953, on the grounds of Luray High School. With David Shirley as its first president, there were over 50 exhibits displayed inside. The LHS band played, and there were fire trucks, farm animals, Little Ashby—"World's Smallest Man," Boy Scouts serving food, bingo, pony rides, and shows. Over 10,000 came and enjoyed their fair. (Lillian Coleman.)

Mollie Zerkel, seen with husband, Lemuel, and grandson Lenferd B. Zerkel (far right), began collecting keepsakes in 1857, opening the first location of the Luray Museum in 1905. Her collection of over 3,500 pieces included, among others, a tintype of President Lincoln, a "Tom Thumb" boot, the rope used to hang John Brown, and Stonewall Jackson's own private camp stove. The museum was widely regarded as the finest Civil War collection in the South. (Chester Ramey III.)

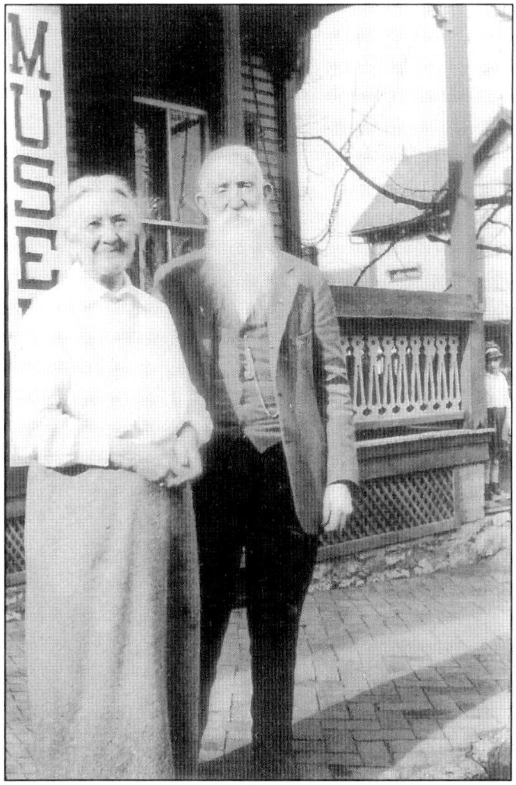

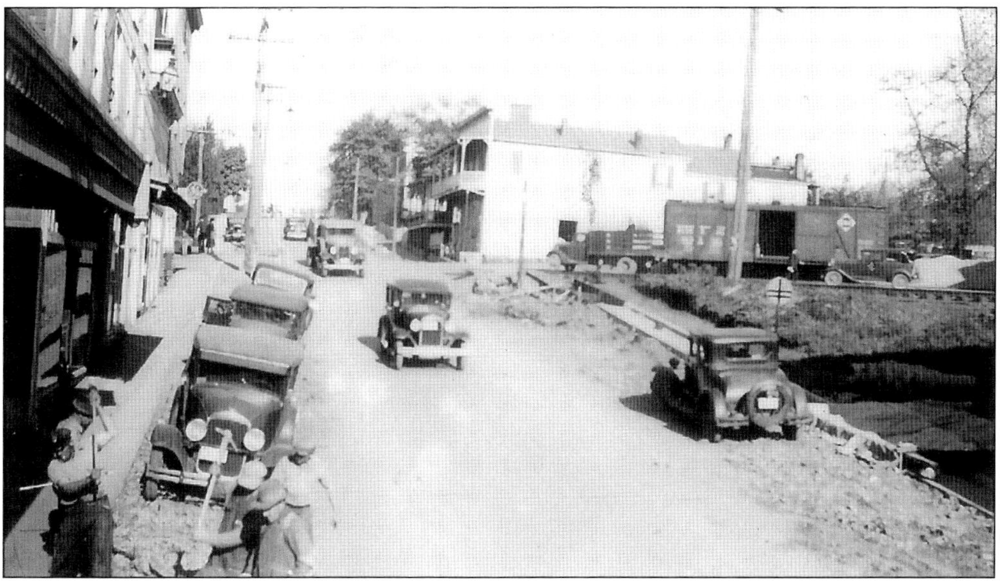

Luray merchants considered the improvements of widened, macadamized streets and concrete sidewalks, seen in this 1938 image, a godsend. A town order forced the removal of the street-side porches that had long given shelter and quaintness. A lone boxcar rests on the now-removed Zirkle Street sidetrack. Both road and rail traffic shared the street. The S. O. Judd Storehouse, at center, and its upper-floor home to the 1890s Luray Military Academy, was removed in 1991 for the present Luray Fire Department. (Bonnie and Sonny Wood.)

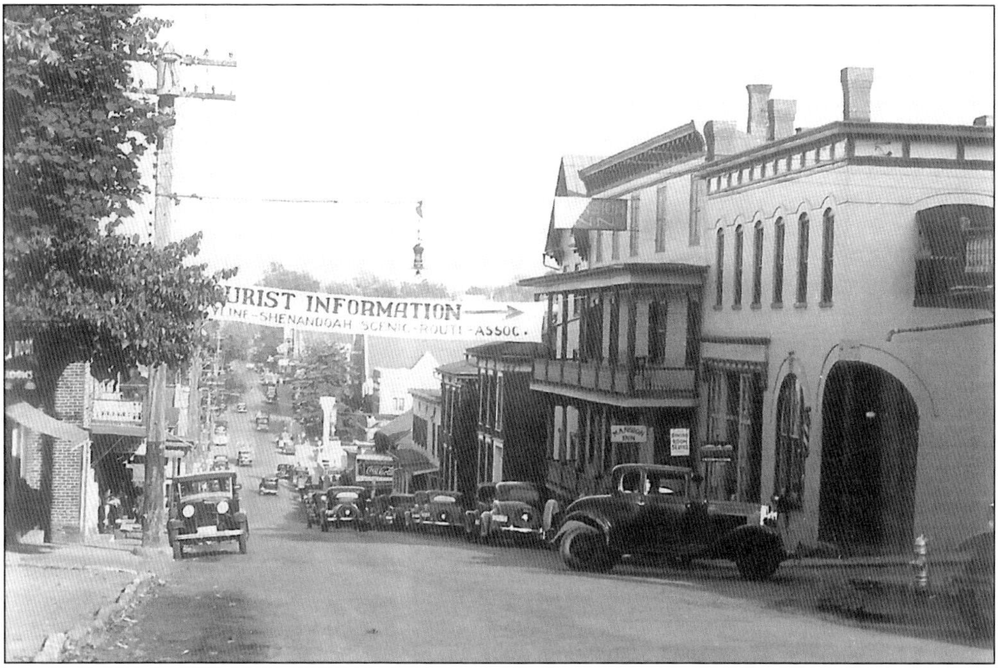

By the mid-1930s, Luray was well established as a popular tourist destination. With the automobile's emergence, the Skyline-Shenandoah Scenic-Route Association opened in the old 1890s Luray Post Office, at right. Both sections of the former Mansion Inn are seen here. (Dan Vaughn.)

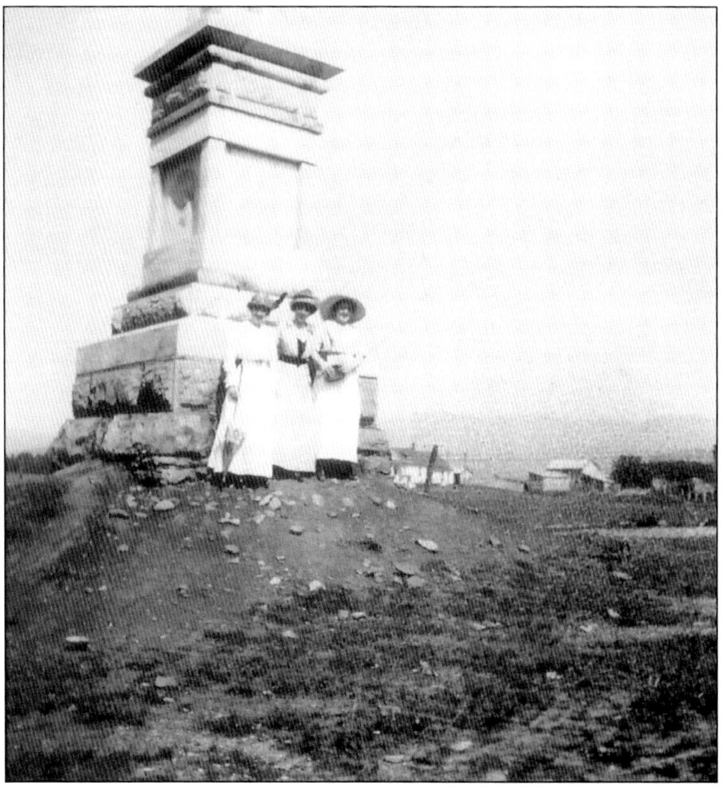

Dr. A. M. Henkel, donating a lot in Luray's East End to sculptor Herbert Barbee in 1895, requested the improbable feat of erecting a Confederate monument by January 1, 1896. It was to be the focal entry point of a proposed Henkel Woods Park. Many favored a triangular road to encompass the statue. Needless to say, the envisioned park did not materialize, nor did Monument Road to form the triangle. Ironically, another monument with roads on three sides appeared on Broad Street two decades later. (Jean Kite.)

Here a work shed and scrap marble linger, and today a solitary Henkel Woods oak, left intentionally, still stands beside the monument. Names of those killed in the Civil War were placed in a "casket" that forms the cornerstone of the marble memorial's base. On July 21, 1898, with 2,000 in attendance, it was unveiled by 11 ladies representing the Confederate states. Sadly, for unknown reasons, the local Confederate veterans were not present at the event. (Dan Vaughn.)

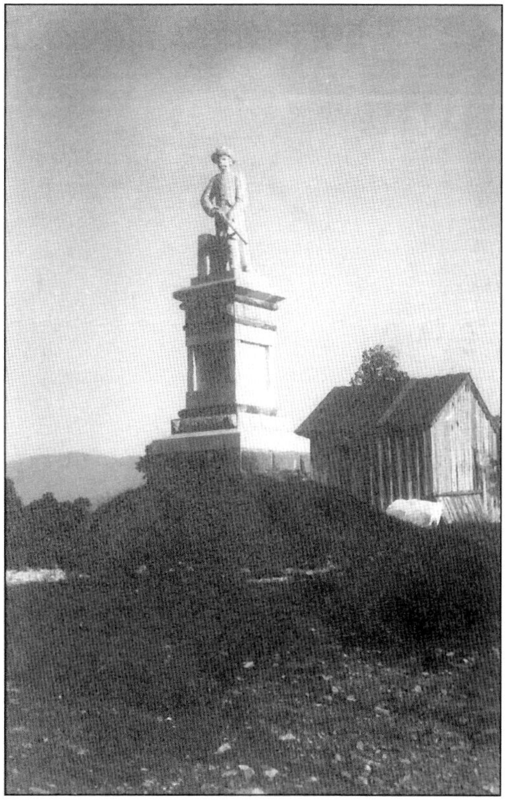

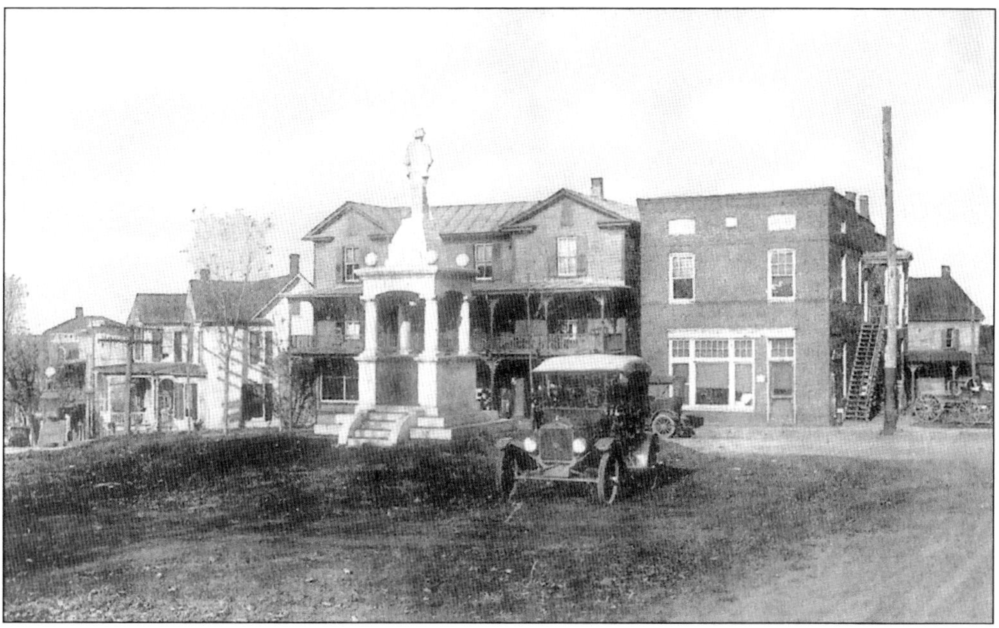

Broad Street's Confederate Soldier Monument, facing the now-removed Commercial Hotel, was erected in 1918 after the 1849 Mount Carmel Baptist Church was razed. Adjacent to the Luray Post Office, the Broad Street, Campbell Street, and Virginia Avenue triangular plot has become a point of reference for both locals and tourists alike. (Dan Vaughn.)

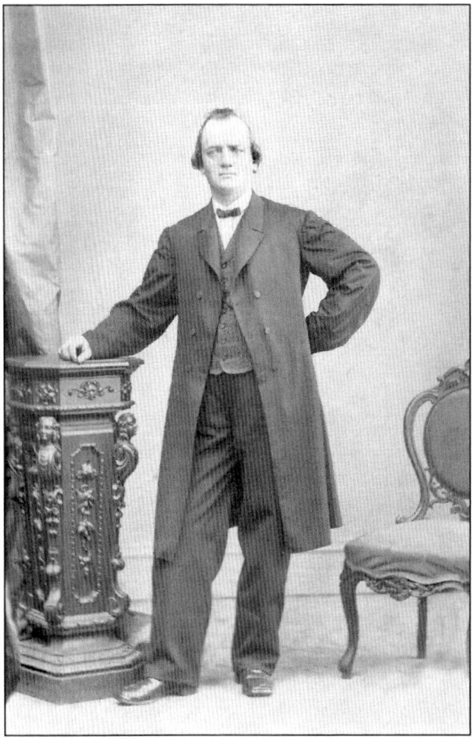

William Milnes Jr., born in England, came to the United States and migrated to Shenandoah by 1866. The following year, he, with brother-in-law Thomas Johns and others, purchased 32,000 acres, including the Forrer Iron Works. Milnes gave land to build churches and railroad shops and employed hundreds in his industrial ventures. After attracting the Shenandoah Valley Railroad (SVRR) here, he became its president. On February 12, 1884, Shenandoah Iron Works was renamed Milnes, Virginia, in honor of the town's former U.S. congressman. (Charles Stevens.)

Documenting Shenandoah's hydroelectric power dam's construction, a photographer records his visit to the town at the Forrer home on Long Avenue. Around 1918, are, from left to right, Melvin Alexander, Bill Alexander, Robert Alexander, and Elsie Rose Alexander. Built in 1855 by Daniel and Henry Forrer, the mansion originally contained 26 rooms, bricks imported from England, and a glass observatory (at top). Shenandoah lost a truly historic dwelling when it was razed in the 1970s. (Laura Rosazza.)

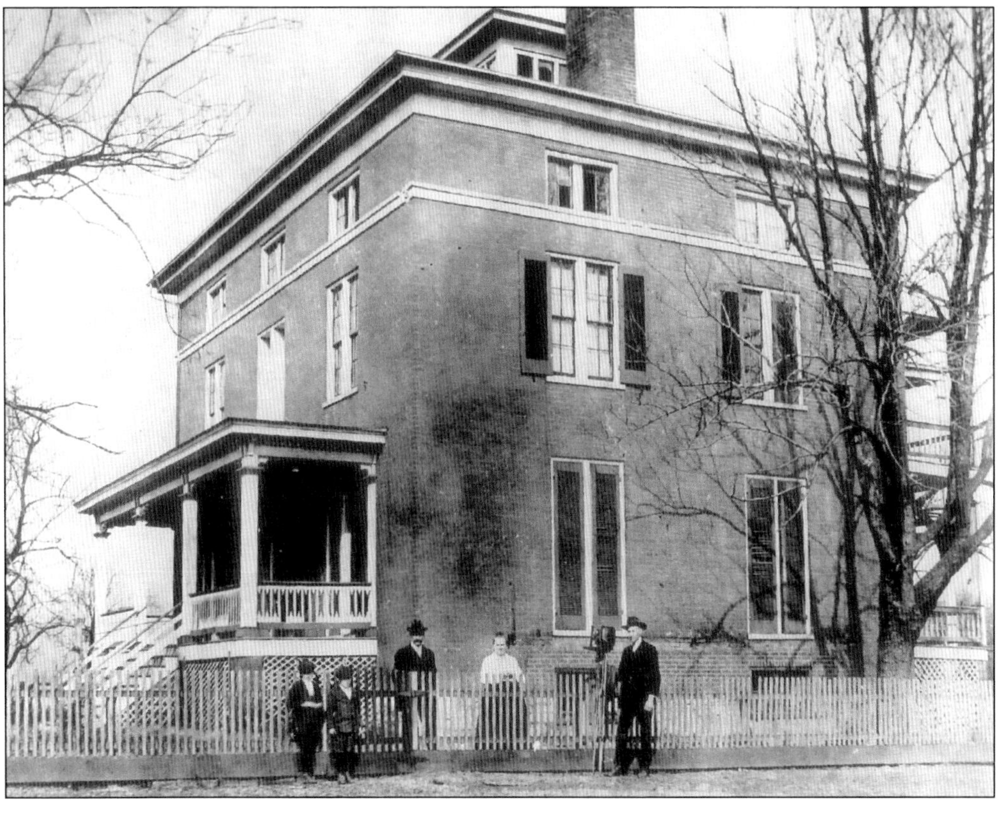

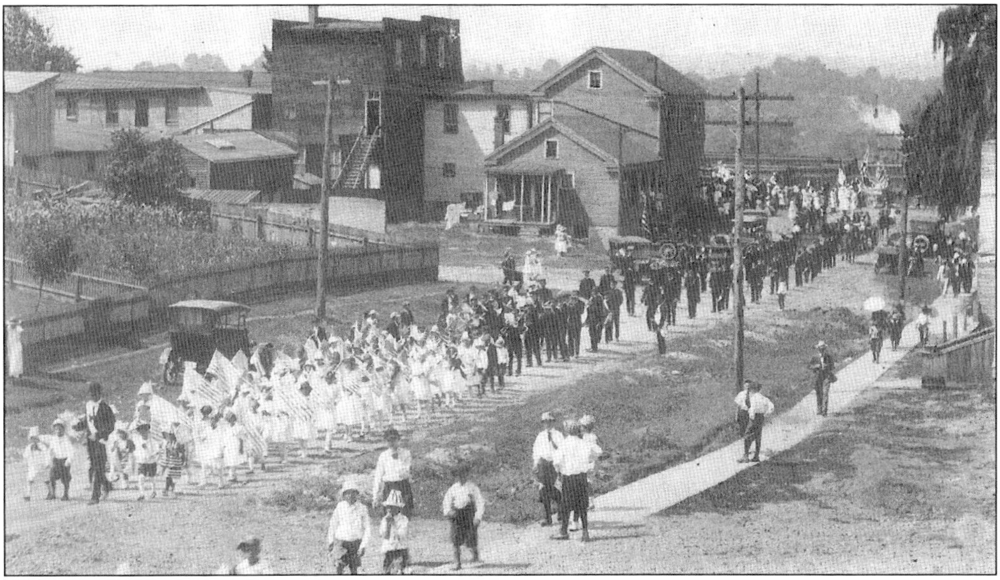

Rev. Warren Baldwin (left) leads a troop of young celebrators up Virginia Avenue in this 1917 exhibition of an Independence Day Parade in Shenandoah. At top center is Foster Brother's Storehouse, facing the town's commercially laden First Street, with Joe Taylor's Shoe Repair Shop at its rear. (Dan Vaughn.)

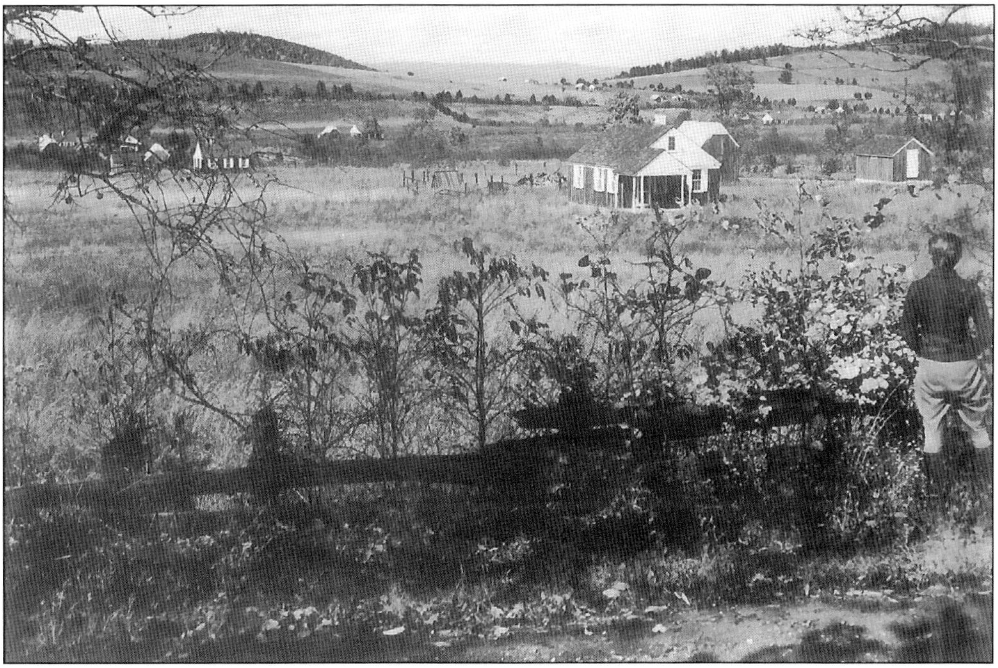

The Ida Valley Homesteads Project accommodated families evicted from their homes during the formation of the Shenandoah National Park. L. Ferdinand Zerkel, J. R. Mims, and Fred T. Amiss were in charge of the project, which included 343 acres on the Kathryn Saunders's farm. This October 20, 1937, photograph, taken from the original Ida Road, looks west over Ida up Hollow Run. Civilian Conservation Corps trucks moved the first families here on this day. (Page Public Library.)

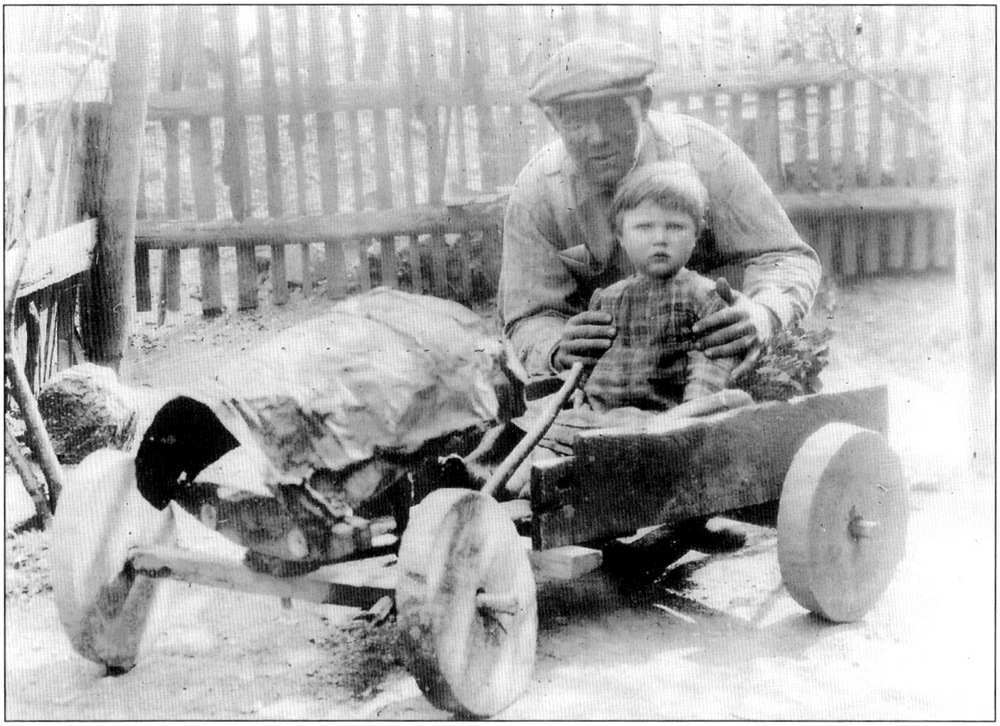

This Tanner's Ridge child may have been considered comparably poor, but his dad's imagination and creativity were priceless. During the Depression, "make do" was a commonly heard phrase. All learned its meaning. (St. George's Episcopal.)

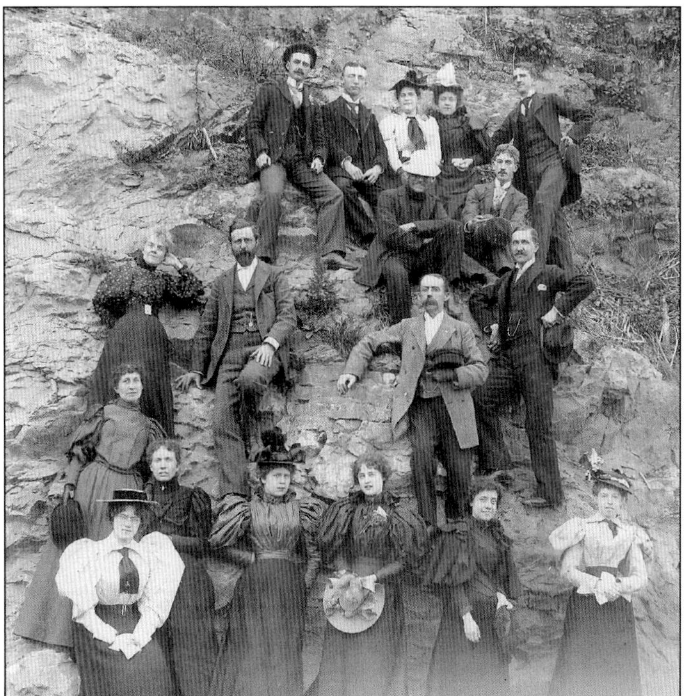

Silas Wright photographed this 1894–1895 session of the Monday Club, Luray's popular music and literary social group. Local poet Lena Carrington Rust was its charter member. From left to right are (first row) Ada Mae Reed, Fannie Rhodes, Fannie MacFarland, Bessie Binford, ? Winslow, and Bessie Broaddus. Behind Reed is ? Stafford; (second row) Mary Roller, Dr. L. H. Keller, John Roller, and Judge E. T. Booton; (third row) Horrace Morrison and Will Rust; (fourth row) Fred Amiss, Rev. ? Oberley, Annie Lauck, Ruth Laughton, and John Booton. (William and Frances Menefee.)

Two

TURN OF THE CENTURY

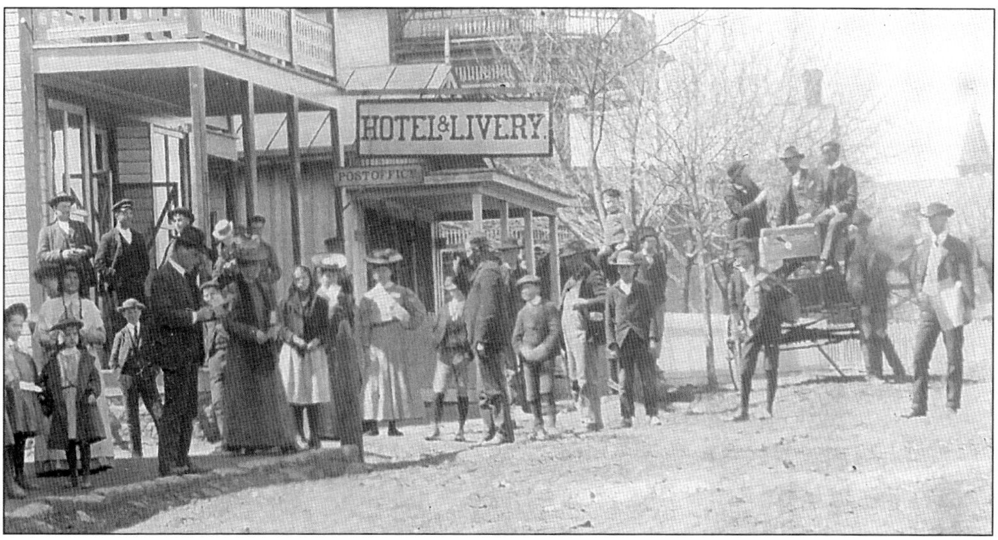

A crowd of well-dressed individuals assembled on this *c.* 1900 winter day outside the Hotel Stanley. D. L. Mauck built the hotel in 1893, and by 1904, Virginia state senator Amos K. Grim of Stanley had assumed ownership. With its own livery, the Stanleyton Post Office, and the railroad just beyond the photographer's back, this was a busy location. (Gaylon Waters.)

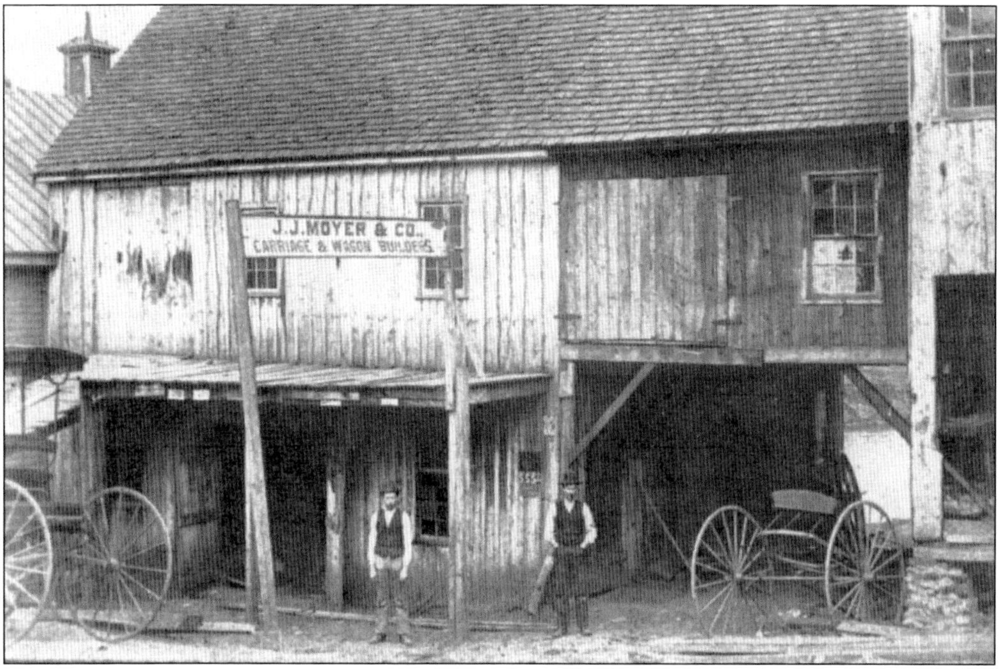

John J. Moyer and his brother M. Lee, of J. J. Moyer and Company, operated this business in the horse-and-wagon era. Their great-uncle, Abram Moyer, was first of that name to acquire the wagon-and-carriage enterprise. In 1911, relational successor Luther J. Moyer advertised "tightening" of buggy tires and his patented Moyer Buggy Brace. Built in 1899, the building was destroyed by fire on January 30, 1933, marking the end for wooden structures with Luray's new building code. (*PN&C.*)

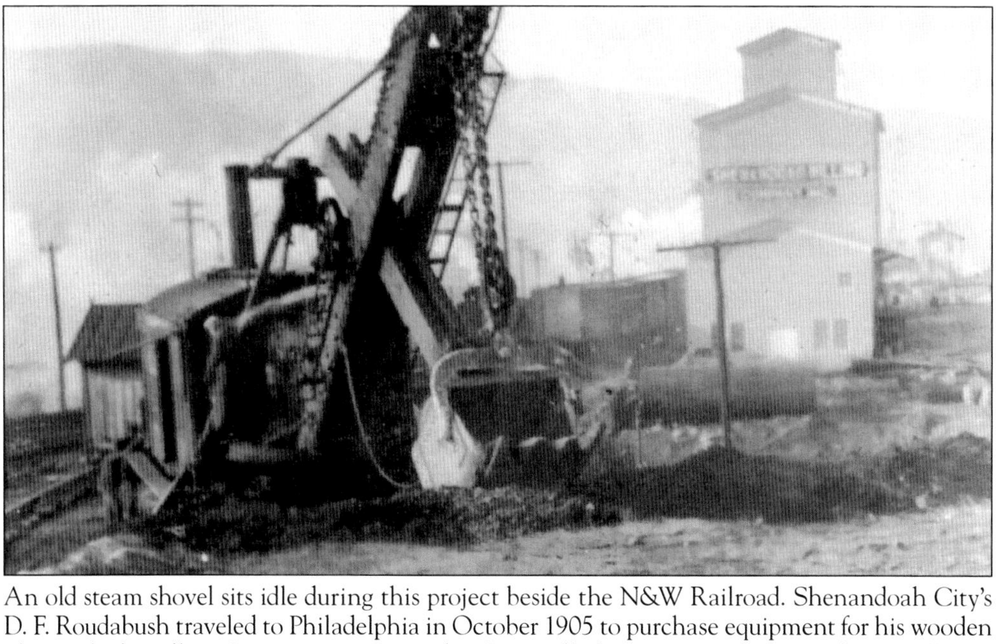

An old steam shovel sits idle during this project beside the N&W Railroad. Shenandoah City's D. F. Roudabush traveled to Philadelphia in October 1905 to purchase equipment for his wooden Shenandoah Milling Company, seen at right. Originally built as a water-powered gristmill, and only producing about 30 barrels a day, it burned in 1925. (Ruth Staples.)

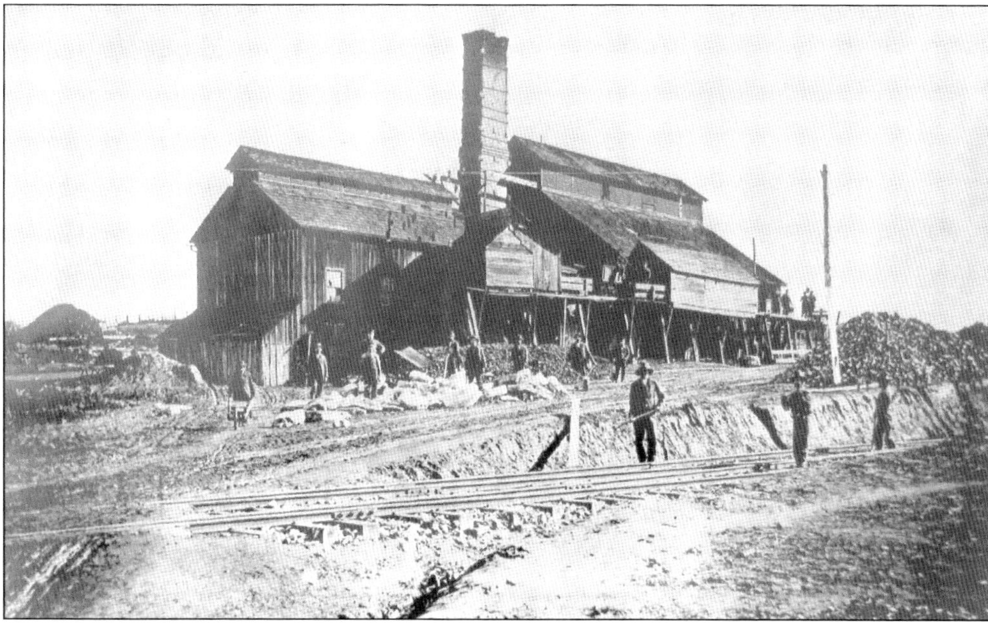

The original Shenandoah Iron Works charcoal furnace had an 8-by-33-foot stack and a Player hot-blast attachment. It could produce 60 tons of pig iron per week. Milnes's company laboratory is at left, just out of view, in this 1871 image. Charcoal, at right, borders the newly laid spur rail. A 3-foot-square brick "cooling" tunnel, 10 feet underground, still remains at the site. (Buddy Comer.)

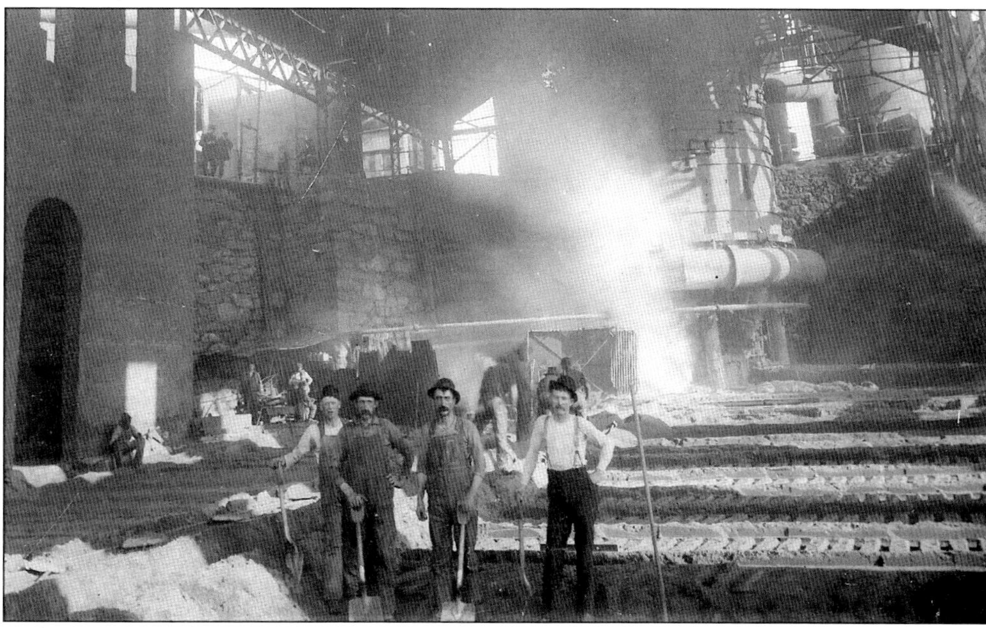

Built in 1882, Milnes's Big Gem at Furnace No. 1 produced 10 times the output as the old forge. With peak production of 135 tons a day and a workforce of 400, the 16-by-70-foot stack was overworked. With site excavation by James Pulliman, James Haney was in charge of construction. David Gray of Page laid the stone as well as bricks from Coffman's Brick Yard. Here workers clean the foundry floor where up to four "let-outs" (casts) were poured daily. (Irvin Judd Jr.)

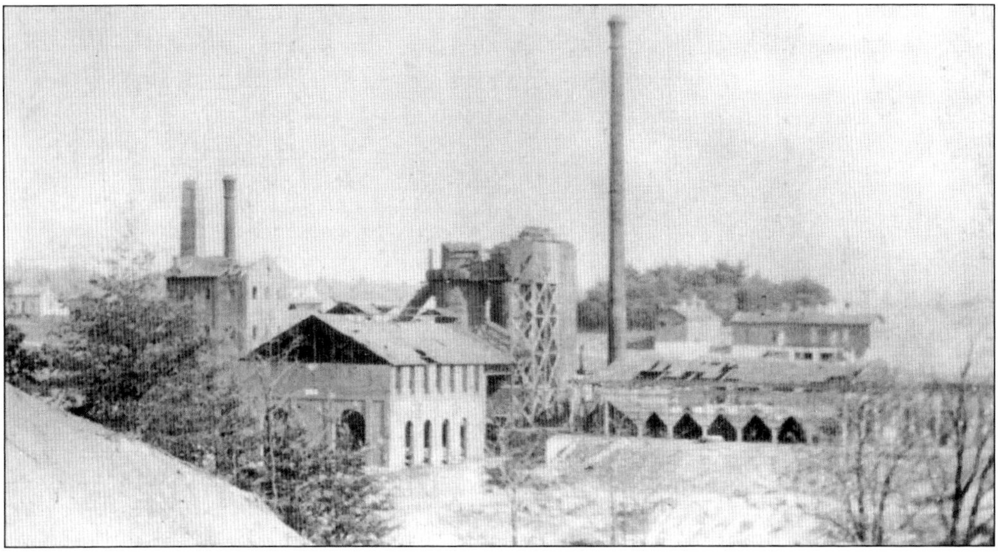

The Shenandoah Iron Works in the first place caused the railroad's attraction, thereafter depending on it for transporting finished goods. Unfortunately, its hand-in-hand arrangement was its demise when both fell into receivership in the mid-1880s. In addition, a principal ore bank failed in 1903. With the pay dirt gone, Big Gem's, and indeed the entire of the ironworks', days were numbered. The coke-fired, iron-smelting furnace discontinued operations in 1907. A five-mile spur rail westward across the river to Massanutten Mountain, proposed in 1899, never materialized. (Irvin Judd Jr.)

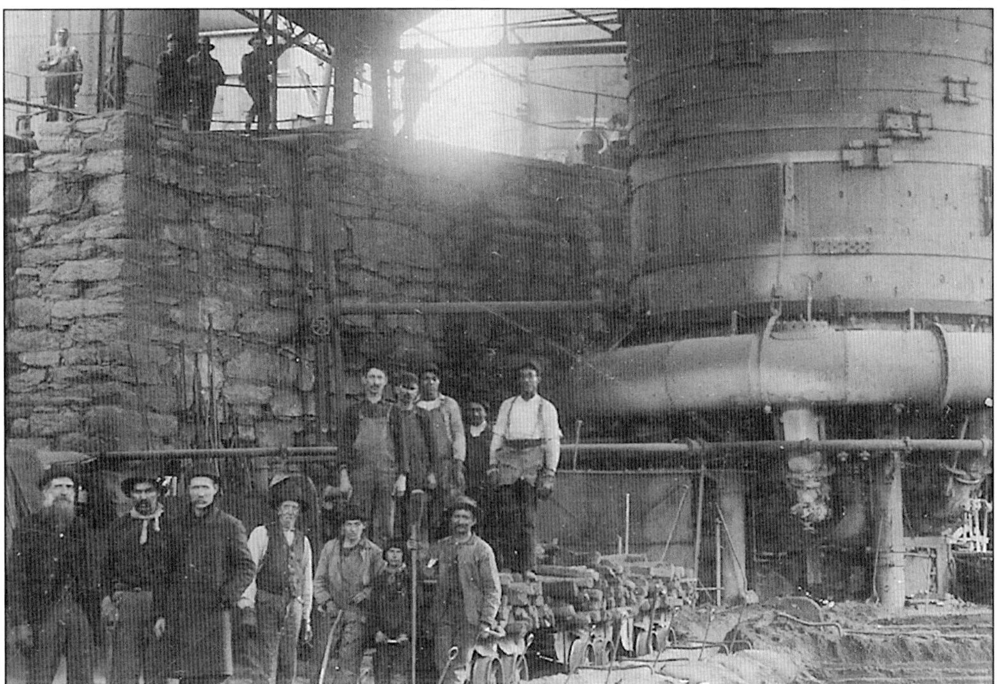

Iron furnace workers are dwarfed by the sheer size of the stack at Shenandoah's Big Gem. Rail carts of cooled "blooms" (uniform-sized ingots) await loading onto flatcars on the N&W spur line that connected it with Shenandoah Yard. Iron ore was first mined at Milnes in 1836 by brothers Daniel and Henry Forrer. A man by the name of Nicholas first broke ground. (Irvin Judd Jr.)

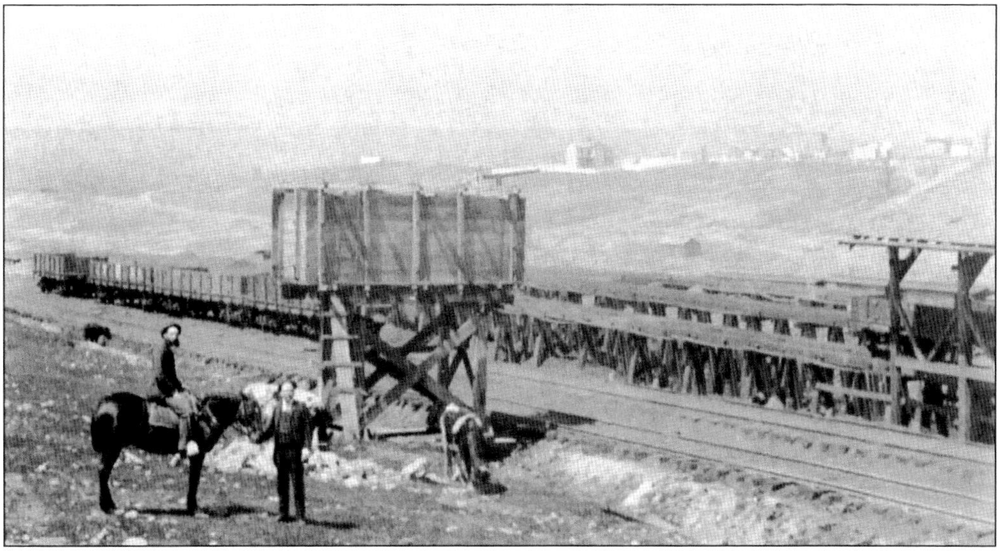

By the time this picture was taken on the grounds of the Shenandoah Iron Works, the fires of Furnace No. 1 were nearly extinguished. Operations shut down by 1907, but activity continued, being leased to local blacksmiths and machinists. Looking toward Shenandoah across the spur rail, Nates Lank, at left on horse, poses with an unidentified gentleman. An elevated railcar work station stands at center. (Charles Stevens.)

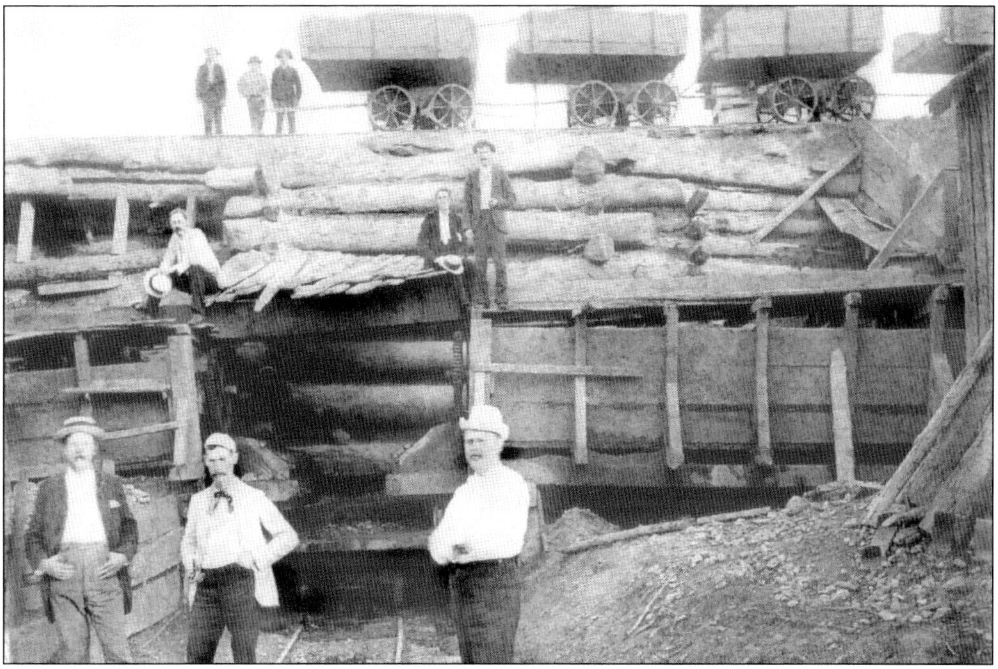

Shenandoah Furnace Company's mine superintendent, Charles J. Stevens, stands at left in this c. 1890s image of Fox Mountain Mine. In 1887, a mine collapse buried five men alive—four were rescued. Also miners were temporarily stunned when lightning conducted by the mine's minerals traveled down the shaft. Just outside Page on Fox Mountain's North Slope, it was Shenandoah's greatest iron ore producer since first opening in 1836. During its 1880s peak, the seven-mile shortline transported up to 100 tons of extracted concentrates daily. (Charles Stevens.)

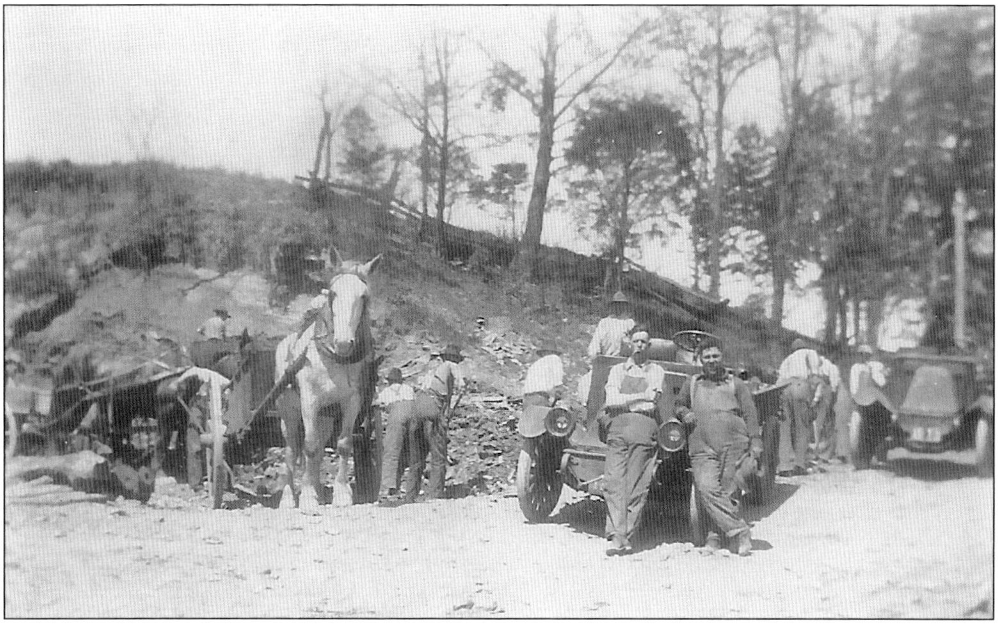

On June 2, 1921, "Road Building Day," citizens of Luray made history with national attention when volunteers turned out en masse at White House Bridge to make Massanutten Mountain Road passable. Coordinated by the Luray Board of Trade, businesses closed down and proprietors and laborers alike worked side-by-side under overseer Joseph Duncan. Those who couldn't join the force paid others to work or furnished trucks and teams. (*PN&C*.)

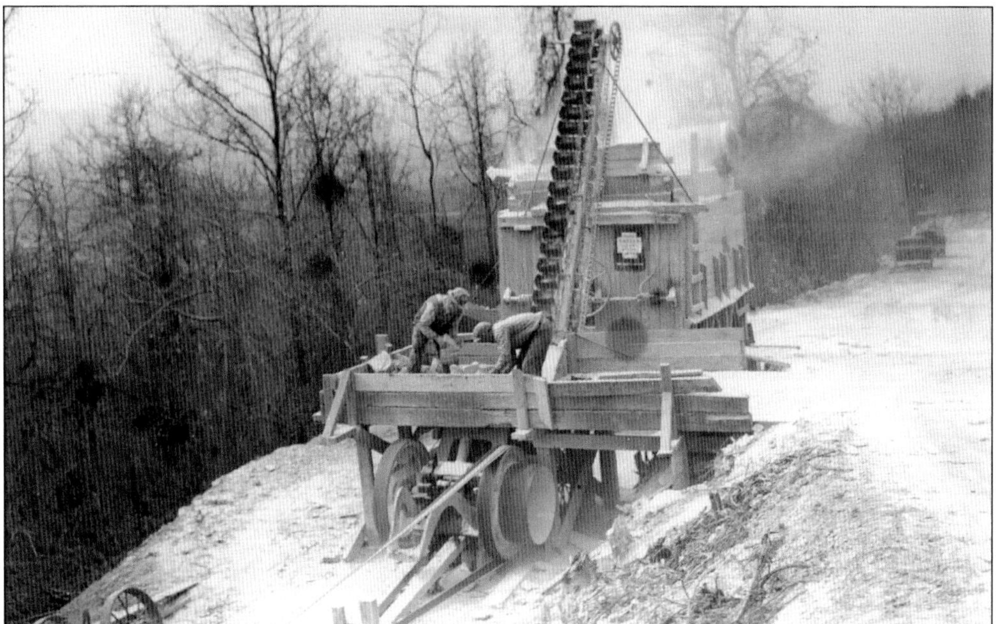

The Town of Luray had purchased a rock crusher as early as 1895. Formerly the board of supervisors had control of roads in the county, but in 1918, the Virginia State Highway System was initiated. These men, operating this portable rock crusher in Page County in this 1938 Works Project Administration (WPA) project, gave manifestation to the term "manual labor." (National Archives.)

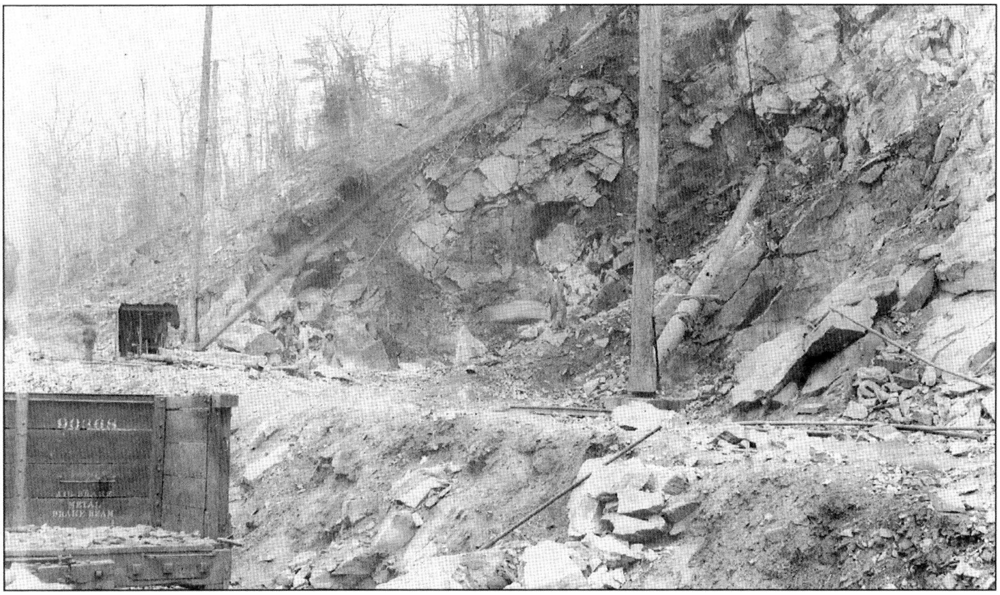

Precious metals discovered along Blue Ridge's western slopes brought mining operations by the droves to Page during the late 1800s. Shenandoah's Iron Works, East Liberty's Watery Branch Mine, Stanley's Oxford Ochre and Eureka Mining Company, Marksville's gold, Ida's Dunchee mines, Kimball's Cornelia Iron Mines, Rileyville's Bonanza Mines and this outcrop of the Compton Mines, where cantilever assemblies were erected to load spur rail cars, all represented the interest. (Mary Ann Painter.)

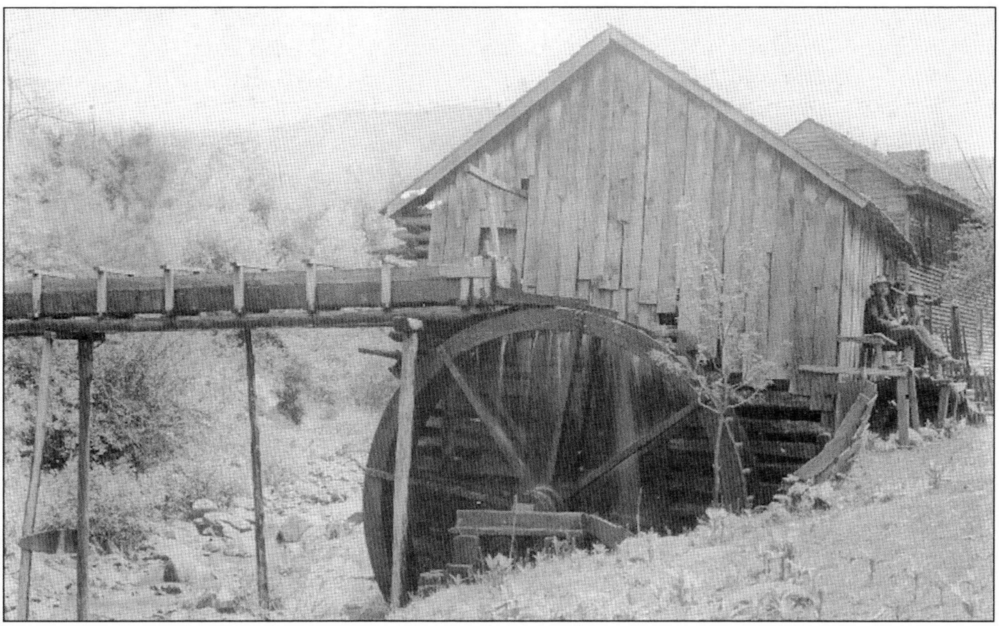

These men, at right, relax outside the old Dora Gray Mill in Pine Grove. An 1882 *Page Courier* issue made the assumption that "soon, there wouldn't be an old burr mill in the county." At the time of this mid-1920s picture, burr-type mills were giving way to the new roller process, and steam and electric power had all but eliminated the gristmill's picturesque overshot waterwheels. (St. George's Episcopal.)

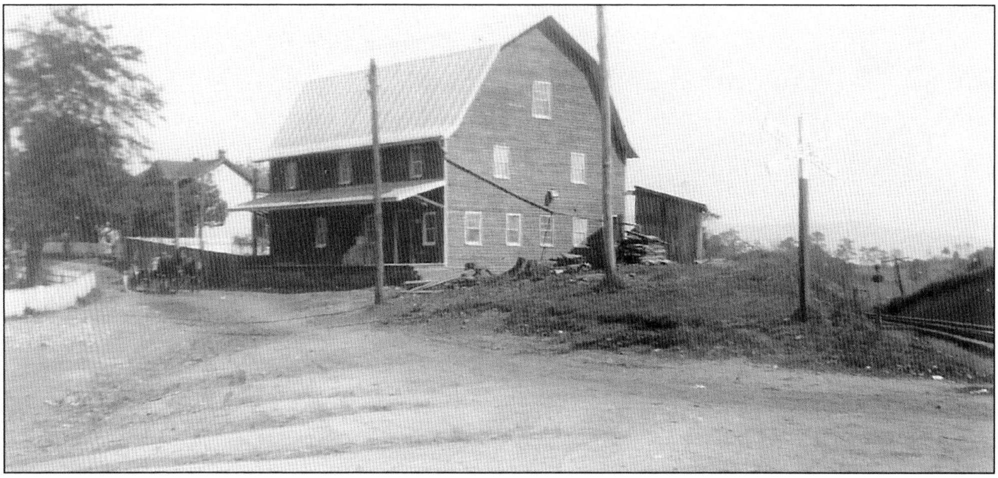

A lone horse with buckboard wagon approaches the loading dock at Wood's Mill in Rileyville, located next to the N&WRR. Proprietor Hugh Wood also ran a popular general merchandise store across the street. Fire, an unforgiving culprit claiming four mills in Page in 1887 alone, would unfortunately strike here as well. (Nora Belle Comer.)

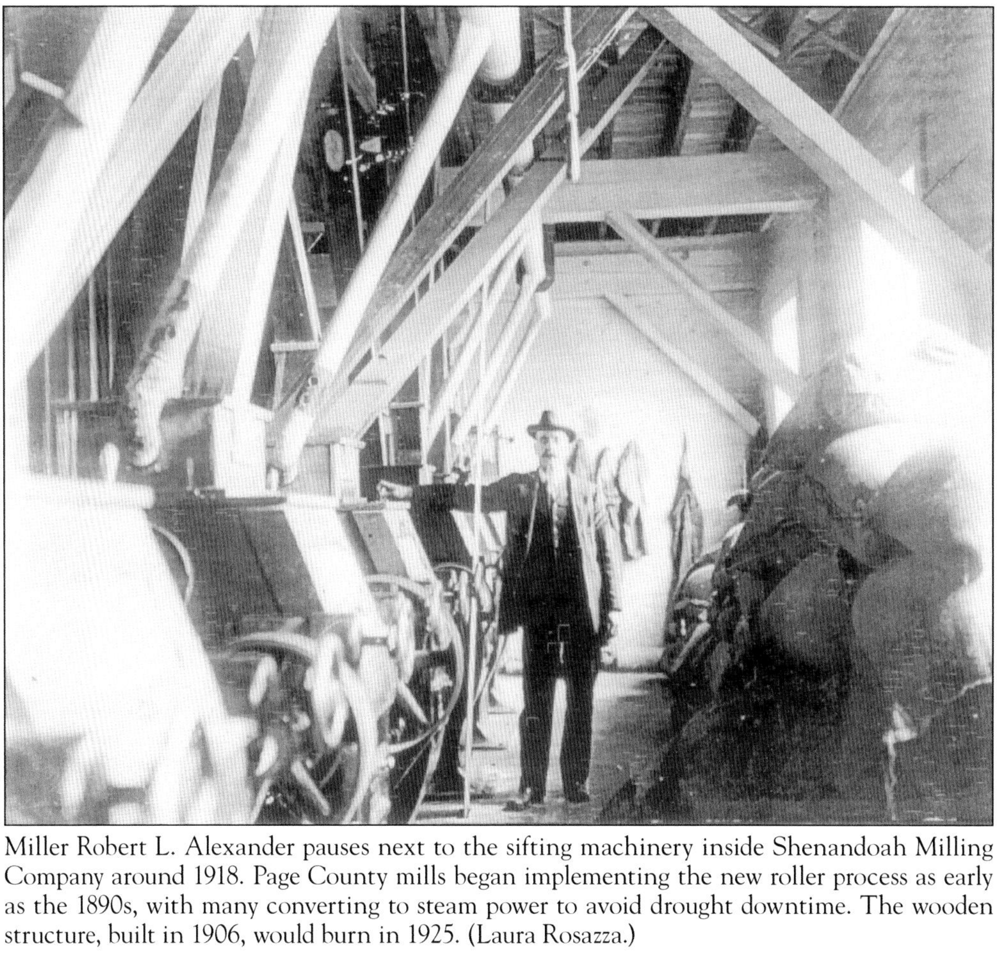

Miller Robert L. Alexander pauses next to the sifting machinery inside Shenandoah Milling Company around 1918. Page County mills began implementing the new roller process as early as the 1890s, with many converting to steam power to avoid drought downtime. The wooden structure, built in 1906, would burn in 1925. (Laura Rosazza.)

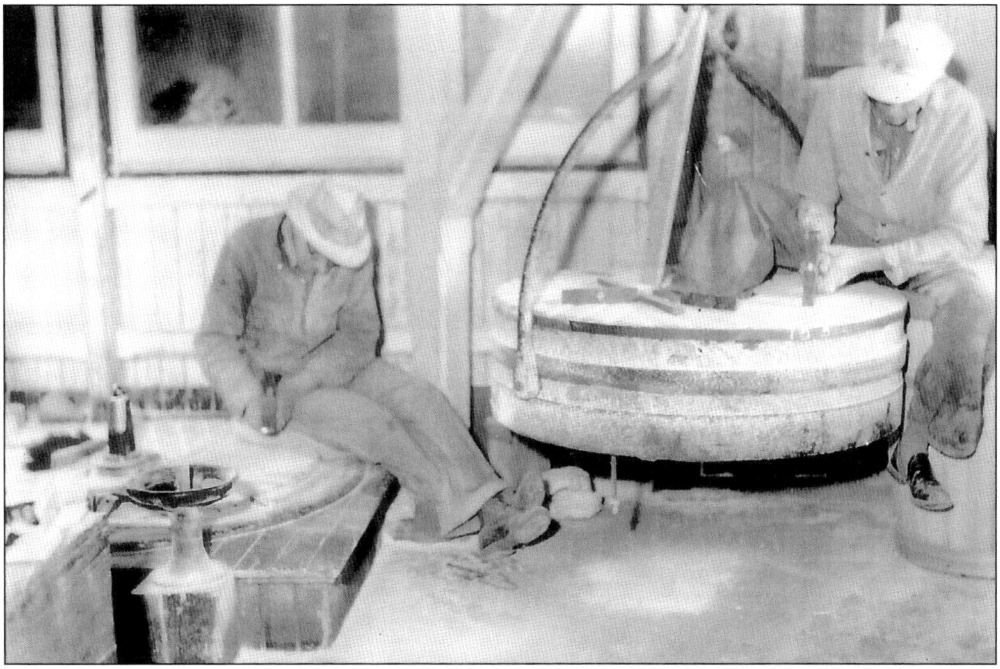

Melvin E. Alexander (left) and Sam Mauck laboriously clean and sharpen burrstone wheels inside Page Milling in 1937. The wheel was then flipped back over and repositioned on its stationary counterpart on the left. A test run with ink determined high spots. (Page Public Library.)

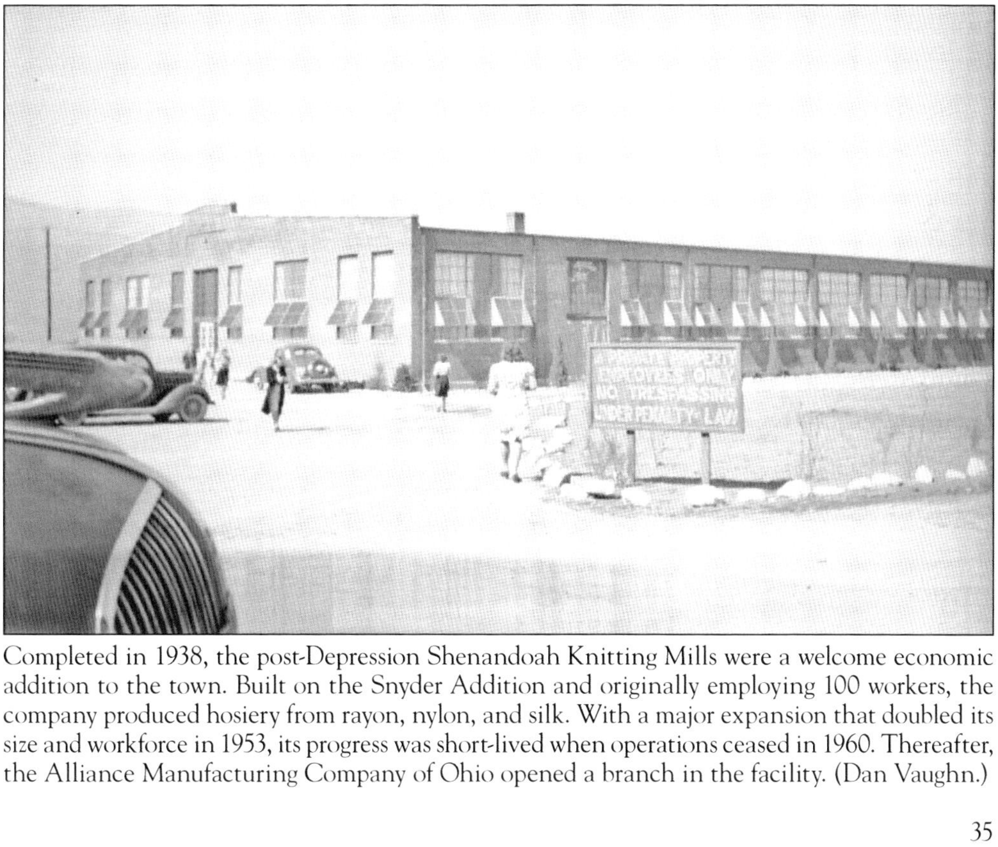

Completed in 1938, the post-Depression Shenandoah Knitting Mills were a welcome economic addition to the town. Built on the Snyder Addition and originally employing 100 workers, the company produced hosiery from rayon, nylon, and silk. With a major expansion that doubled its size and workforce in 1953, its progress was short-lived when operations ceased in 1960. Thereafter, the Alliance Manufacturing Company of Ohio opened a branch in the facility. (Dan Vaughn.)

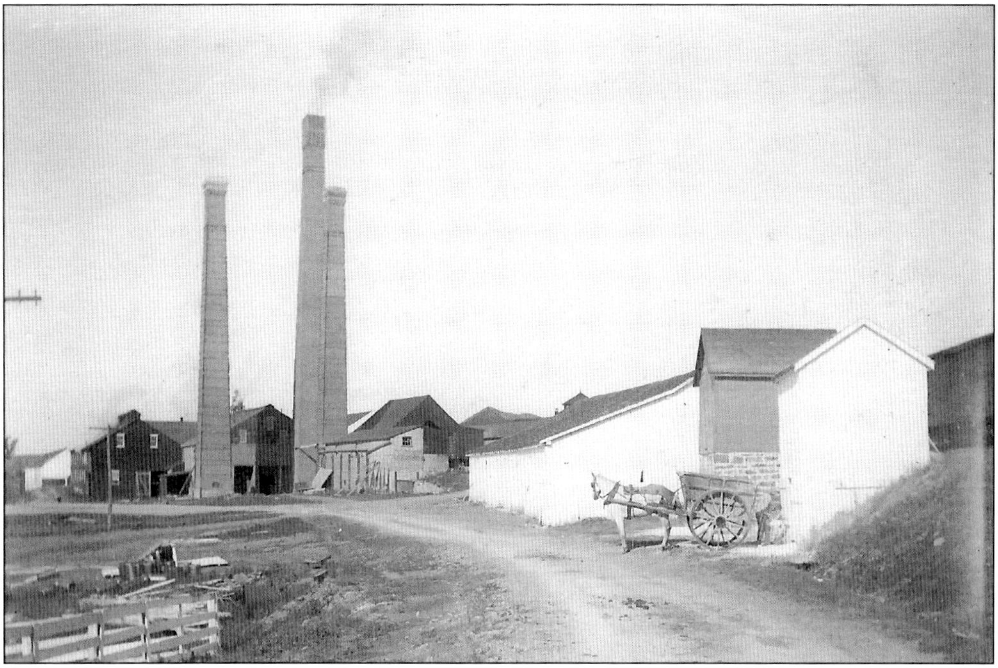

On September 16, 1880, Lafayette Griffith broke ground to begin construction of Deford Tannery. A strike in December 1880 was refused by Captain Bechtal, the foreman, with workers resuming duties for 75¢ a day. It was completed on August 20, 1882, with such superior quality by its finishing rollers that many local tanneries had their leather finished here. A premium exhibit was on display at the 1907 Jamestown Exposition. (Mildred Stirewalt Coleman.)

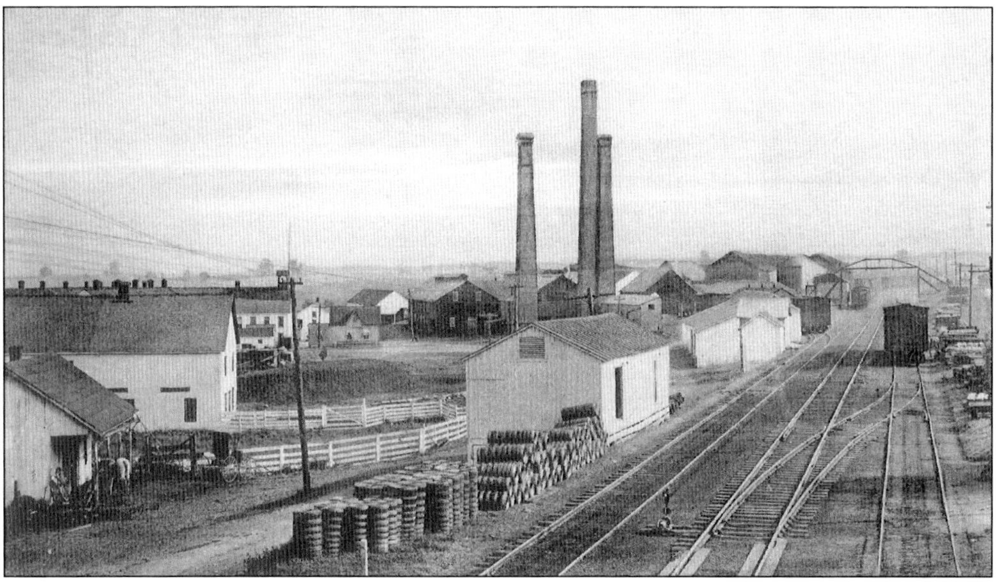

Deford Tannery was reported as not only the largest tannery in Virginia but in the United States. With its capacity to produce 1,000 hides a day, the *Luray Times*' inaugural edition of August 22, 1890, gave it the grandiose title of "largest in the world." Headquartered in Baltimore, the company also operated in Covington, Virginia. N&W sidetracks, passing under the 1892 arched bridge at right, were mostly removed in the 1960s. (Dan Vaughn.)

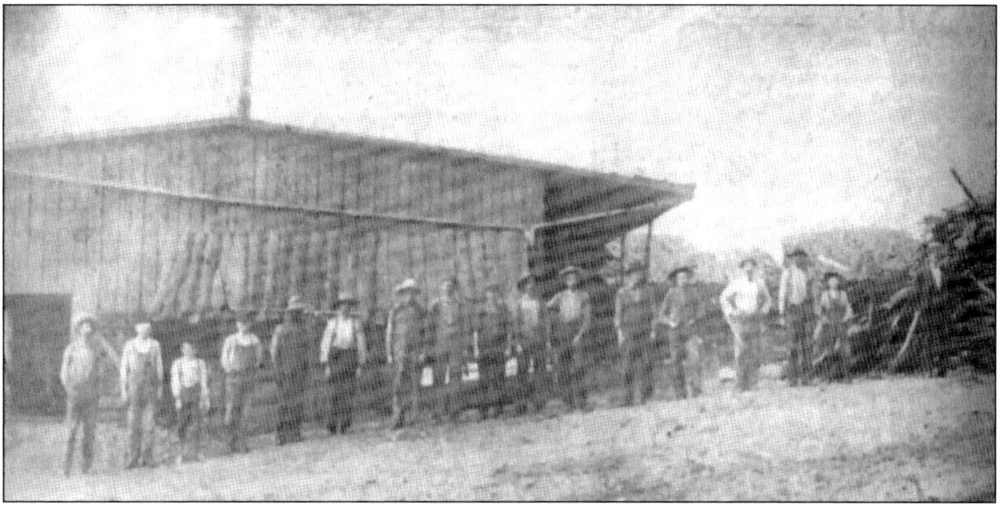

W. H. Shuler of Stanleyton advertised to buy any quantity of bark between Luray and Furnace No. 2. The Stanley Bark Mill processed and shipped this bulk commodity via the Shenandoah Valley Railroad to Luray Tannery, greatly relieving the burden placed on local wagon teams. Here employees pose outside the very basic structure in 1902. (*PN&C*.)

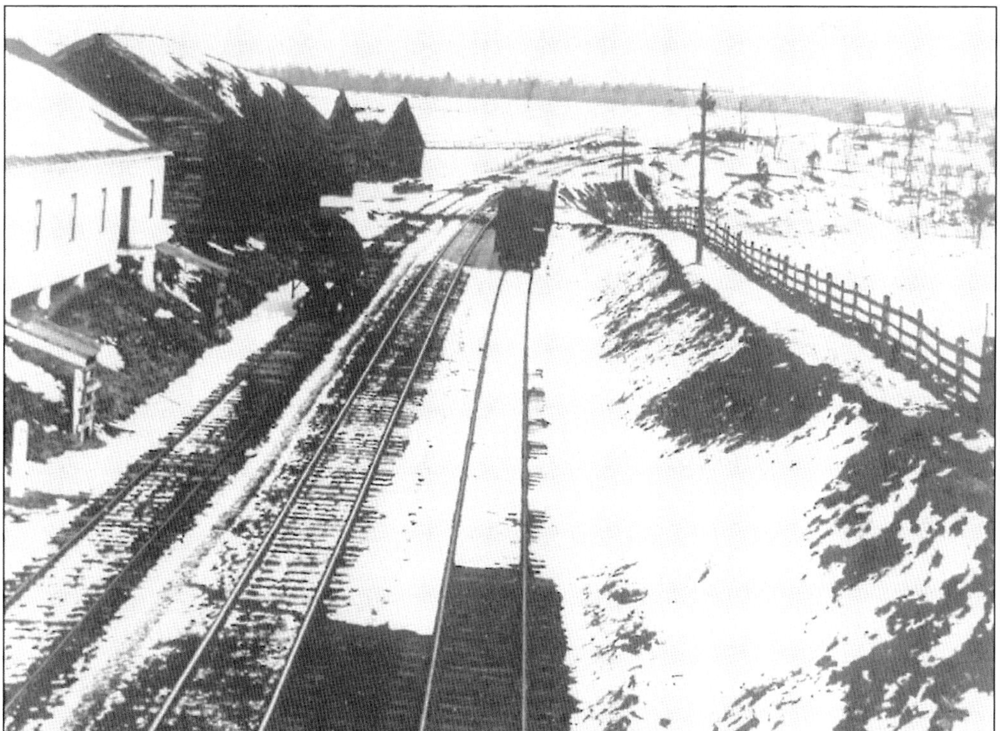

Tan bark was used in such large volume here that it became an issue in having sufficient quantities for continuous operations. Large parcels of land were purchased, not only in Page but in Madison and Shenandoah Counties as well, for nothing more than bark peeling rights. With the 50 tons needed ground daily, Deford installed their own bark mill by 1900. The bark ricks are seen at left. (Dan Vaughn.)

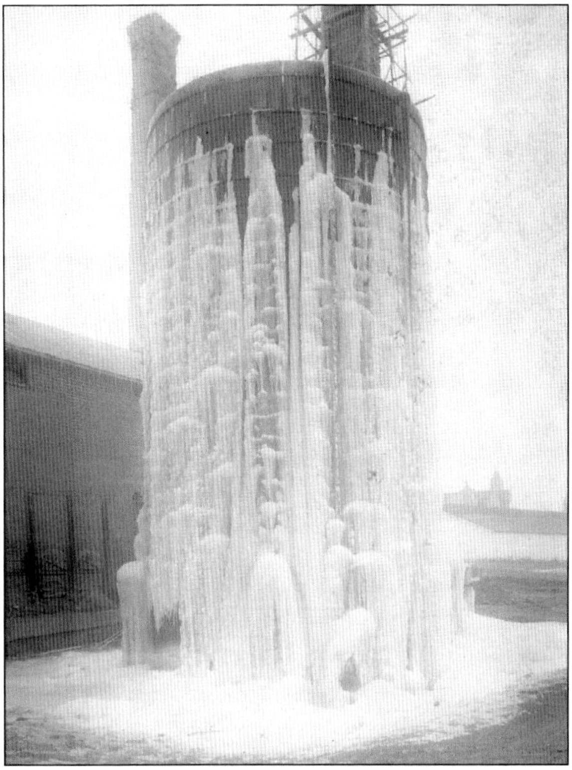

This wooden water tank at Deford Tannery, extruding water frozen in a cascade formation, puts on a picturesque display in 1893. A steel tank, erected thereafter, provided decades of service for this local industry. When it was dismantled in January 2007, the singular skyline vestige remaining was the last of three smokestacks, one of which was under construction, at top, when this image was taken. (*PN&C.*)

The Great Depression showed little favoritism, and in a forced sale through bankruptcy, the tannery was purchased in 1938 by the Federal Reserve Bank of Richmond. In 1940, Arthur Blaut reopened it as the Virginia Oak Tannery, and wartime needs were once again a priority. Men lined up for employment in this Wallace Rhodes image around 1920. (*PN&C.*)

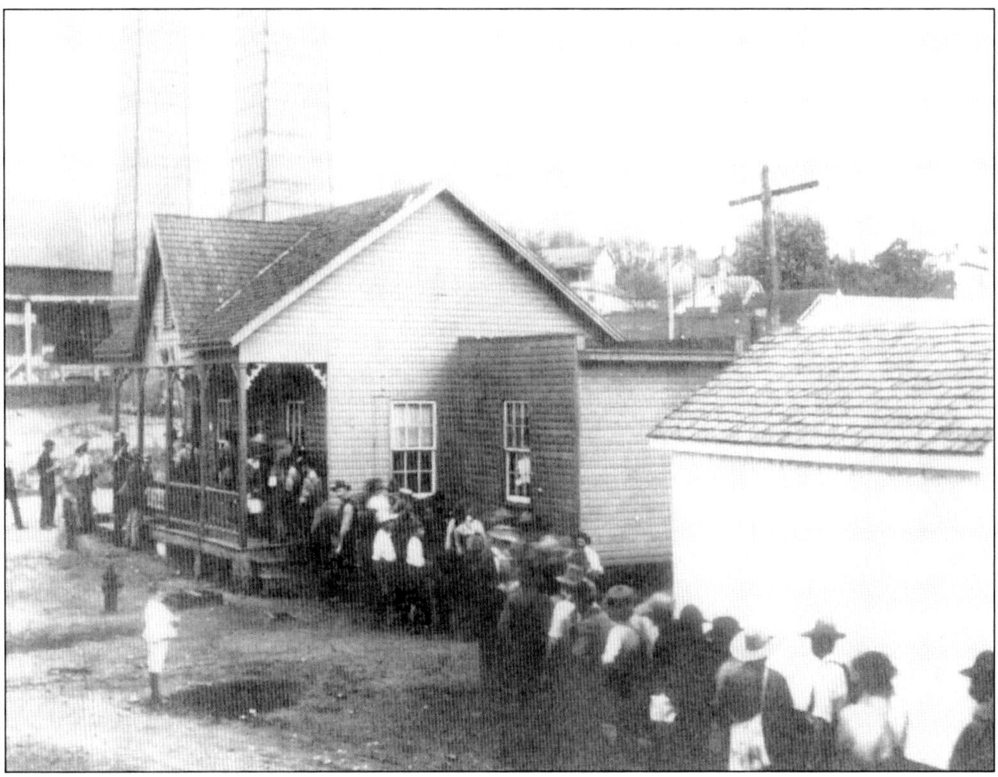

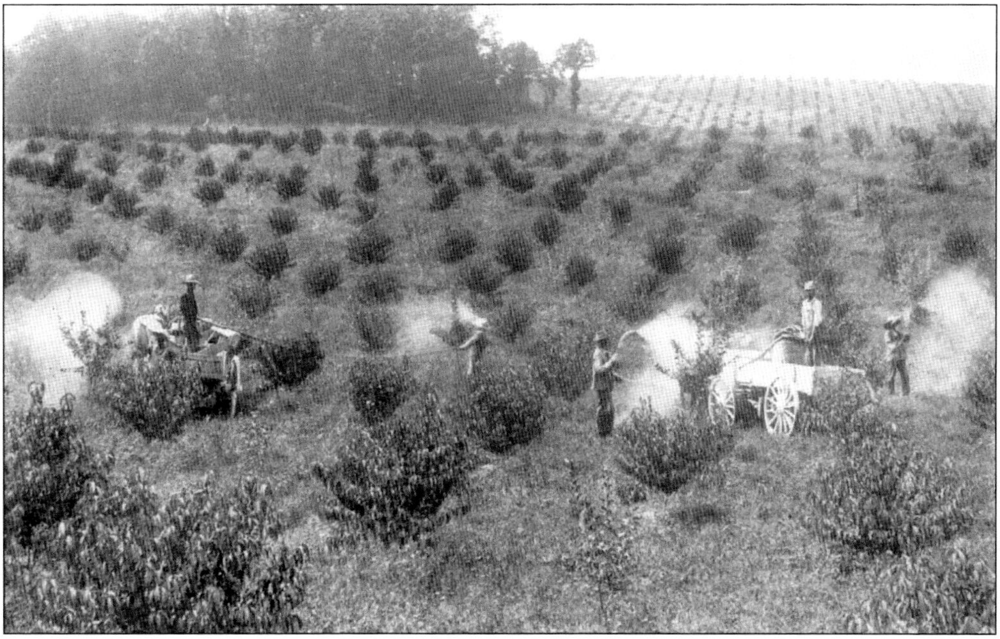

The Valley Land and Improvement Company provided the beginnings for the Deford Orchard Company when planting 4,000 pear trees in 1891. Adjacently, Joseph F. Stover planted 1,400 apple trees by 1894. In this 1913 image, manager C. E. Rhodes has laborers spray for San Jose scale to satisfy Page County fruit inspector S. L. Batman. Thomas Deford would ultimately name the business Luray Orchard Company, which remained unchanged when sold to M. E. Roudabush. (Dan Vaughn.)

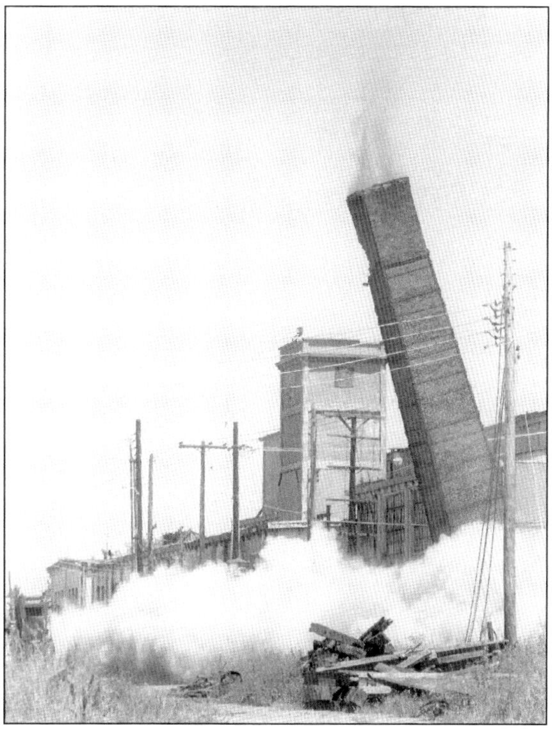

Built in 1882 by Ochs and Company of Allentown, Pennsylvania, and after 105 years of towering 90 feet above Luray, the oldest of three smokestacks constructed here met its end on August 14, 1987. Lightning damage is seen near the top. S. W. Strickler of Leaksville had delivered the bricks from Henkel's kiln to the tannery in 1889 for another stack that was razed in 1937. (Dan Vaughn.)

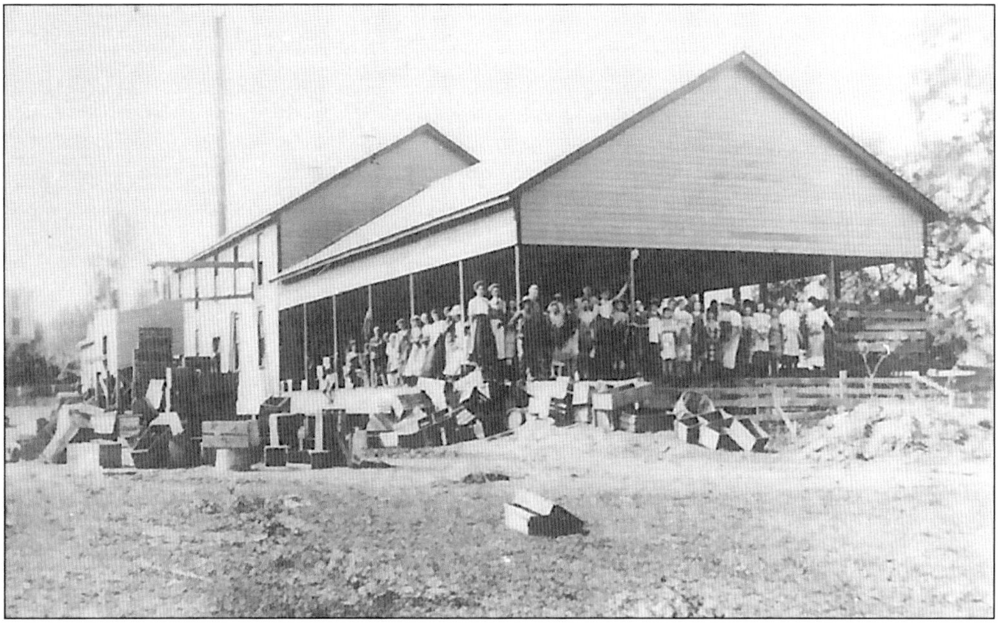

In 1903, F. M. Jones, W. H. Griffith, W. M. Rosser, and F. W. Weaver formed the Luray Canning Company. Built in 1906 by the Southern Construction Company, this cannery, Page County's earliest, operated on Luray's North Hawksbill Street. In 1914, it was purchased by I. N. Dovel, who continued the business in the same structure until it burned in 1950. (Dan Vaughn.)

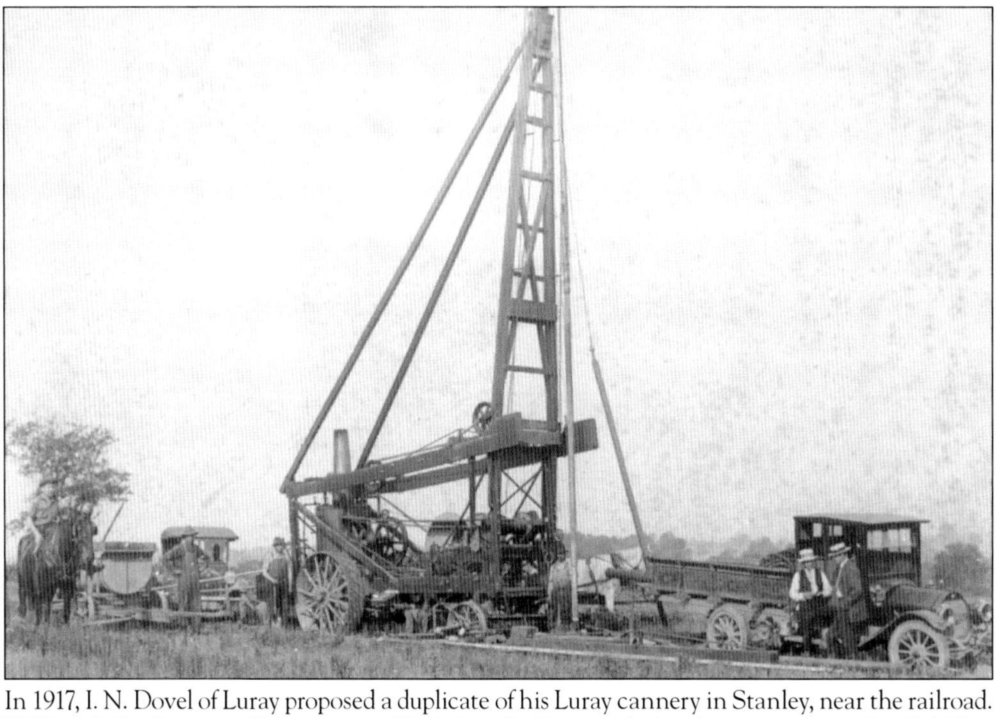

In 1917, I. N. Dovel of Luray proposed a duplicate of his Luray cannery in Stanley, near the railroad. William J. Gochenour of Mauertown, Virginia, a DuPont explosive demonstrator and well driller, was in charge of drilling an artesian well for the plant. At a depth of 20 feet, an ochre stratum, running 100 feet down, was struck. The venture was purportedly abandoned. (Melvin Miller.)

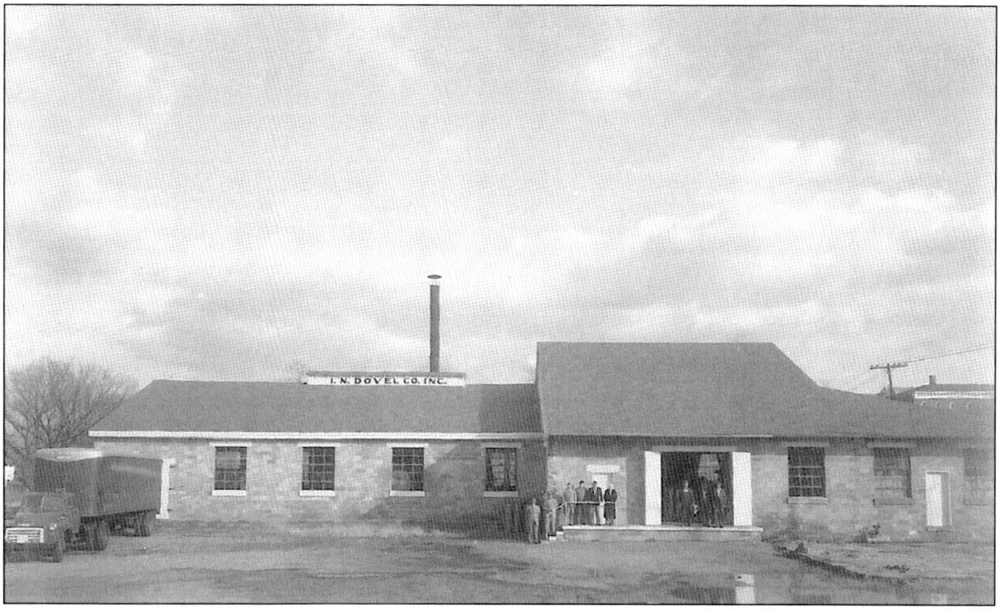

I. N. Dovel, rebuilding, continued the operation and renamed it Hawksbill Cannery, a brand that became the company's trademark. In 1952, Dovel's son, I. Randolph, pioneered canning dry land cress and in 1955 was still the only factory in the world to do so. Five hundred acres were planted that year. With the need and uncertainty in employing hundreds seasonally, he purchased Virginia's first automated bean picker in 1960. (*PN&C.*)

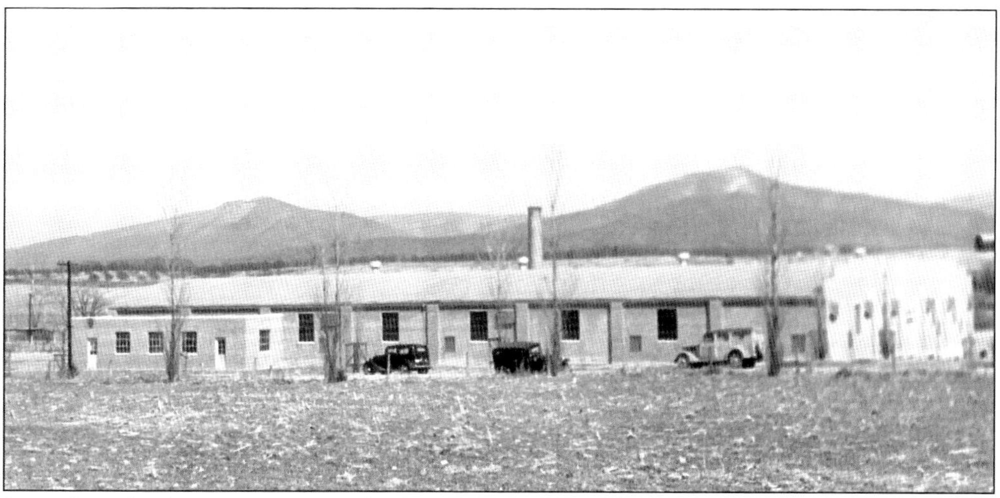

Luray Textile Corporation opened on March 28, 1941. The company "threw" (twisted) yarn into thread, a preparatory process in the manufacture of fabric. In May 1942, a large order was received for nylon thread for use in parachutes. With five expansions and a peak workforce of 450, the plant flourished until the 1970s, when inexpensive imports and changing technology caused its closure in 1985. The workers themselves were so close-knit that a reunion still exists after more than 20 years. (*PN&C.*)

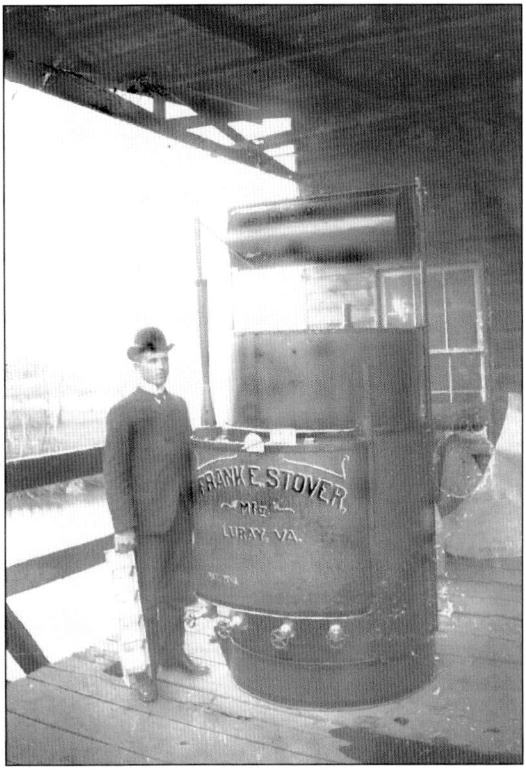

Revamping his acetylene gas apparatus and refining his appearance was Frank E. Stover's last attempt to capture the confidence of Luray. But his idea of gas lighting came at a precarious time in inventive history, when the alternating current principal of electric lighting took prominence. For decades after his venture's demise, Town of Luray employees unearthed his two-inch underground gas lines. Hawksbill Creek is seen at left in this glass-plate image. (*PN&C.*)

Debris accumulates beyond the spillway of the Shenandoah River power dam west of Luray. Pictured on the dam, from left to right, are John N. Black, James M. Black, Andrew Black, and an unidentified worker. Interestingly, Frank Stover, the project's initiator, previously designed a water-powered elevator for use in his F. E. Stover Hardware Store. (Nick Black.)

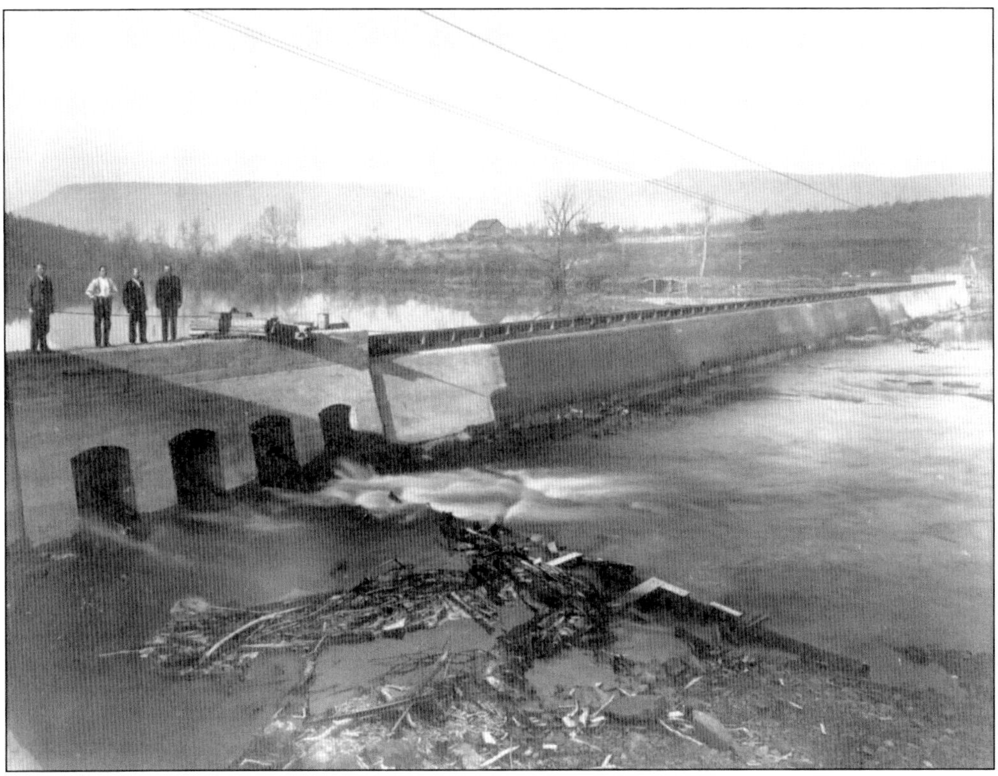

Renaming his business Luray Gas and Electric, Stover constructed a hydroelectric power dam, but after encountering difficulties, he was forced to sell to his competitor Charles Landram of the Shenandoah River Light and Power Corporation. Landram completed the project in December 1906, with the first current entering Luray on February 14, 1907. Initially a timber dam was built, but it was found faulty, with a concrete version constructed thereafter. Wanting more power, and with an engineer's advice, Landram precariously added a five-foot wooden extension, rendering the whole structure unstable. It proved catastrophic when it toppled during a freshet. The in-house Luray Electric Company and Deford Tannery electric plants somewhat remedied the situation, but it was M. E. Roudabush's newly constructed power plant at Newport that mainly provided during the emergency. Roudabush's Page Power Company would buy out Landram. With another dam in Shenandoah, a fourth was proposed at Overall but never built. Below, inside the powerhouse, engineer James Black looks Lilliputian among the plant's mechanical workings in this 1907 Wallace Rhodes image. (Right, Nancy Lee Shifflett; below, Gaylon Waters.)

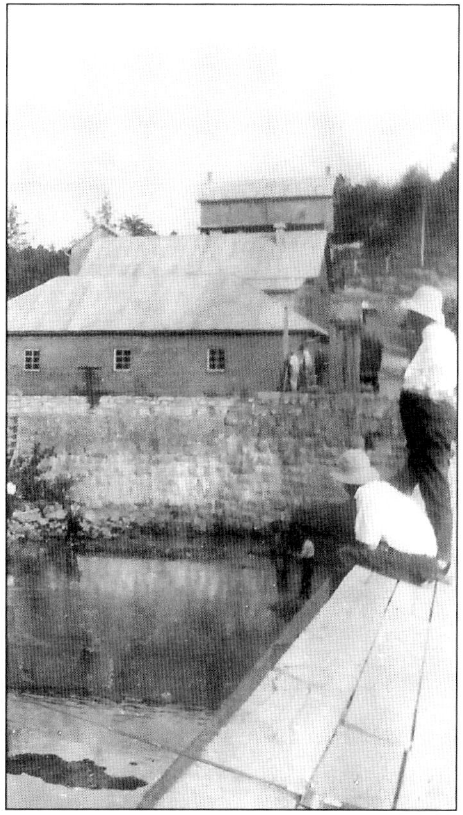

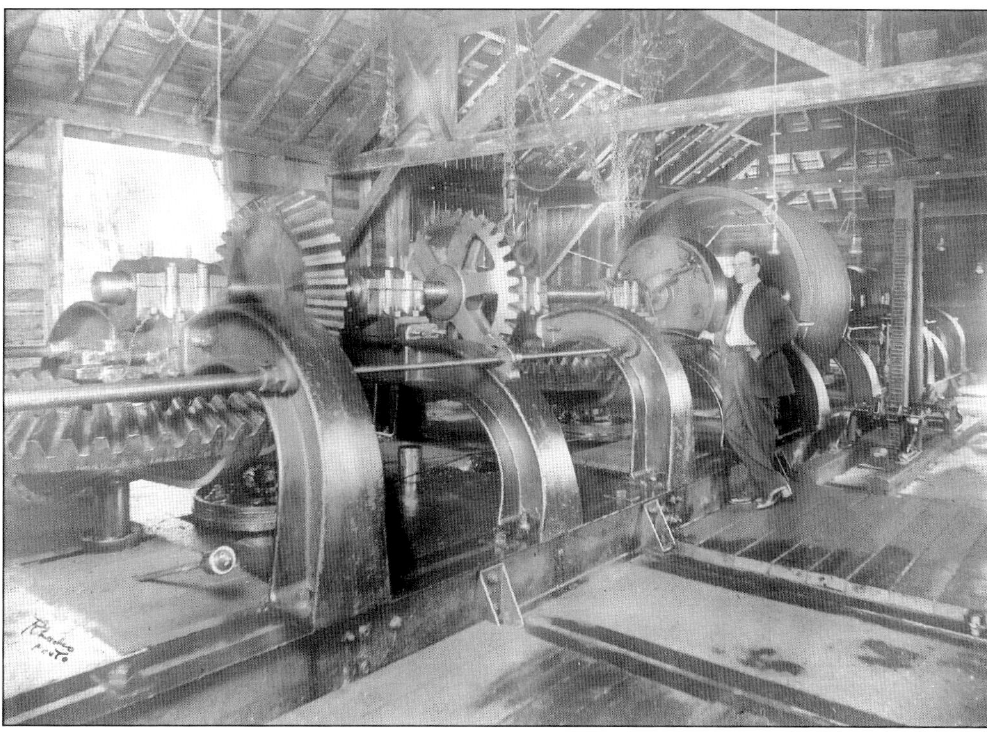

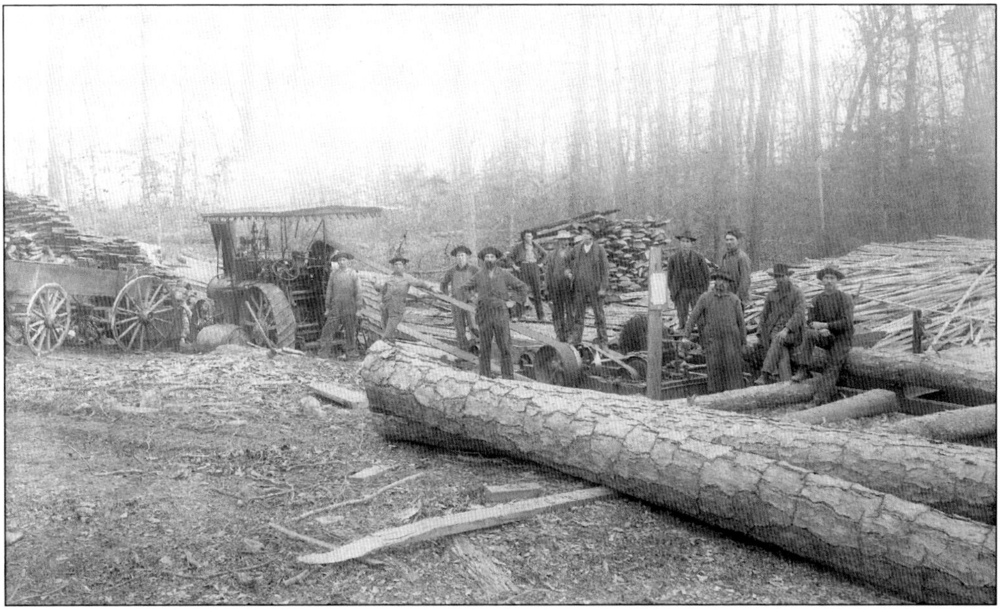

Jacob D. Frazier (center) was in charge of this 1910s sawmill operation on the Cletus Brubaker land outside Luray. The Geiser Peerless steam traction engine greatly increased productivity of this laborious profession. In January 1905, Frazier and his men sawed 31,000 feet of lumber in just six days in the Joseph Spitler woods. (Harry Price Jr.)

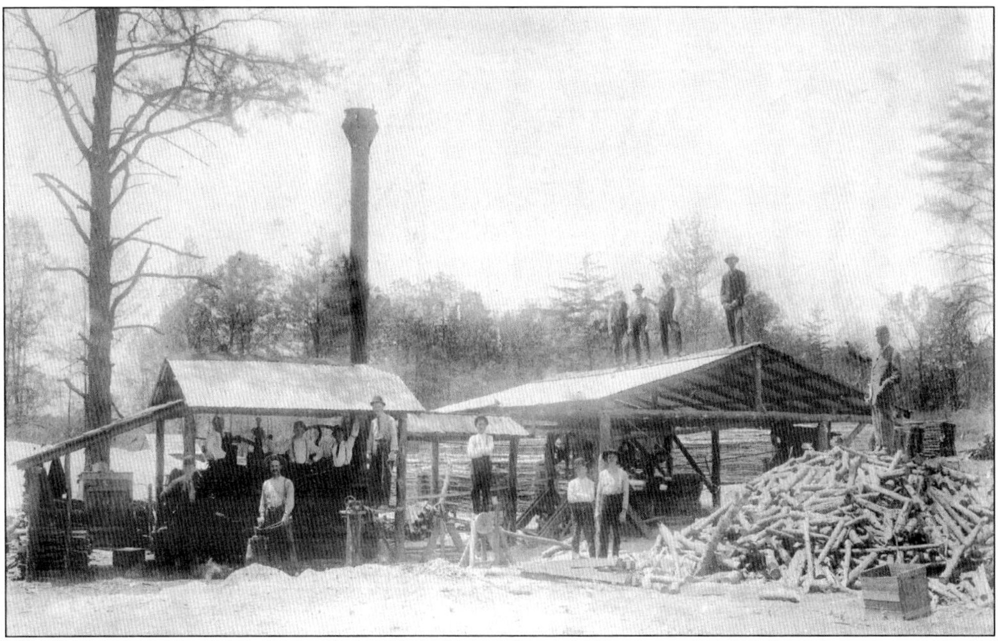

An 1884 *Page Courier* stated, "Page has too many sawmills." But with fires came the need. Luray ultimately passes a fire ordinance prohibiting the use of flammable materials in reconstruction. Pictured outside Stanley are, from left to right, (on the ground) Ward Owens, Walter Jenkins, Frank Parks, Dan Taylor, Harry Parks, Bob Breeden, H. Taylor (at grindstone), Sonny Sours, and Walt Berry; (on the roof) Homer Jenkins, Marvin Jenkins, Mahlon Jenkins, and Carl Jenkins; (on the woodpile) N. Weakley. (Gaylon Waters.)

Three

COMMERCE STREET

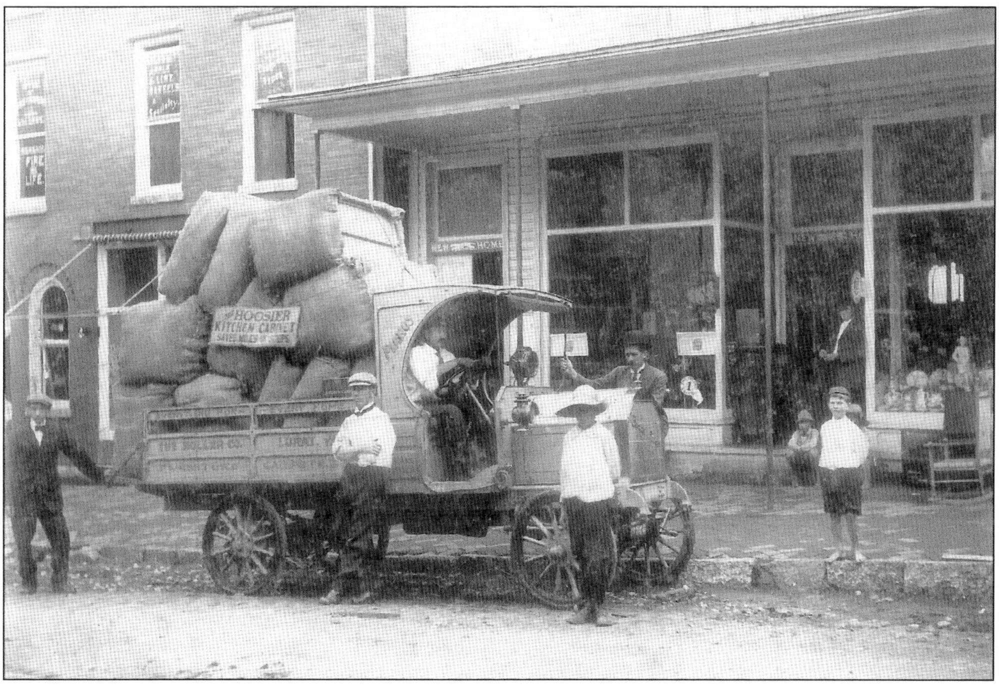

The Roller Company's John A. Roller, seated in the right-hand-drive, "C"-cab truck, encouraged business by offering deliveries, such as the load of Hoosier kitchen cabinets in this fascinating c. 1912 image. Joseph Franklin Kibler leans, arms folded, against the wooden-spoke, rubber-treaded B. F. Board truck. A souvenir of Herbert Barbee's East End Confederate Soldier Monument is displayed at right, while at center, behind the cab, is the doorway leading to the Luray Opera House. (Marleen Hansen.)

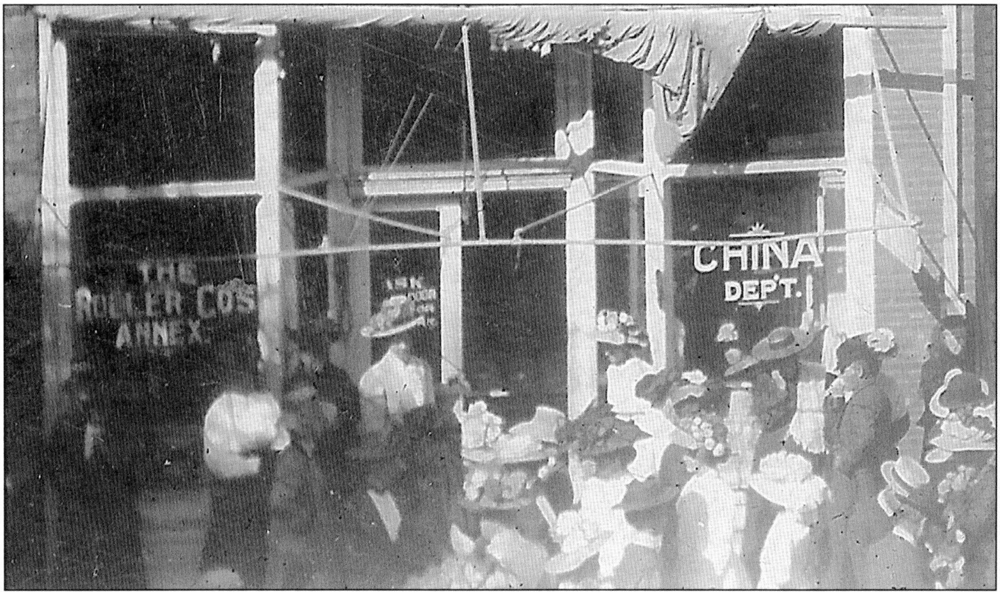

Patrons flocked to the Roller Company on this September 28, 1909, Roller Days event on East Main Street. The store opened May 27, 1905, in the old Luray YMCA, expanding thereafter with this First National Bank Building annex one door west. Taking over the Sachs and Company Storehouse at the time, they were suited for the housewife as they advertised having "everything for every house," including Bouldier player pianos, carpet, and cookstoves. (Ann Vaughn.)

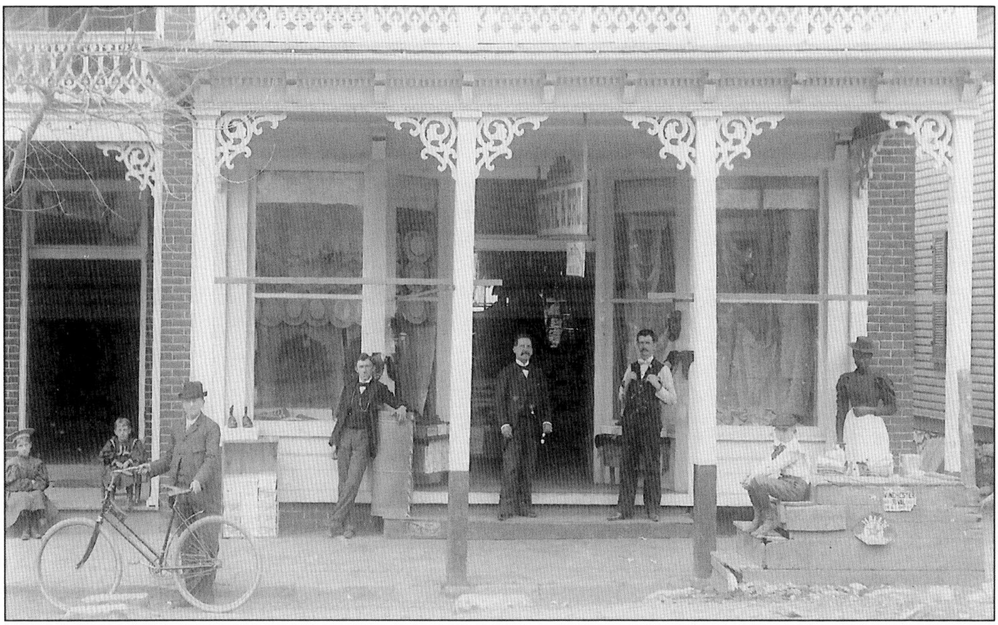

In 1881, C. B. Woodward sold this house (the current Luray Copy Service) to Grove and Brother of Massanutten for $725 to operate a general merchandise store. Merchants John W. Grove and brother Charles H. had originated in Massanutten in 1873, and they advertised their store as the "Crystal Palace" of London's Great Exhibition popularity. John's two sons, Arthur and Harry, continued the store's success, with his daughter, Julia Anita Grove, ultimately operating an antique shop here until its closure in 1976. (Dorothy Grove.)

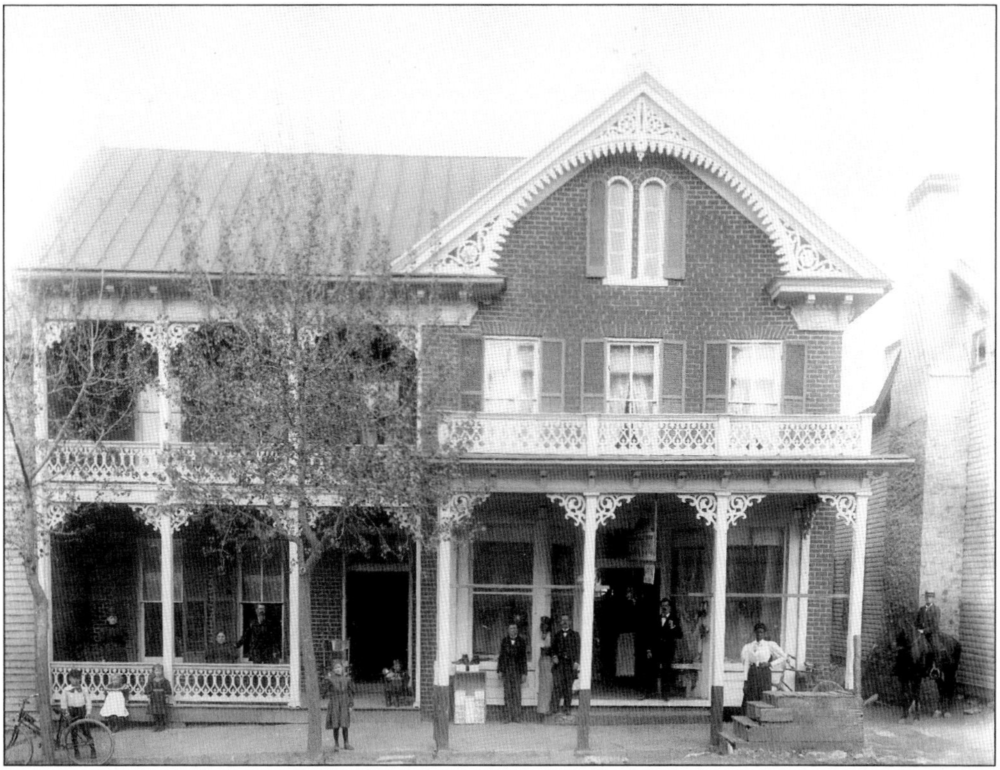

This vintage scene revives recollections of Luray's Main Street around 1900, when elm and maple trees lined the thoroughfare and stone steps were laid for street crossings. In this classic image of Grove and Brother are, from left to right, Harold Elon Grove, three unidentified, Laura Brumback Grove, John W. Grove, Jessamine Lee Grove, Julia Anita Grove, William G. Fitch, Charles H. Grove, Hugh W. Cary, Mitty Lewis, and Arthur Ashby Grove on a horse. (Dorothy Grove.)

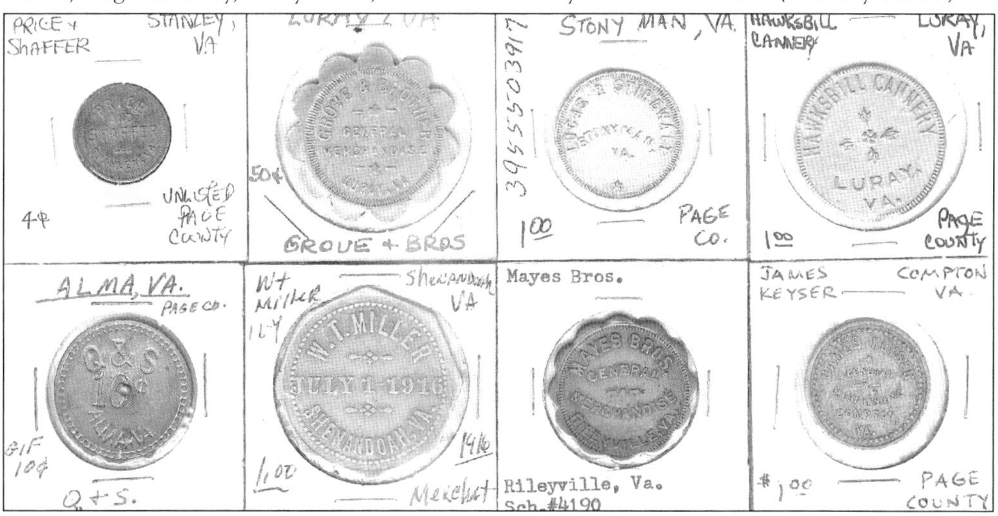

To increase business and promote loyalty, local merchants began the issuance of trade tokens. Made of aluminum, brass, bronze, tin, and even pasteboard, they were used as a form of in-store credit redeemable only at the store listed. More than 30 merchants used this very creative barter-like system throughout Page during the first half of the 20th century. (Dan Vaughn.)

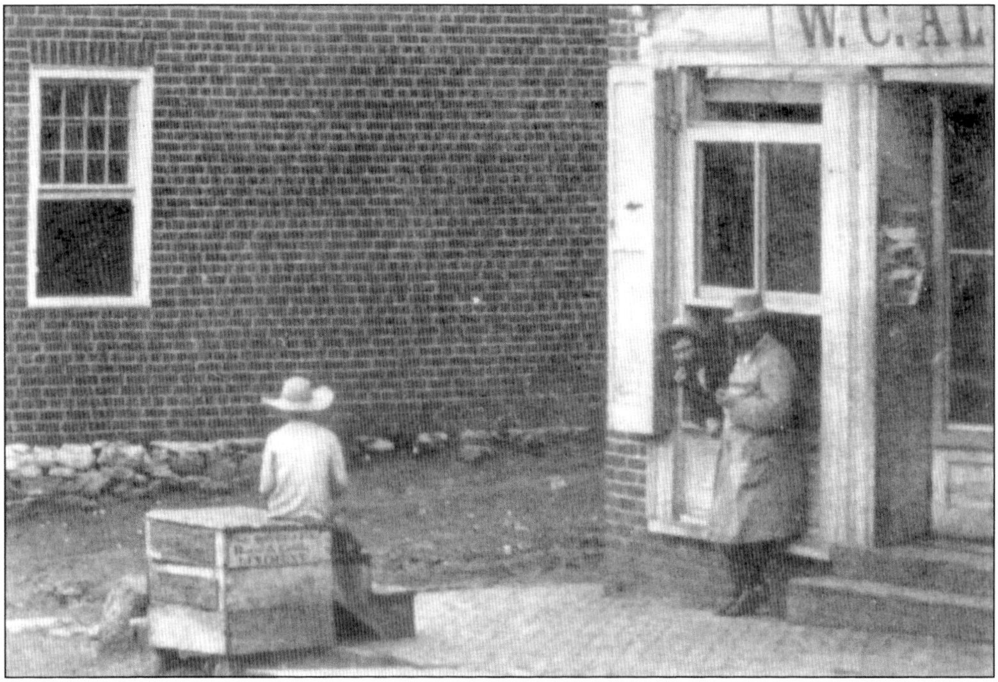

With the number of staged photographs during this era, one wonders what the specific subject was here. Taken in the 1880s, it may be the only existing image of the William C. Alther General Merchandise Store on West Main Street, where Luray Caverns prediscovery conversations took place. Caverns codiscoverer Benton Stebbins visited here often for information since he had just recently moved from Easton, Maryland. (© *Discovery of Luray Caverns, Virginia* by Russell H. Gurnee.)

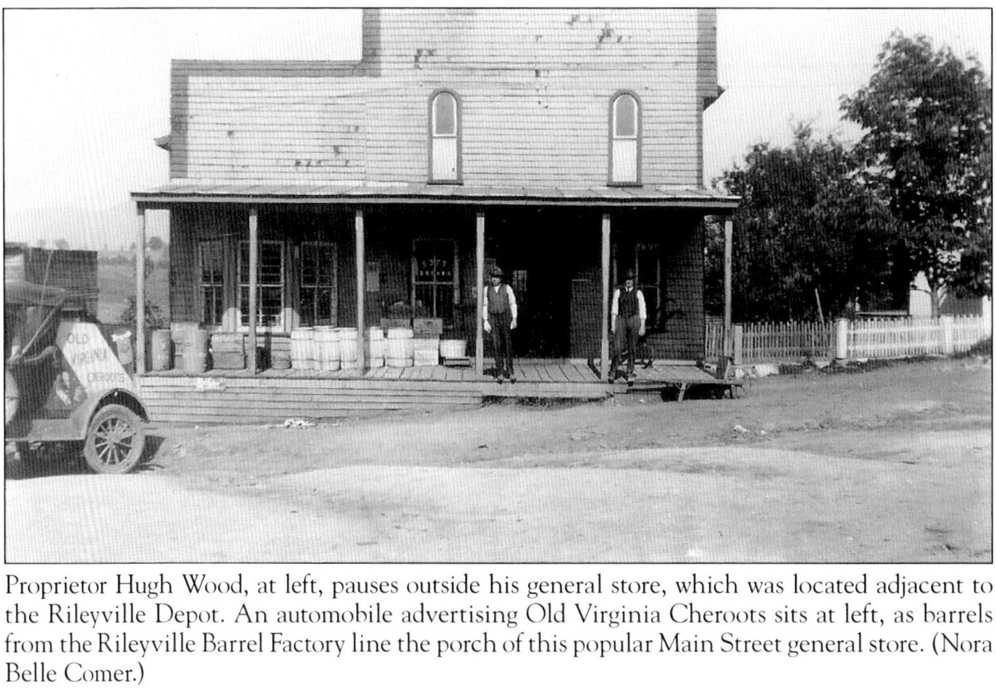

Proprietor Hugh Wood, at left, pauses outside his general store, which was located adjacent to the Rileyville Depot. An automobile advertising Old Virginia Cheroots sits at left, as barrels from the Rileyville Barrel Factory line the porch of this popular Main Street general store. (Nora Belle Comer.)

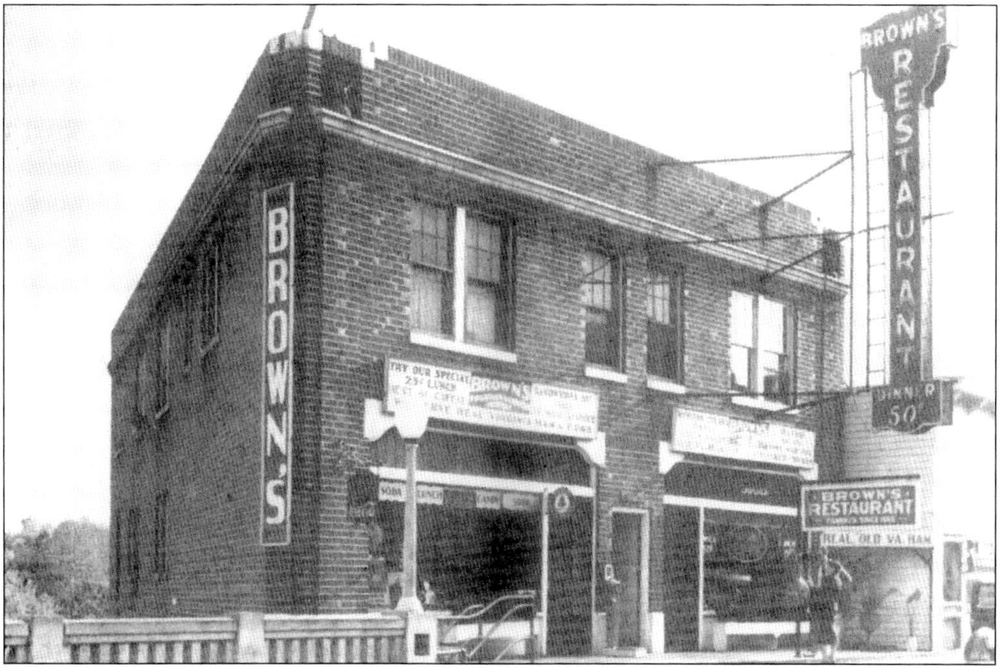

In 1915, brothers James M. and Thomas C. Brown ran a meatpacking business on West Main Street before opening Brown's Restaurant. In November 1938, a coon hunter's banquet was held with the main entrée unlisted. In 1940, the popular business moved across West Main to its current location. Chinese cuisine was added in 1973 to the now almost century-old mainstay. (*PN&C*.)

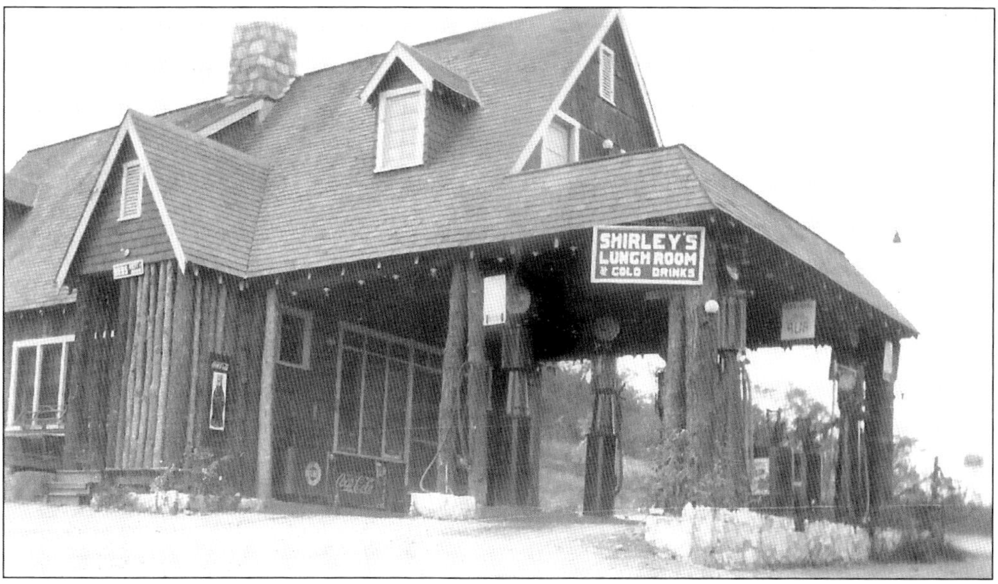

Built in the 1920s, Shirley's Lunch Room capitalized on New Market Gap's automobile crossing. Run by brothers Tom and Zach Shirley, the non-electric establishment offered bare necessities of gasoline, cold drinks, and wood stove–grilled sandwiches. The short-lived eatery was later purchased by the National Forest Service and converted into the present-day visitor's center. In 1956, Massanutten Mountain's three-lane expansion forced the removal of the diagonally located Kauffman's Restaurant. (Lois Foley.)

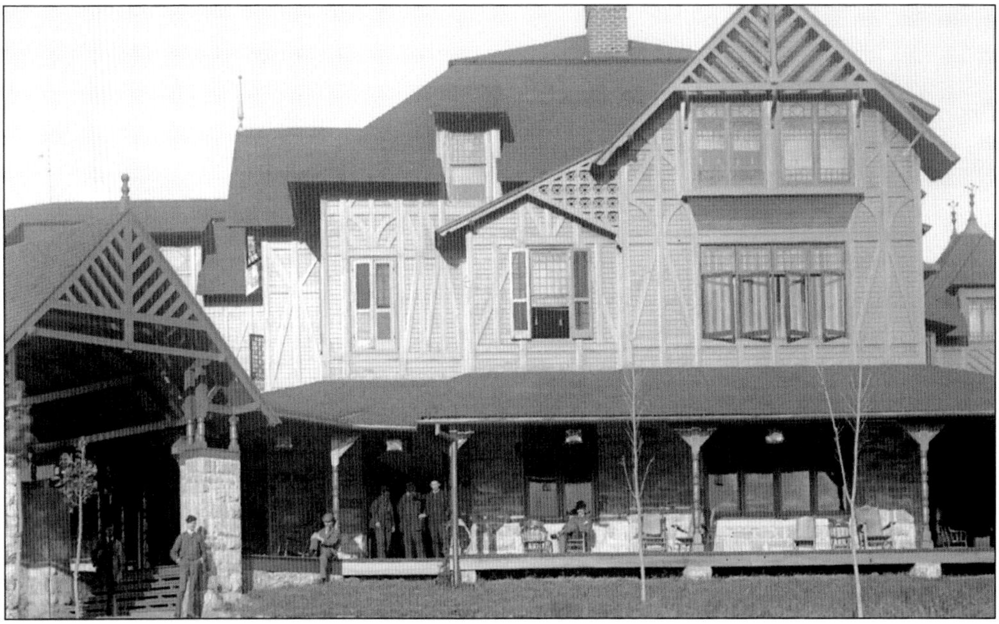

Construction of Luray Inn began May 2, 1881, with its opening a mere four months later. With large locomotive lamps, inn contractor Julius Holmes worked his crews day and night until completion. Among the exorbitance at the time of this 1886 view was electricity, trainloads of ice from Gettysburg, telephones, two-horse lawn mowers, and an automatic iron gate. Oddly enough, the inn contained a "smoking room" in a time when fires were almost a continual event. (George Eastman House.)

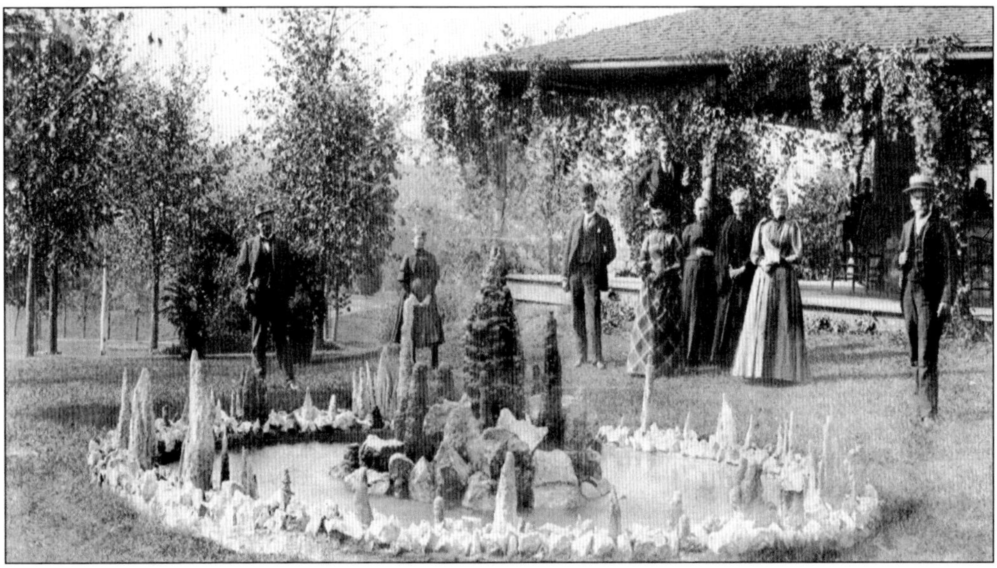

In fall 1882, Excelsior Nurseries of Rochester, New York, landscaped the grounds with royal oaks of England, Japanese maples, maidenhair trees, and American elms. A vine-covered piazza fronted the building's entire length. On May 29, 1883, the inn's first marriage was performed when William Burner and Elizabeth Brubaker were united in matrimony. Added in August 1890, this fairyland-like fountain, fed by Siebert's Spring, was popular with both children and adults. (Curtis Harrell.)

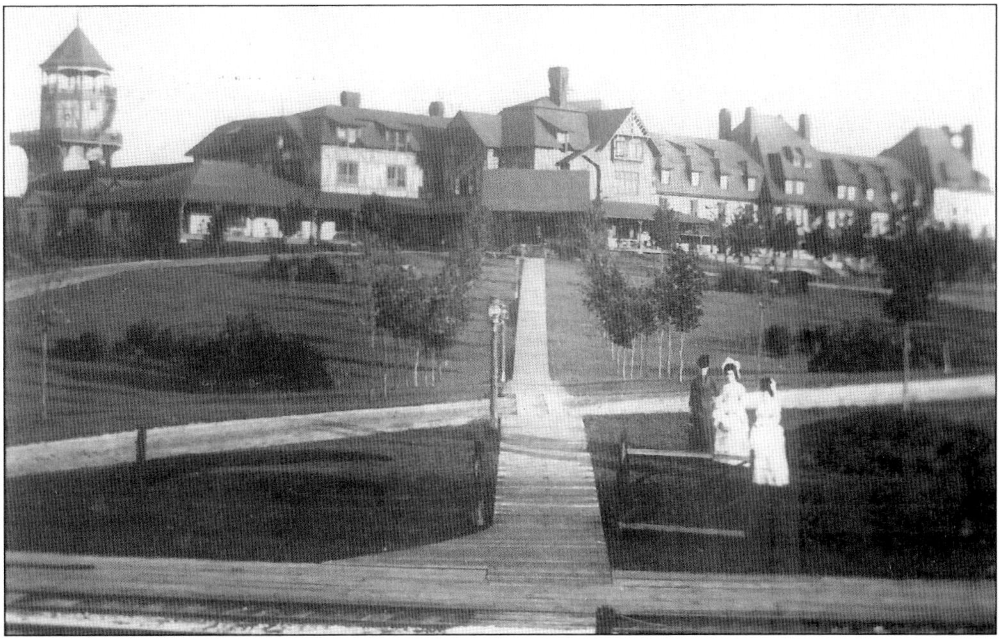

When SVRR had Philadelphian architect George Pearson design this Queen Anne and Tudor–style hostelry, its purpose was to serve as a staging area for excursionists to the newly discovered Luray Cave. They profited two-fold, royally—for a season. The elliptical loop drive, macadamized with white sand in 1884, was bordered with American elms, while the plank walkway, lined with kerosene lanterns, directed visitors to the inn, 200 yards uphill from Luray Station. S. K. Wright took this *c.* 1888 photograph. (*PN&C.*)

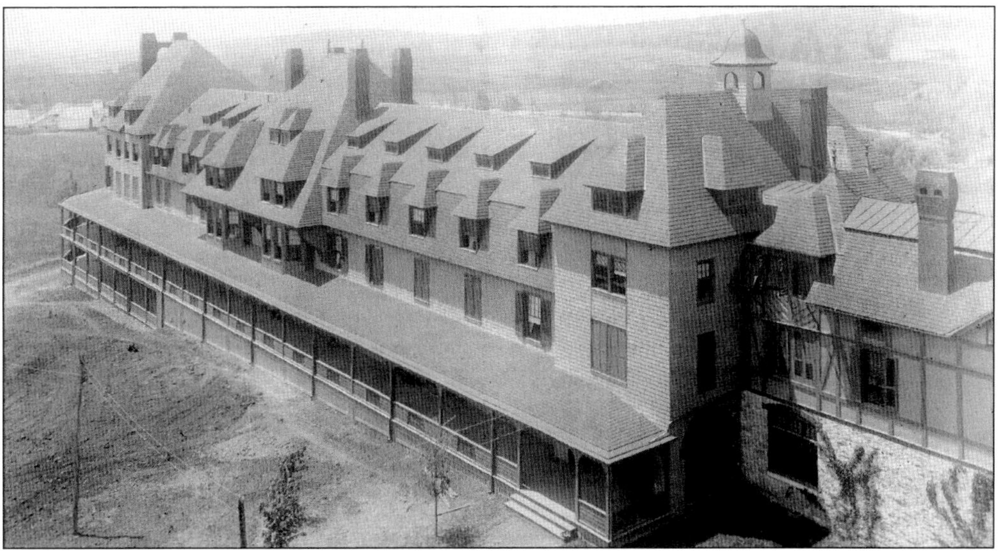

In 1887, a 100-room addition, newly built here, juts 245 feet southward, perpendicular to Luray's Main Street. Its enormous mansard roof, fitted with nooks, turrets, and dormers, was covered with slate, as seen in this eastside (rear) view. Cypress shingles from Alabama clothed its upper floors' exterior, while native limestone, comprising the first story, was quarried locally. An automatic sprinkler system, contemplated following the addition, most unfortunately never materialized. (Warren and Penny Smith.)

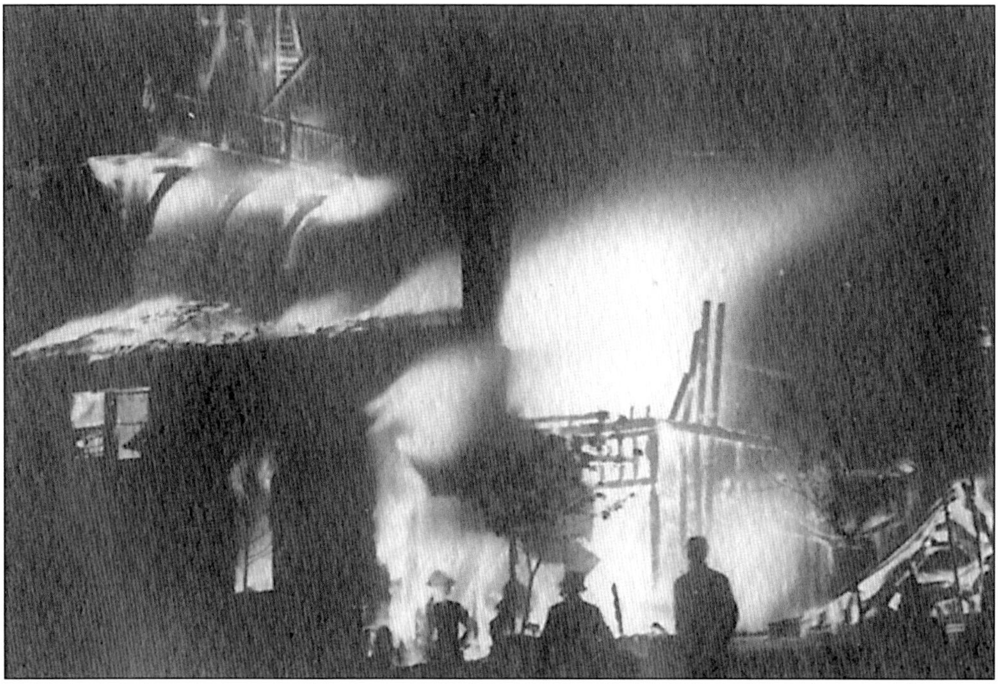

English capitalists, meeting at the inn with SVRR's Frederick Kimball and Joseph Sands, discussed an expansion. Sadly, the ink reporting the successful meeting had barely dried in *Page Courier*'s November 5, 1891, issue when disaster struck. The Hawksbill looked like liquid fire, and newspapers were read two miles away in its glow. This Silas Wright photograph, one of only two known images of the inn's fire, was a constant reminder to night watchman C. H. O'Neal. (*PN&C.*)

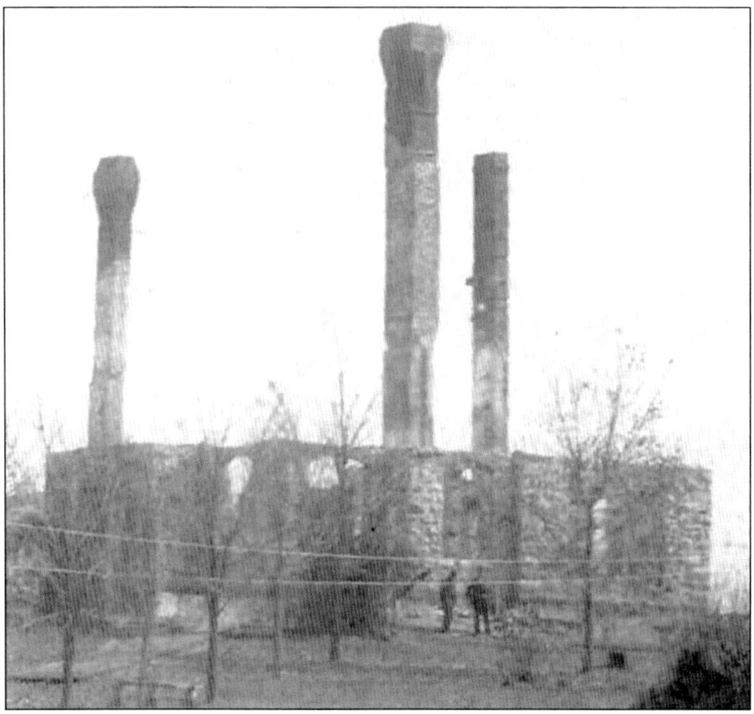

This image needed no description, for it spoke all too loud in its stark silence. The elm trees, leafless in their dormancy, seemed to empathize with the inn in the tragedy on this November 1891 afternoon. Two unidentified gentlemen at center ponder the fire's destruction, for architect Pearson's efforts were gone, never to be repeated here. The stone wall would later be crushed to macadamize Main Street. (*PN&C.*)

The inn, burning under more than questionable circumstances considering the widespread severity of the 1890s depression, was nonetheless gone. Something resembling the Luray Singing Tower under construction was all that remained of the old inn tower. E. J. Reed posed here in July 1900 with the remnant, left, seemingly for sentimental reasons. The loss to the town was monumental, for they had prided themselves on their "Castle on a Hill." (Dan Vaughn.)

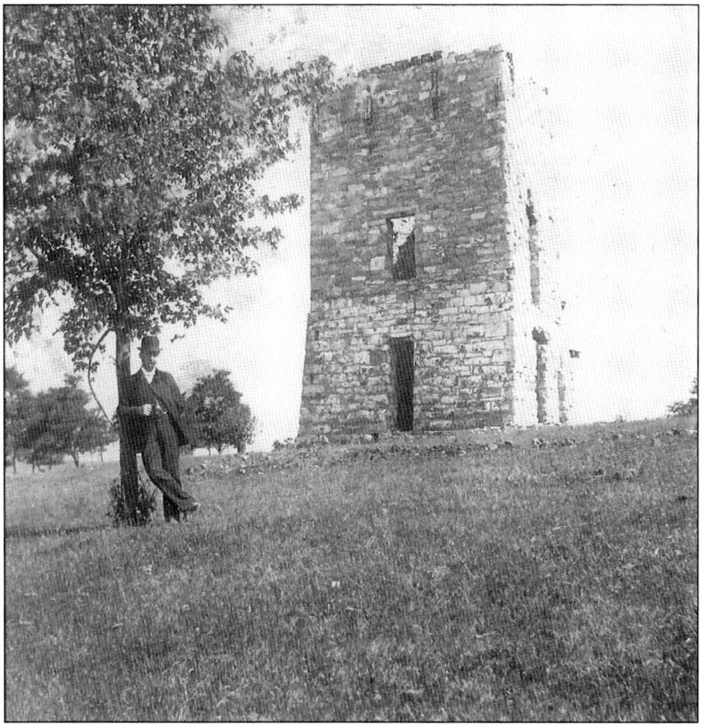

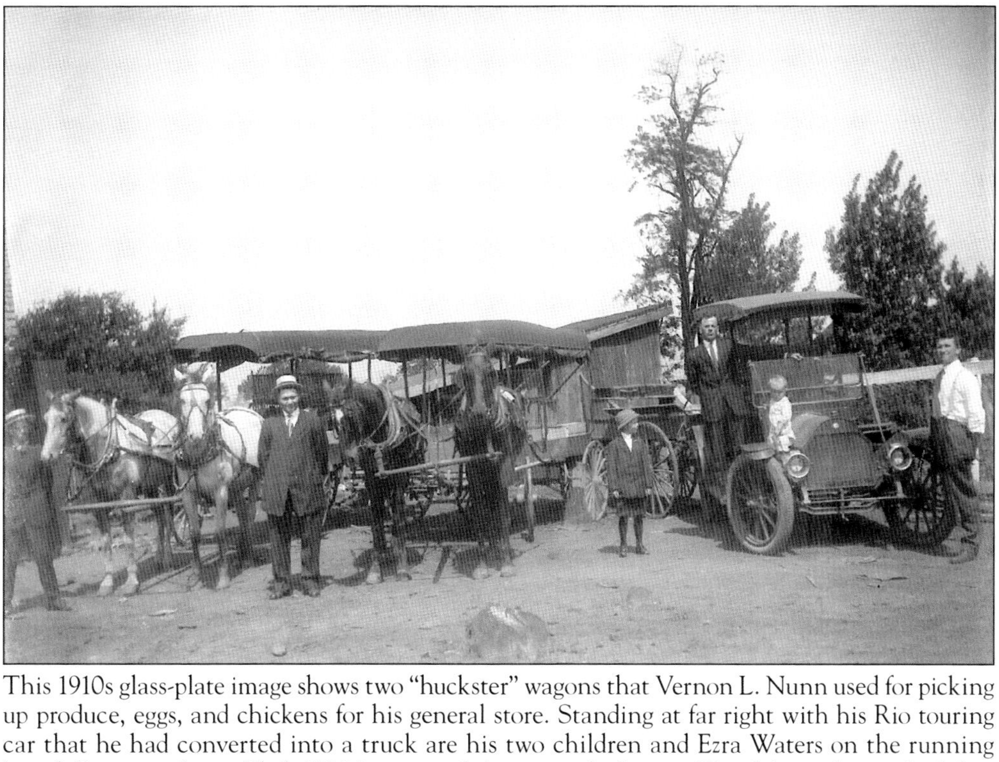

This 1910s glass-plate image shows two "huckster" wagons that Vernon L. Nunn used for picking up produce, eggs, and chickens for his general store. Standing at far right with his Rio touring car that he had converted into a truck are his two children and Ezra Waters on the running board. Store employee Clyde W. Nunn stands between the horses. The delivery boy at far left is unidentified. (*PN&C*.)

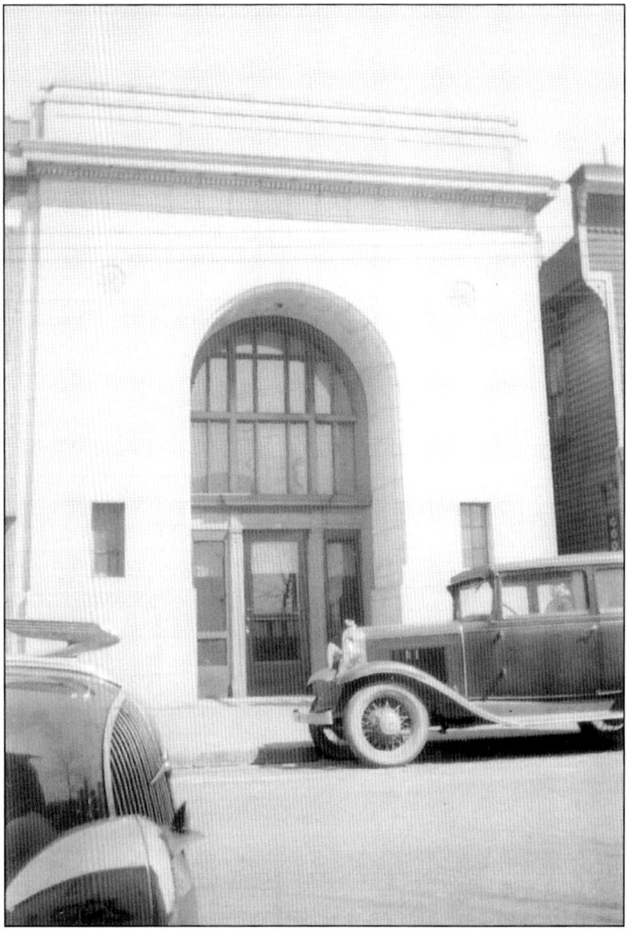

In 1891, *Page Courier* spoke on behalf of the need for a bank in Shenandoah City. Established in October 1903, it nationalized on October 21, 1918, to become the First National Bank of Shenandoah. Its first president, George W. Kite, had a competent core of Shenandoah's prominence under him. (Dan Vaughn.)

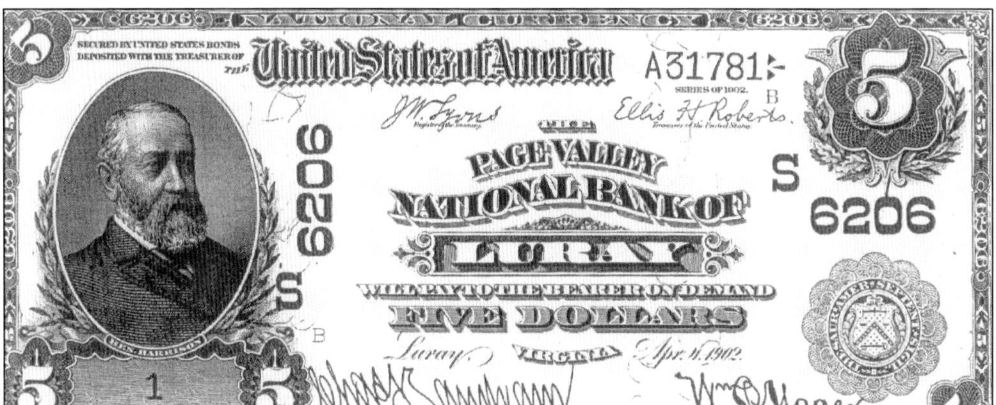

Nationalized in April 1902, the Page Valley National Bank issued this serial No. 1, $5 denomination in the Third Chapter of national currency notes (1902–1922). National ("hometown") Notes instilled trust and were secured by U.S. Treasury Bonds in the pre-FDIC days. Bank president William O. Yager, along with cashier Charles Landram, an original founder, signed the note. The First National Bank of Luray and the Farmers and Merchants Bank of Stanley also issued local notes. (Page Valley Bank.)

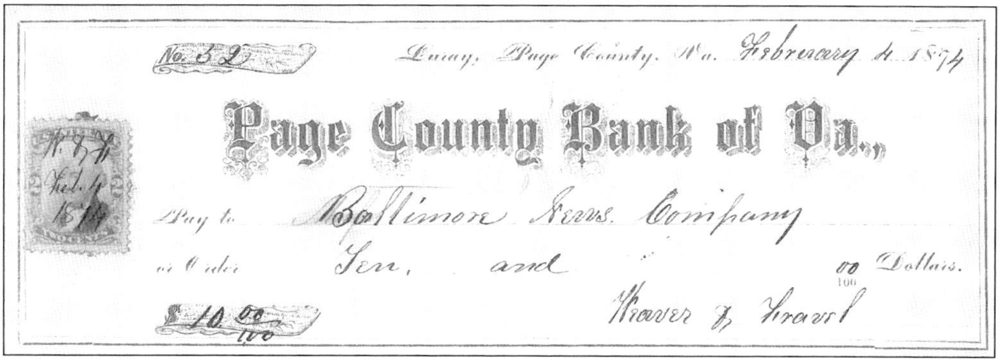

The Page County Bank of Virginia, a forerunner not only to the Page Valley and First National Banks, but also to the earlier private banks of J. V. Jamison and Brother, N. A. Rust, and the D. F. Kagey Company of Luray. Very little is known about this local bank, Page County's first. A gilded sign was hung, giving it a city-like appearance. Locating on Luray's West Main Street, it formed during Reconstruction on January 1, 1873, and had folded by 1880. (Dan Vaughn.)

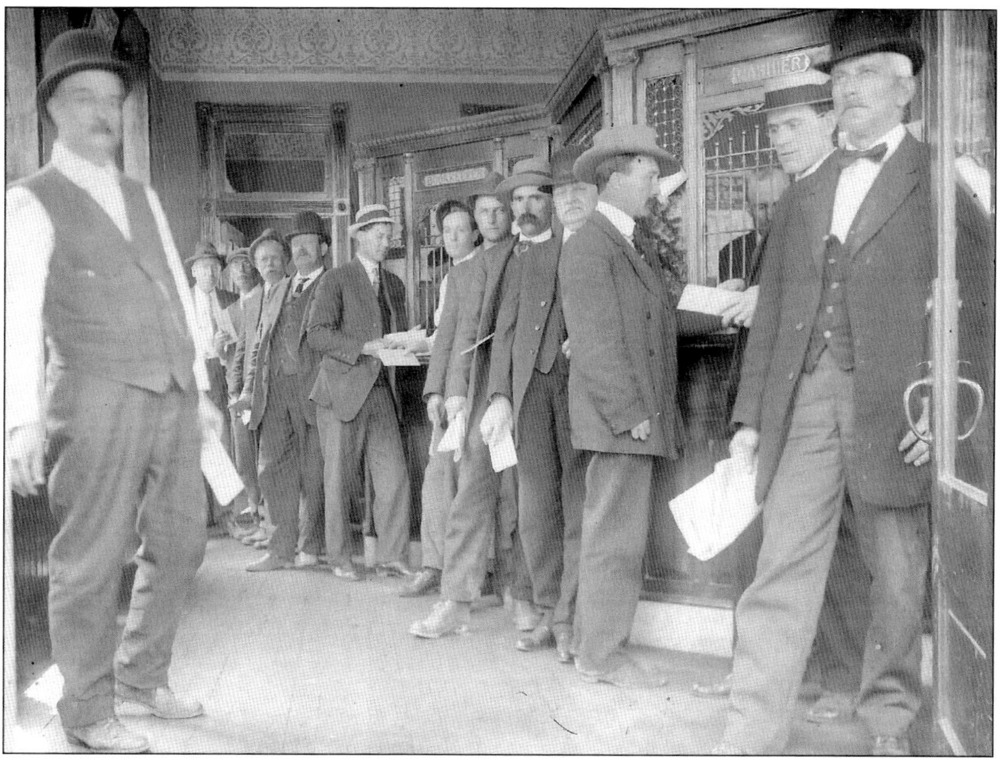

Pictured in the C. B. Foote Building on opening day, December 3, 1909, is the first location (still standing) of Farmers and Merchants Bank. C. C. Louderback hands out shareholder's stock certificates at the cashier's window. At left foreground is Stanley merchant Theodore Shryock. Continuing from left to right are Sumpter Kibler, Ed Manor, C. B. Foote, Benton Shenk, Edward Louderback, Oscar Louderback, William Graves, Lester Kite, David Modisett, Wilbur Miller, Virgil Petefish, and William Shuler. A new bank was built across Main Street in 1912. (Town of Stanley.)

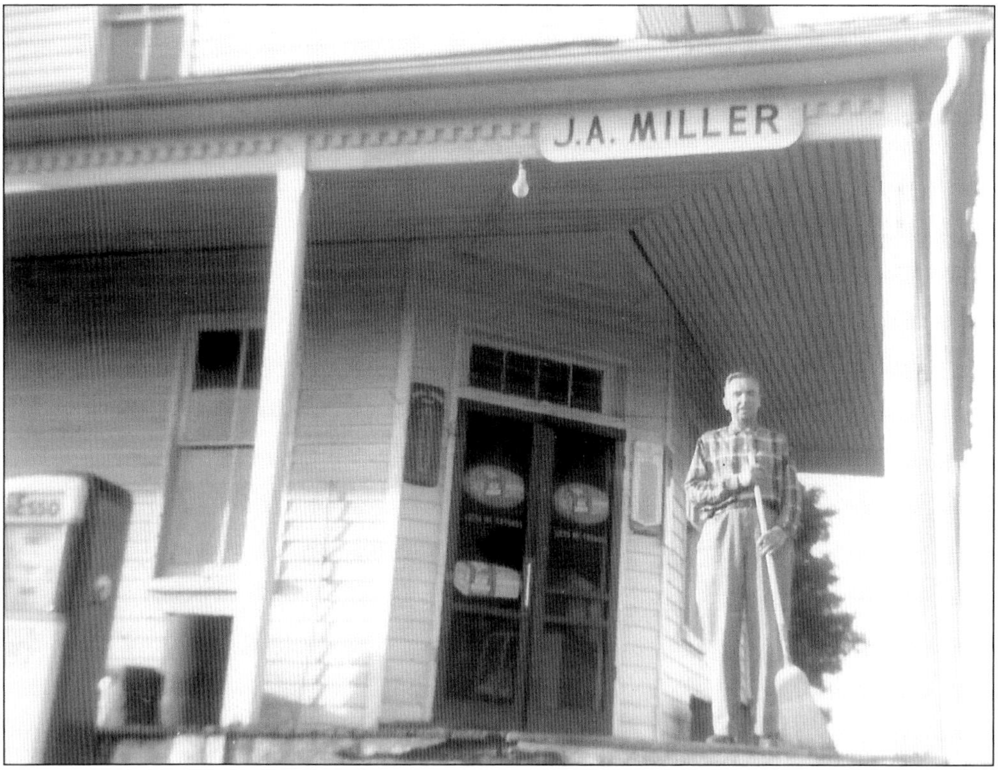

In 1961, John A. Miller and his wife, Edna, purchased this general store in Rileyville from Roy Gochenour. Pictured in September 1963, John poses on the porch of this typical country store. It offered everything from horse collars to penny candy when it opened in the late 1890s, and for 30 years, it served as the voting poll for the Rileyville precinct. (Nancy Waldo.)

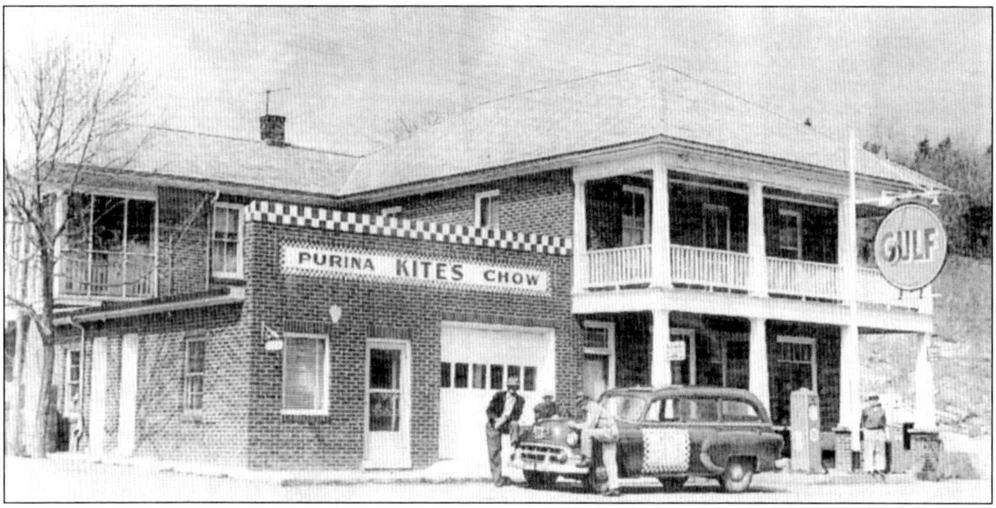

Kite's Store in Newport had its humble beginnings in 1913 in a shed-like structure by brothers-in-law Harry Kite and Carl Foltz. After moving in 1929 to its present location, H. Wilson Kite purchased it in 1936. This 1950s image shows, from left to right, Harry Kite, unidentified, Pete Price, and Charlie Foltz. Current proprietors Bill and Sylvia Deavers continue this quaint local business that is soon to celebrate its first century. (Dan Vaughn.)

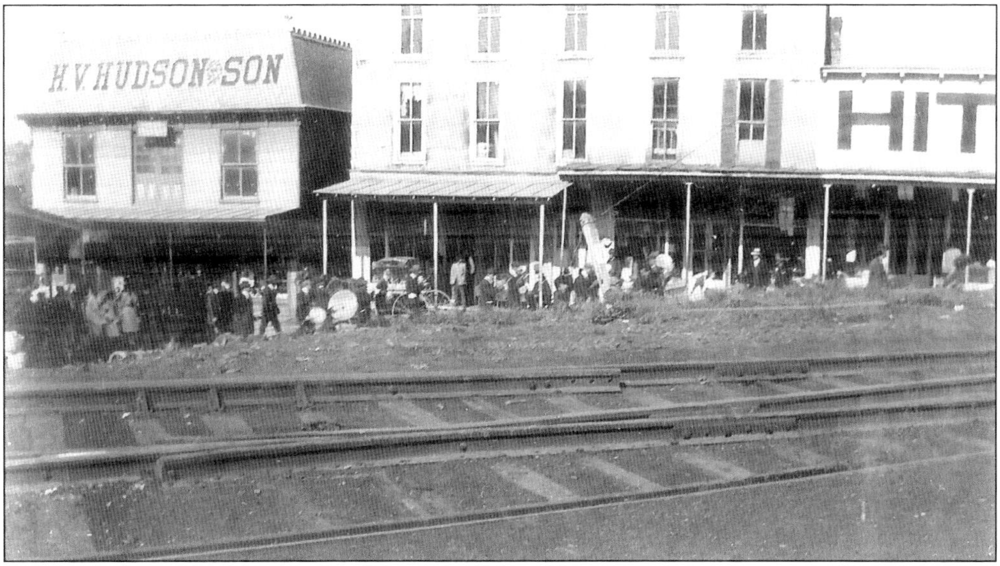

H. V. "Bud" Hudson initially partnered with A. L. Jameson in this catch-all enterprise opened in 1882. By 1887, a second story with metal covering was added. Advertised in 1890 as the "farmer's headquarters," they sold Champion reapers, Oliver chilled plows, Stover windmills, and Frick traction engines, and yet the same advertisements listed beautiful lamps, tea sets, and all kinds of glassware. One could only imagine the store displays. A warehouse built later that year accommodated the farm implement trade. (Naomi Inskeep.)

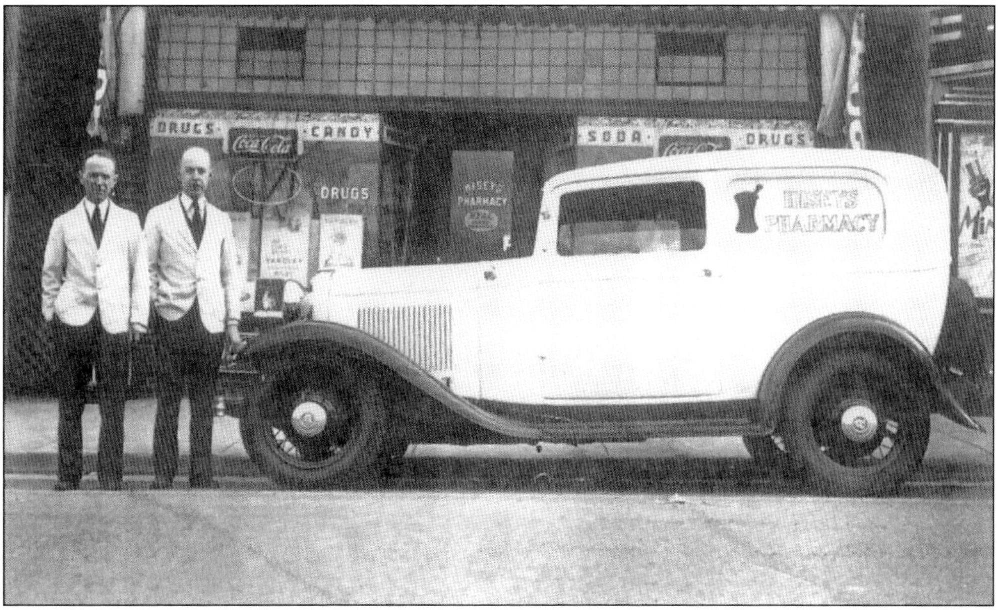

H. Clyde Hisey, at left, and his brother William M. ran Hisey's Pharmacy on Shenandoah's First Street. Pictured in 1948, the pharmacy began operation on November 17, 1919. Their great-aunt, Virginia Page Carder, was the first child born in the newly formed Page County in April 1831 in what was to become the Eagle Tavern and, later, Luray Museum of West Main Street. (*Shenandoah: A History of Our Town and Its People.*)

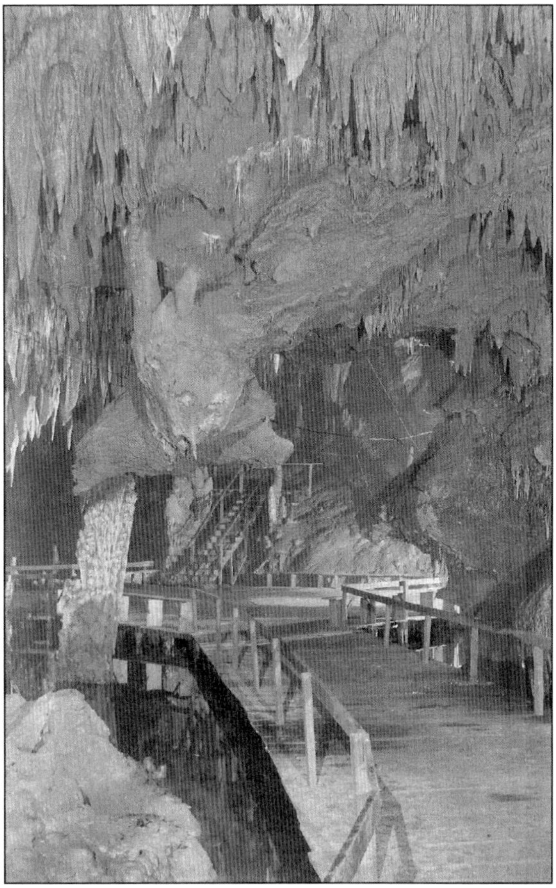

Luray Caverns gained recognition for being the first cave in the world lit by electricity when a Luray Inn dynamo, with a seven-mile circuit, provided lights on September 19, 1881. Earlier, tourists from Warrenton, Virginia, became the cave's first excursionists when they participated in its Grand Illumination, utilizing 1,000 candles on November 6, 1878. Willis Kauffman and Bettie Shenk were the first couple united in marriage in the Underground Wonder. (Dan Vaughn.)

Theodore Booton, with Dr. L. H. Keller's team of white horses, poses beside the caverns' original entrance house in 1884. Caving tools and equipment were initially stored here. Slightly relocated, the structure still stands today. James Crim's Luray Cigar Factory of West Main sold the popular Luray Caverns brand throughout town. Cavern's owner Col. T. C. Northcott offered free admission to Civil War veterans, Confederate and Federal alike, on July 21, 1905. (*PN&C.*)

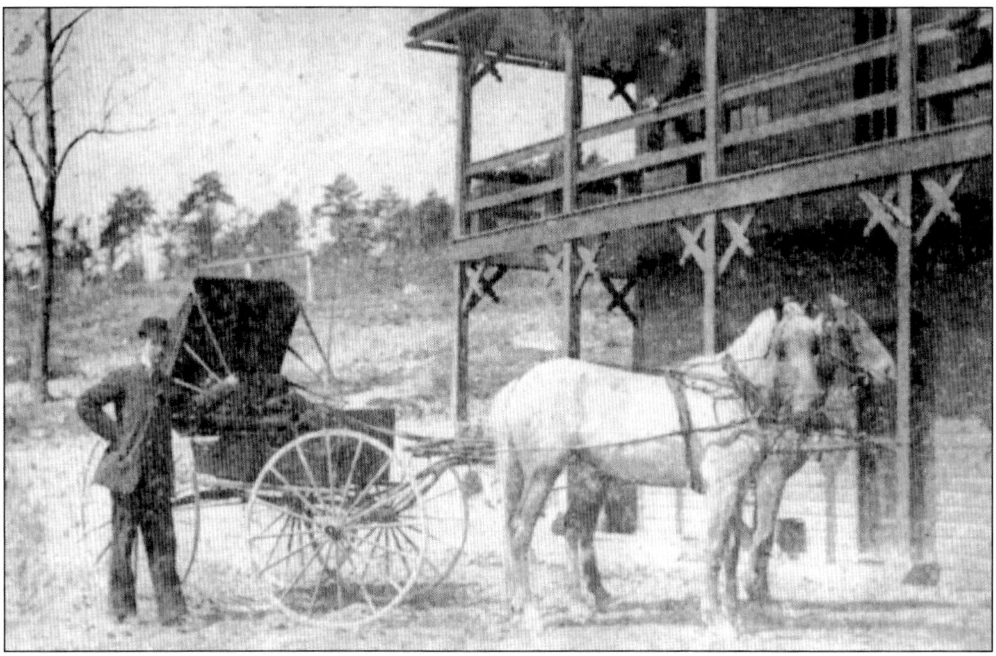

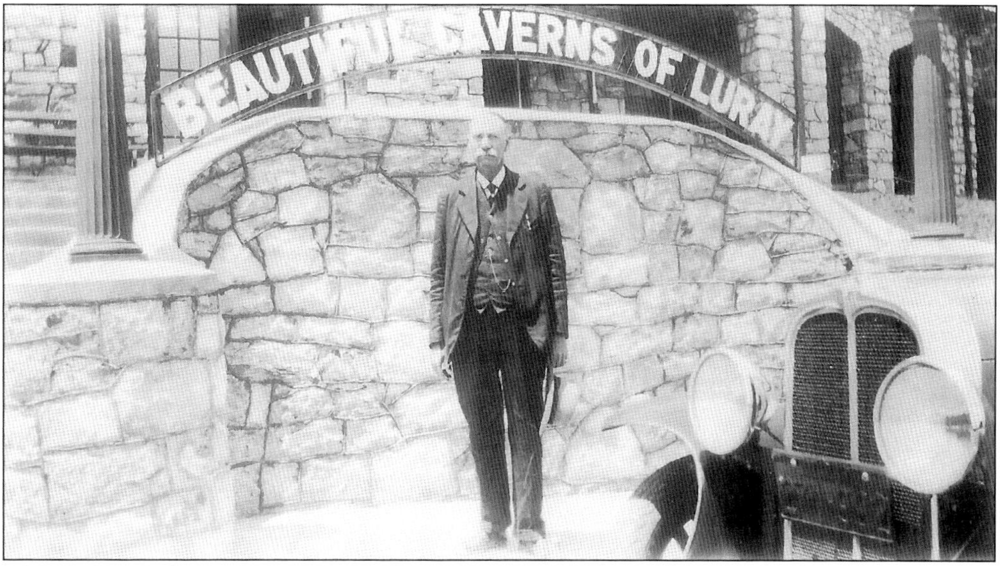

This unidentified caverns guide had the honor of being remembered for his presentation in this June 1931 image. Senior guide Lacurgus W. Shenk began conducting visitors through the subterranean chambers in 1896. Having walked more than twice the earth's circumference underground, his bronzed shoes are now on display. The caverns' first guide, Samuel G. Smith, began tours in 1878, the year of the cave's discovery. Smith received a quarter gratuity from the richest man in America when railroad magnate Jay Gould visited the caverns in June 1888. (Dan Vaughn.)

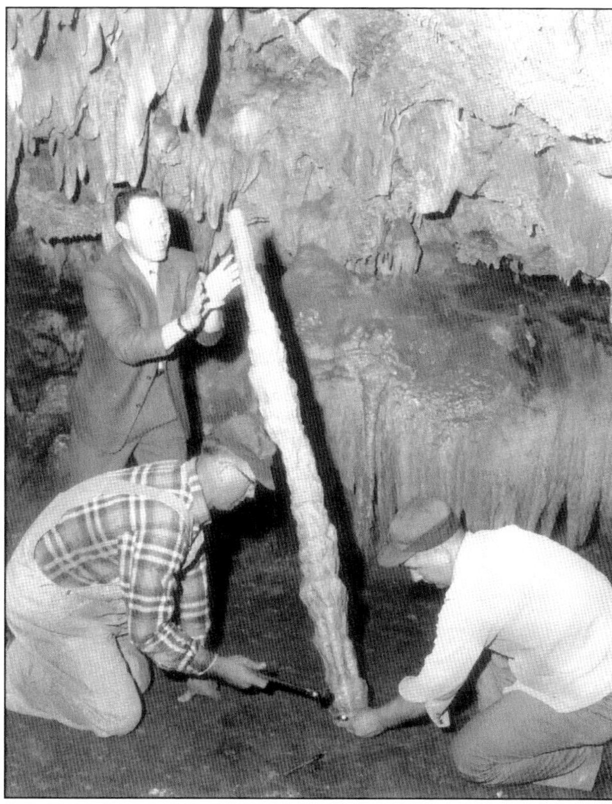

This whimsical 1960 publicity shot shows Luray Caverns' owner H. T. N. "Ted" Graves, standing, along with Reuben Fahnestock, left, and Joe Shenk, chiseling down a six-foot stalagmite. Taken from the Broaddus Lake section, it was donated to the Greek National Tourist Organization in honor of the discovery of a cave in Petralona, Greece. In filming *The Guns of Navarone*, actor Gregory Peck would ceremoniously present the formation to Irene Papas, his Greek costar. (*Richmond Times-Dispatch*.)

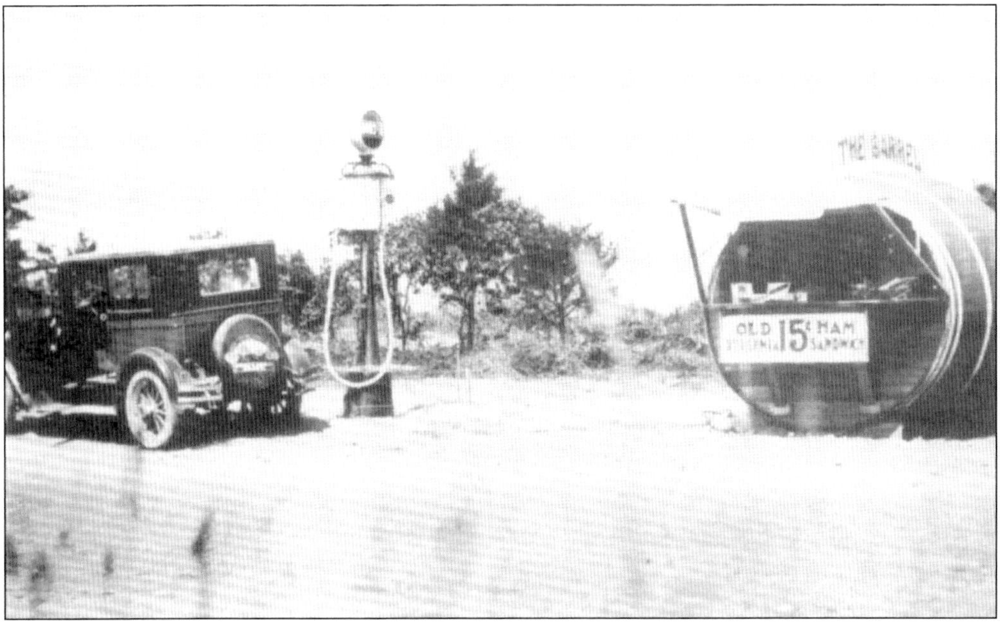

The Barrel was a well-known eating place and gas station in the 1920s–1930s. Operated by Leon and Louella Keyser, it sold travelers an old Virginia ham sandwich for 15¢, a Coca-Cola for a nickel, and gas for around 9¢ a gallon. The stand, pictured in 1927, was located in what was then "Tom's Town" on Lee Highway west of Luray. (Dan Vaughn.)

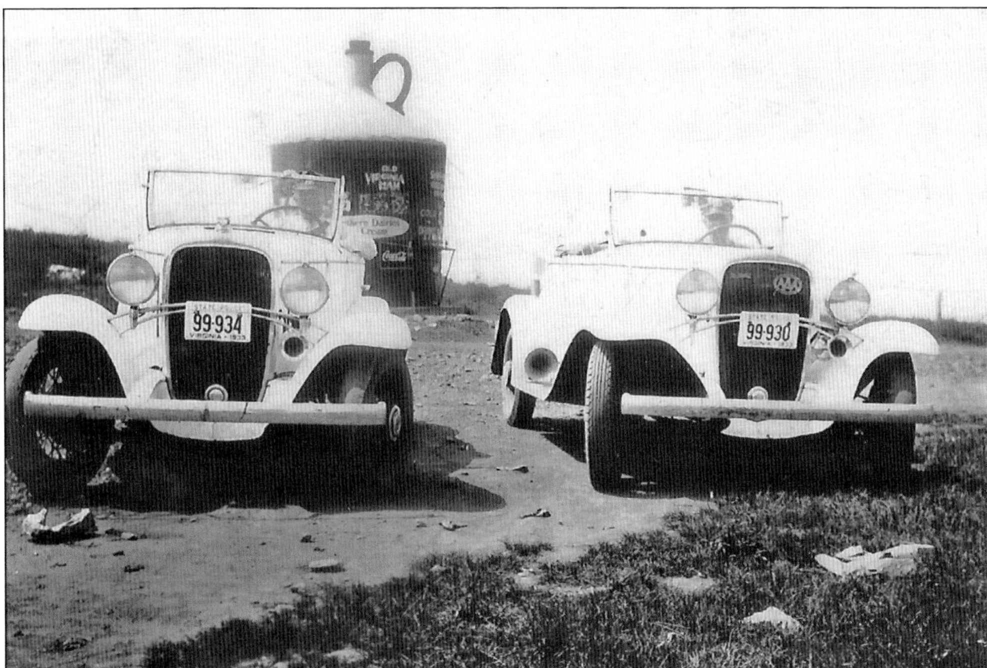

Another refreshment stand called the Jug, located at Thornton's Gap, was operated by Robert Keyser. His brother, Leon Keyser of Luray (left), and Andy Kaiser of Rockingham County posed in 1933. The two Virginia state patrolmen became known as the "Amos and Andy" team. (Lillian Keyser Fox.)

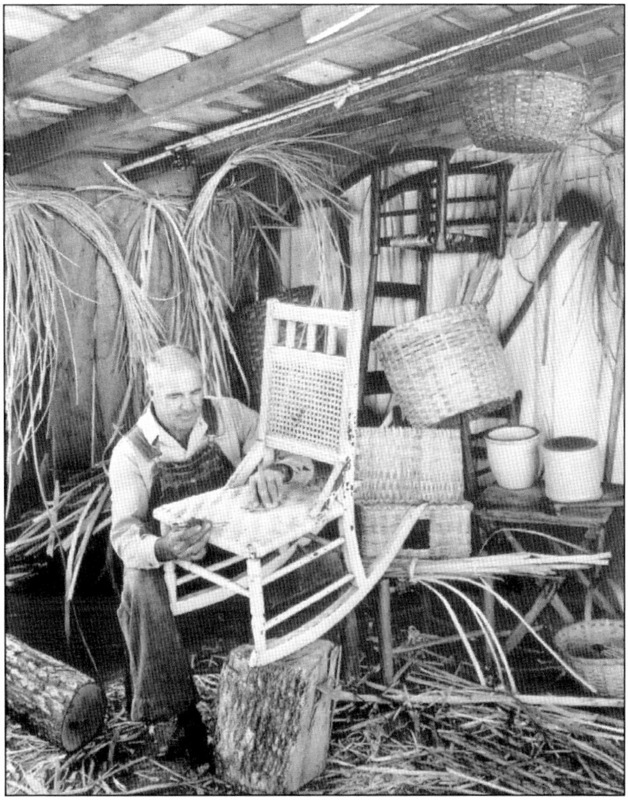

This early-1960s view shows William Cody Cook, a local Luray basketmaker for over 70 years, working at his profession. He was among six generations of the Cook family whose livelihood depended on the trade. William and his wife, Lucy, were professional basket weaving demonstrators in Colonial Williamsburg. Their craftsmanship was widely known. (© Jennifer B. Bodine; AAubreyBodine.com.)

Thelma Judd Fears, seen here around 1963, ran the popular Pumpkin Hill Gift Shop at the base of the Blue Ridge Mountains east of Luray. All types of souvenirs (a French word for memory) were offered here, including cider, baskets, and lawn ornaments. (© Jennifer B. Bodine; AAubreyBodine.com.)

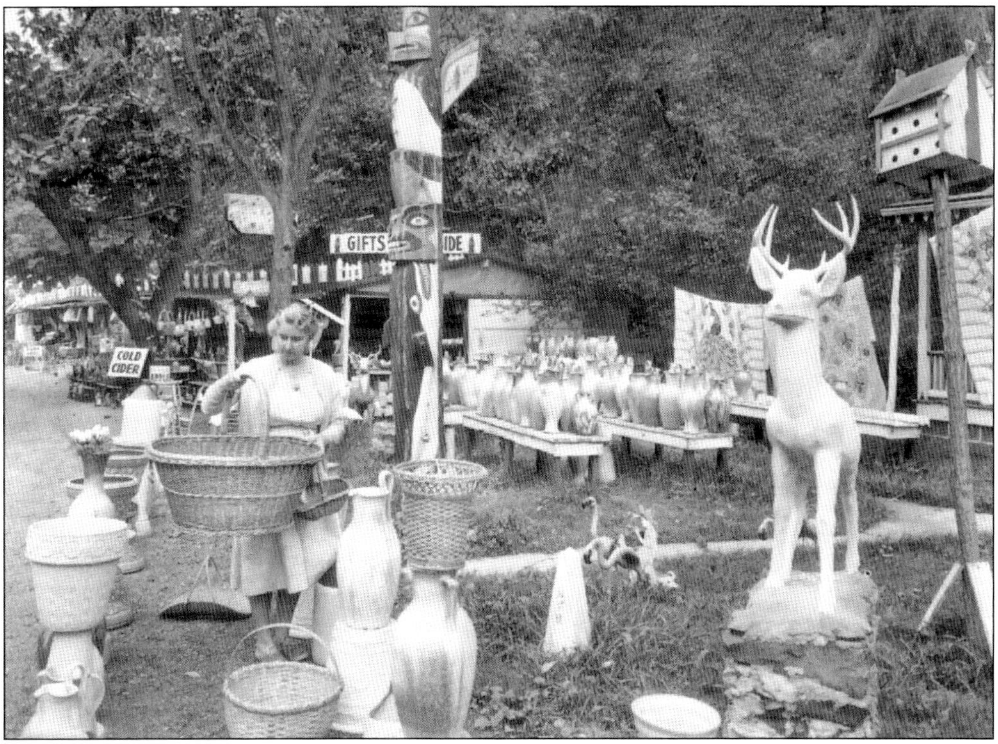

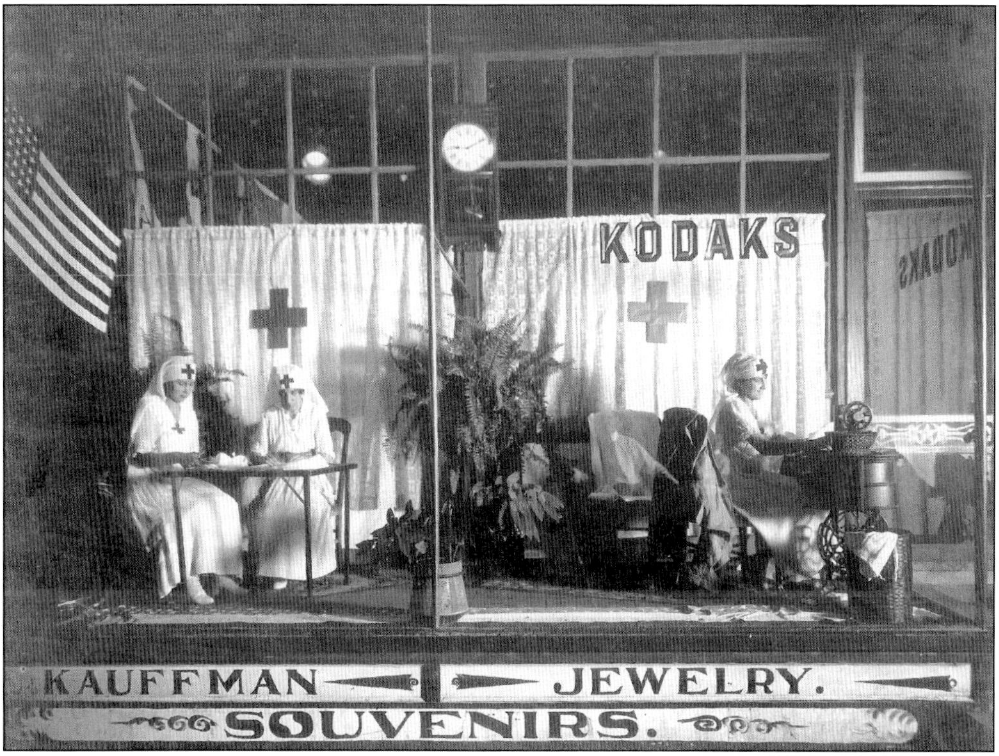

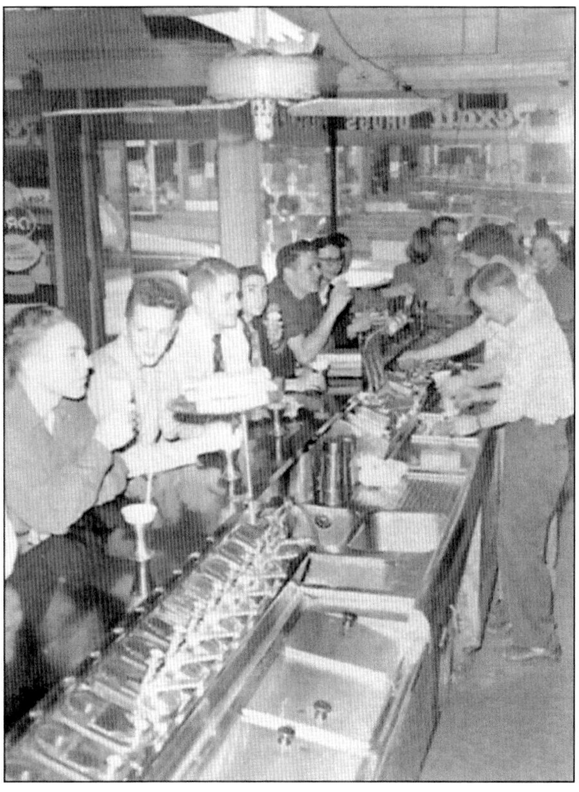

A live window display hosts Red Cross nurses in Dorfie Lindsley "D. L." Kauffman's Jewelry and Souvenirs west of Main Street Bridge in Luray. He sold gold, silver, and nickel cast watches with his own imprint and personal guarantee. In 1911, he advertised "on the Plank Walk, nigh unto the bridge." Opening in the late 1890s, and popular with excursionists, he sold out in 1934, devoting his time to his optical business. (William and Frances Menefee.)

McKay and Son's Drug Store catered to these Luray High School boys in 1953 with its ice cream counter and soda fountain. The business originated across Main Street in 1885 when marble cutter G. W. Haines opened his East End Drug Store. McKay's operated here in the old 1887 Luray YMCA from 1928 to 1968, when the business moved west to its third and final location, the former Butler's Pharmacy. (Dan Vaughn.)

Burgess A. Redman ran a general store in Cavetown, present-day Blainesville. Seen here filling a customer's kerosene can, he sold Shell gasoline for over 40 years at his humble establishment. His first store was built in 1907, and when it burnt in 1927, he rebuilt directly in front, continuing until his death in 1977. The store still stands today, appropriately, at the end of Redman's Store Road. (*PN&C.*)

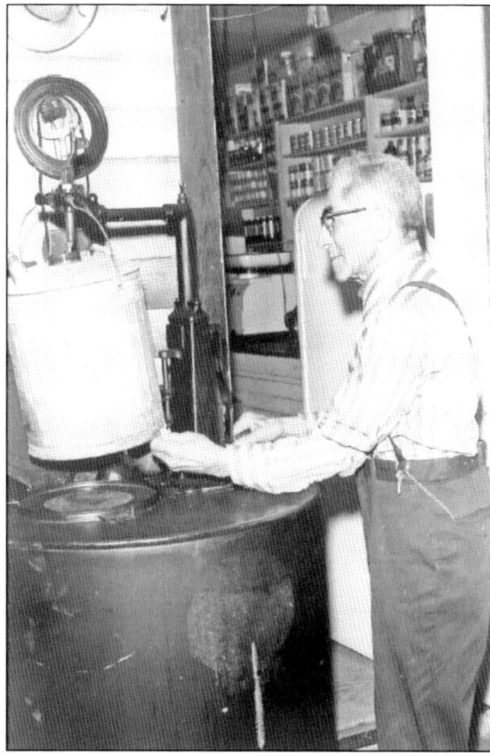

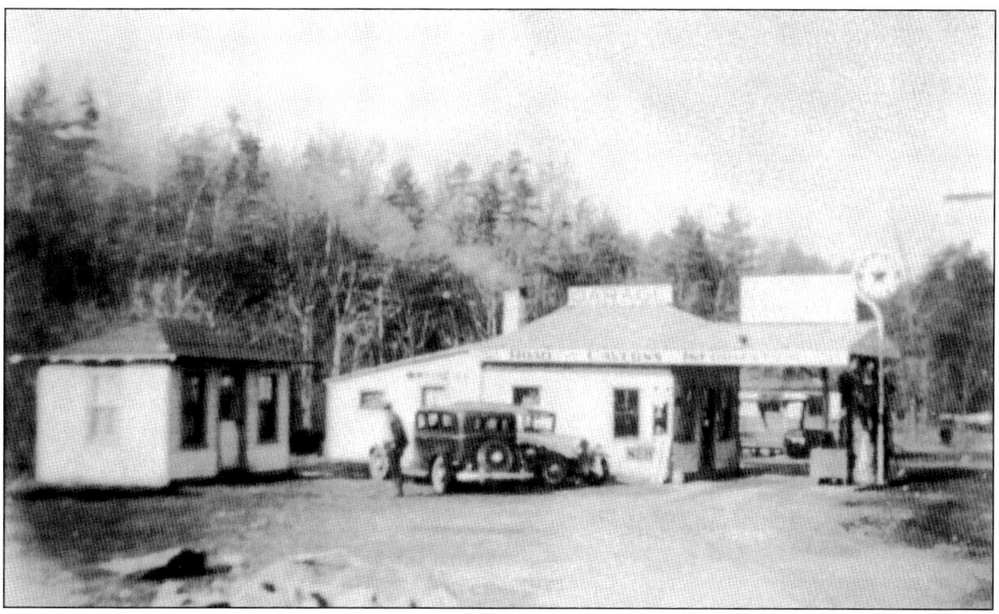

In 1937, Page and Ollie Shenk opened Brookside Restaurant. Charles L. Fake Sr., owner of both Brown's and Pickwick Restaurants, purchased the local eatery in 1965, operating all three simultaneously. In 1976, Lloyd and Katrina Wakeman began serving customers, which they did until 2004, when they sold to present owners Bob and Cece Castle. At the base of the Shenandoah National Park, this popular restaurant, with mountain cabins, has served locals and tourists for over 70 years. (Bob and Cece Castle.)

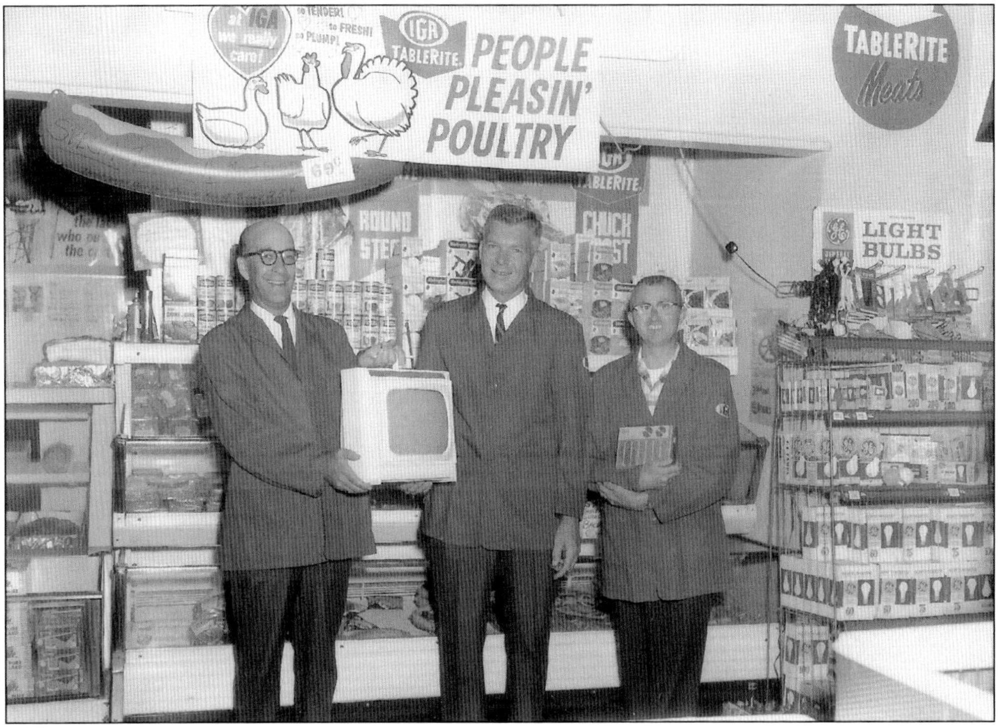

Morris John Dunlap Sr., with his brother William, started Stanley Cash Store east of the N&W Railroad in 1919. Morris later bought out William, and in 1961, his son M. J. "Buss" Dunlap Jr. took over the business, moving westward and renaming it Stanley Food Market. The men pictured in 1967 for this store promotion are, from left to right, "Buss" Dunlap, John Engelman, a Blue Ridge Grocery representative, and Aaron "Sike" Mayes. (Dan Vaughn.)

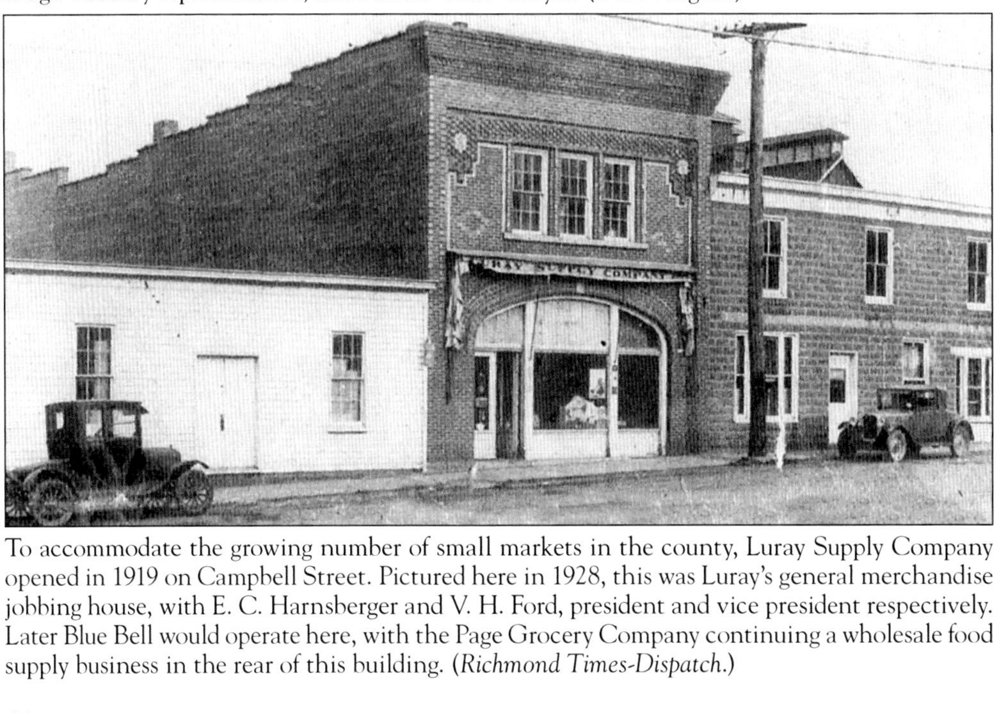

To accommodate the growing number of small markets in the county, Luray Supply Company opened in 1919 on Campbell Street. Pictured here in 1928, this was Luray's general merchandise jobbing house, with E. C. Harnsberger and V. H. Ford, president and vice president respectively. Later Blue Bell would operate here, with the Page Grocery Company continuing a wholesale food supply business in the rear of this building. (*Richmond Times-Dispatch*.)

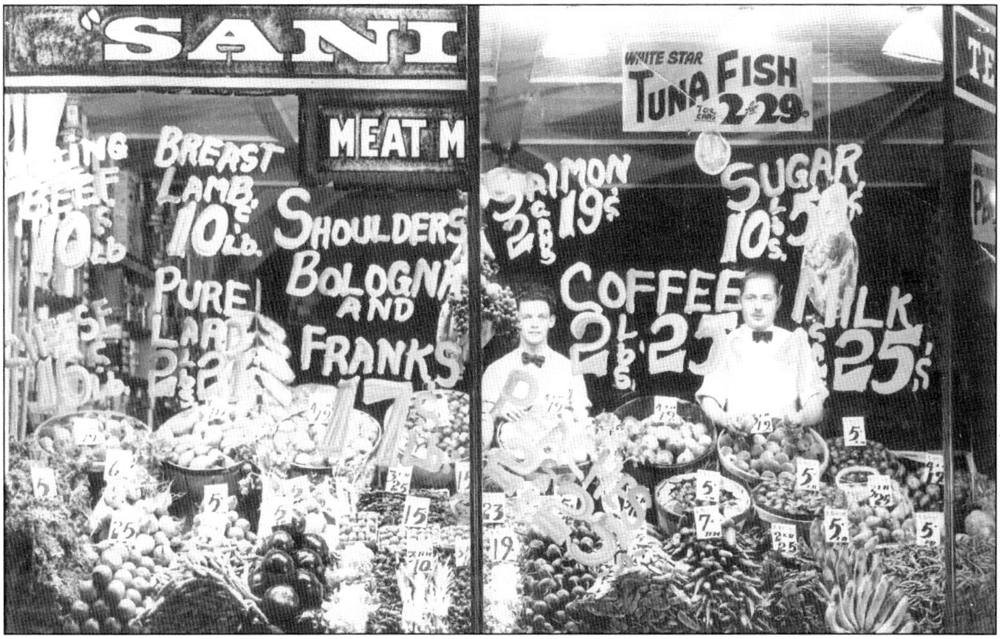

There was no need to ask prices when you shopped at Sanitary Market. A newly replaced glass lacks their name in its entirety but not the daily specials. Johnny Fox, at left, and manager G. R. Anderson Sr. had a large array of produce to choose from at this very popular East Main Street market, which opened in 1932 in Luray. (Iva Anderson.)

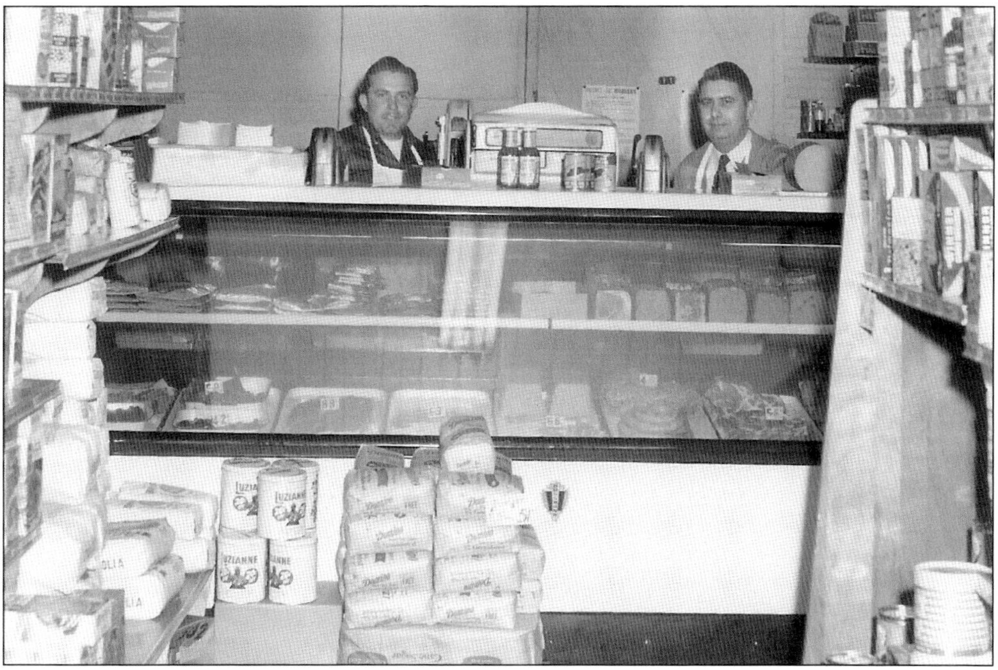

Aylor Grubbs, at right, and his wife, Charlotte, opened this self-serve grocery store on Stanley's Main Street on March 3, 1939. Teddy Housden, a meat cutter, pictured here with Grubbs in 1959, started working here at age 14, continuing for 20 years. When offered the business, Housden declined, but his brother Johnny purchased it and continued to serve the Stanley residents. (*PN&C*.)

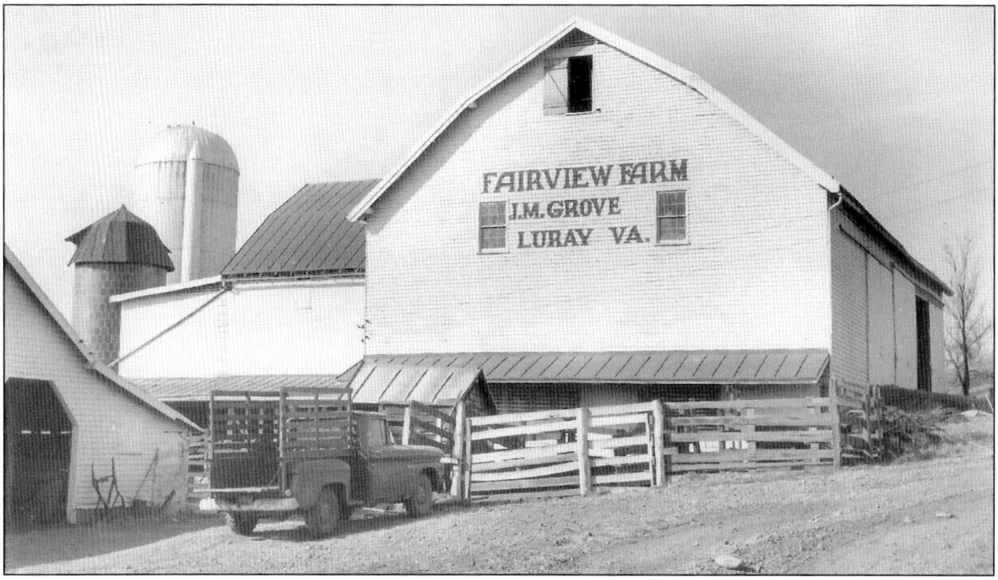

Virginia initiated the Century Farm Program in 1997 by awarding farms in operation over 100 consecutive years by original descendants. Glendon and Ann Grove Vaughn (parents of this author) of Luray were recognized as Virginia's first recipients of the nearly 1,000 statewide by 2008. Their farm, on the Groveton Tract south of Luray and one of the original Page County land grants, has been in continuous operation since 1756. (*PN&C*.)

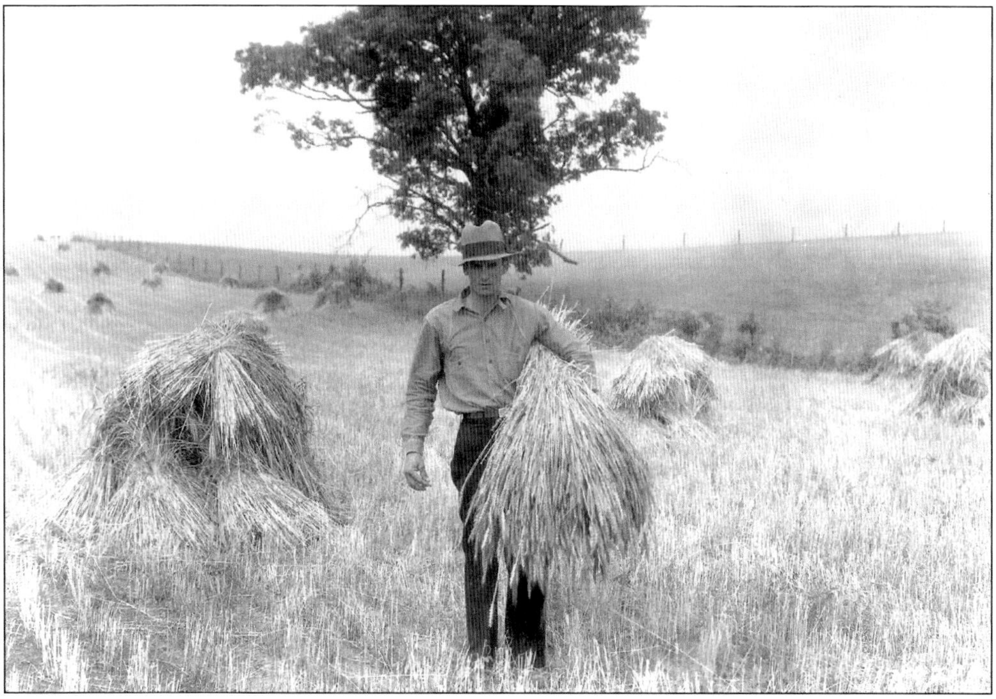

Here, on Fairview Farm south of Luray, posing with a bound shock of wheat, is John Maurice Grove around 1930. Maurice's grandfather, John Pendleton Grove, purchased Page County's first hay baler from Luray implement dealer H. V. Hudson in April 1896. The self-binding reaper used here was just one of many inventions that helped reduce farm labor. (Dan Vaughn.)

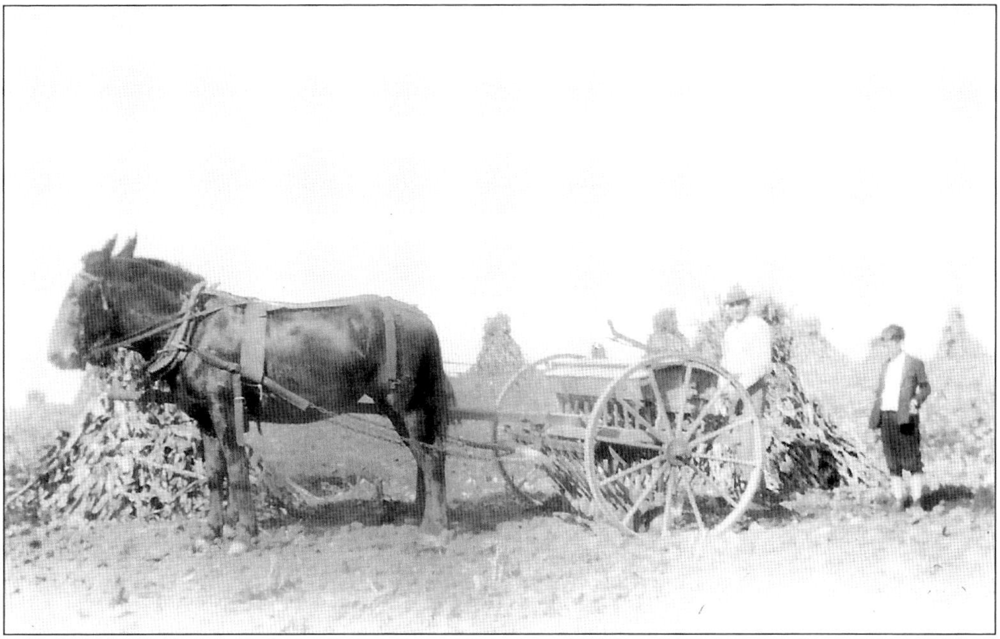

Ben Spitler stands behind a Bickford and Huffman two-horse-team seed drill as young Harold E. Grove watches curiously on the J. Gill Grove farm south of Luray. With shocks of corn standing beyond, Spitler readies the ground for its winter crop of wheat. Luray's Union Exchange, the Luray Alliance and the Grange, in the Massanutten section, were all forerunners of present-day farmers' cooperatives in Page. (Jean Kite.)

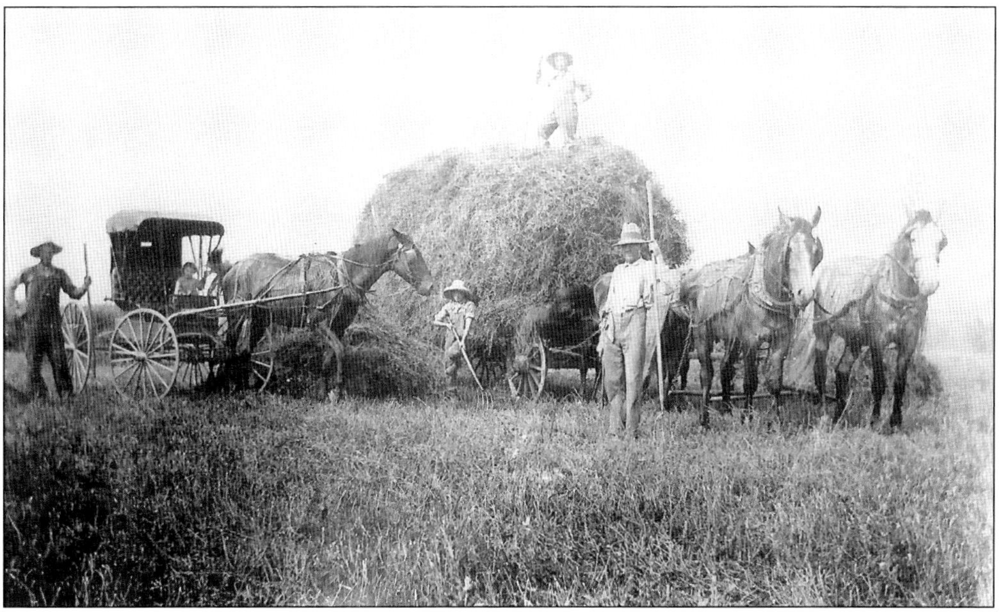

Alfalfa, an Arabic word curiously enough, showed up in the United States around 1860 and in Page around 1900. It was spoken highly of by local farmers. A hay making crew poses in 1914 on the Frank Spitler farm near Long's Store, midway between Luray and Stanley. Page has always maintained a fairly predominant farming community, but in a day of rapid modernization and land development, it is beginning to feel somewhat a stranger in its own land. (Jim and Kay Stilwell.)

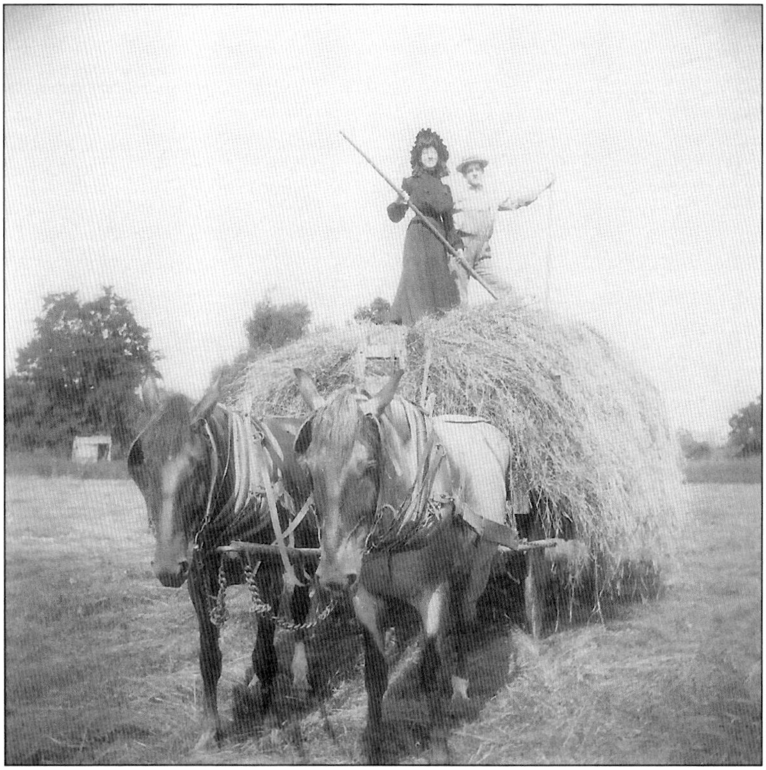

Farming is hard work, and in times past, the lack of modern inventions only added to the hardships. The Bible says in Genesis 3:18, "Thistles shall it bring forth." And it did when the invasive Canadian pest showed up throughout Page County in the 1880s. These horses wait obligingly as Nettie Graham and Ezra Stirewalt pose atop the load of hand-gathered hay in the Stony Man area. (Mildred Stirewalt Coleman.)

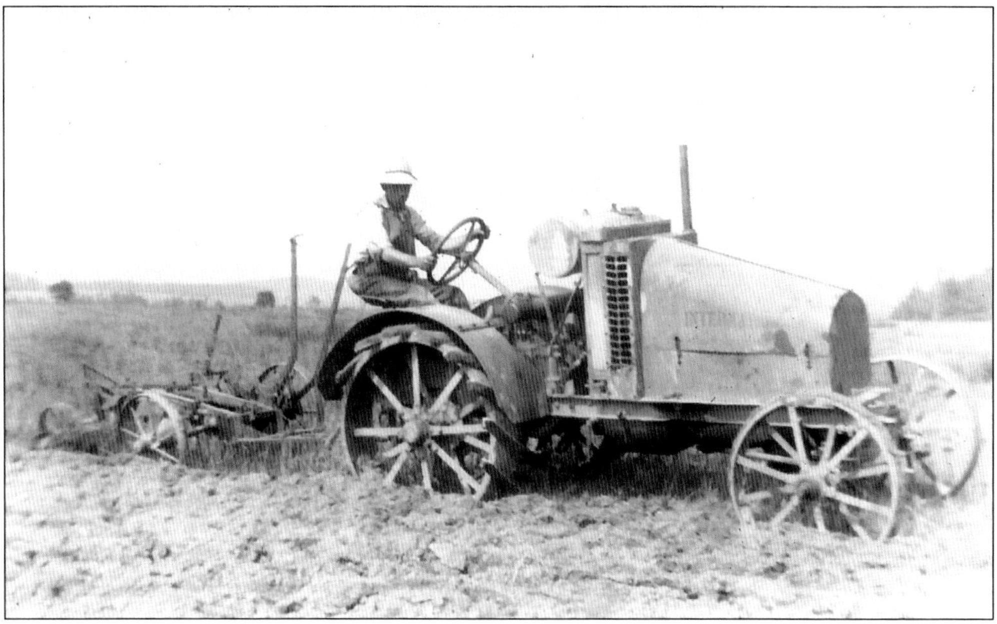

Harold K. Modisett is shown here plowing with an 8-16 International tractor in the Leaksville area in the 1920s. The tractor's invention was a turning point in the mechanization of farming. In October 1939, International Harvester announced that W. F. Judd and Kenneth Stader, proprietors of Stader's Garage in Luray, would handle their full line of trucks and farm implements. Appropriately, the business would be named the Page Implement and Truck Company. (Robert Modisett.)

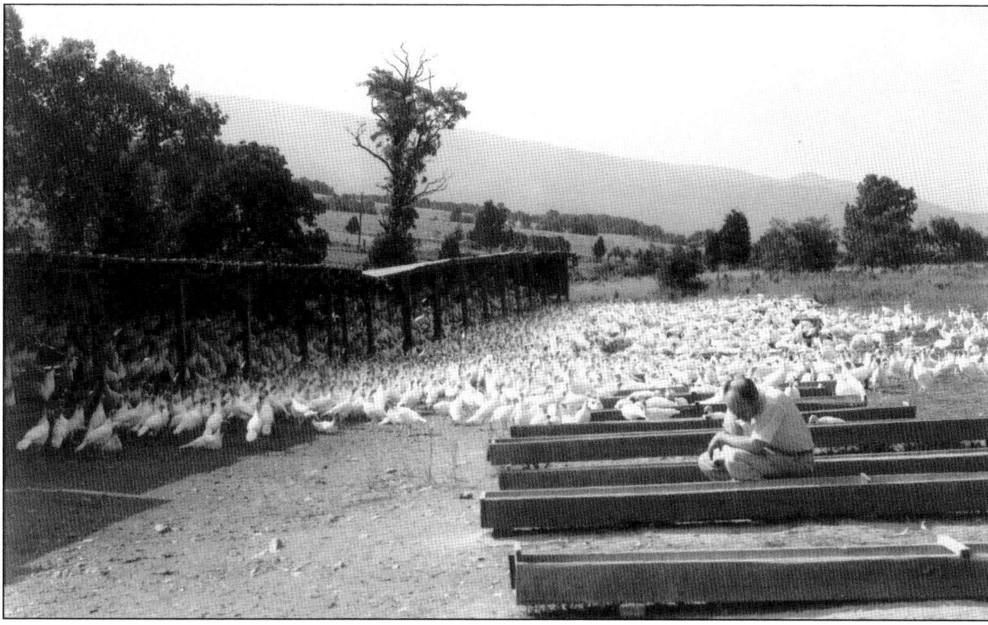

The Page Poultry Show, advertising in 1906, stated, "Held in the Bradley Building, Main Street, Lighted with electricity and kept warm, Open February 15–16, Free to all." This turkey farm outside Luray, photographed in 1954, is a good representation of a "free range" operation. The prize, seemingly, for the finest poultry house in the county goes to Mrs. Lee Long. Burning a coal stove, with lace curtains at the windows, she averaged 100 eggs per day. (Virginia Tech.)

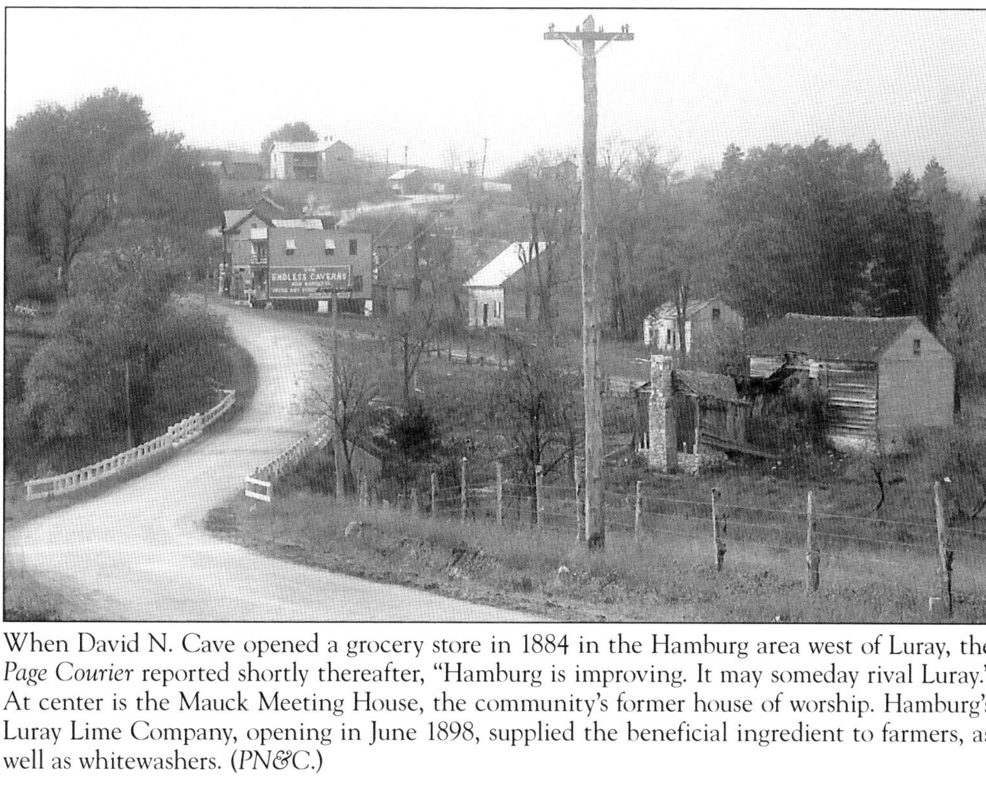

When David N. Cave opened a grocery store in 1884 in the Hamburg area west of Luray, the *Page Courier* reported shortly thereafter, "Hamburg is improving. It may someday rival Luray." At center is the Mauck Meeting House, the community's former house of worship. Hamburg's Luray Lime Company, opening in June 1898, supplied the beneficial ingredient to farmers, as well as whitewashers. (*PN&C*.)

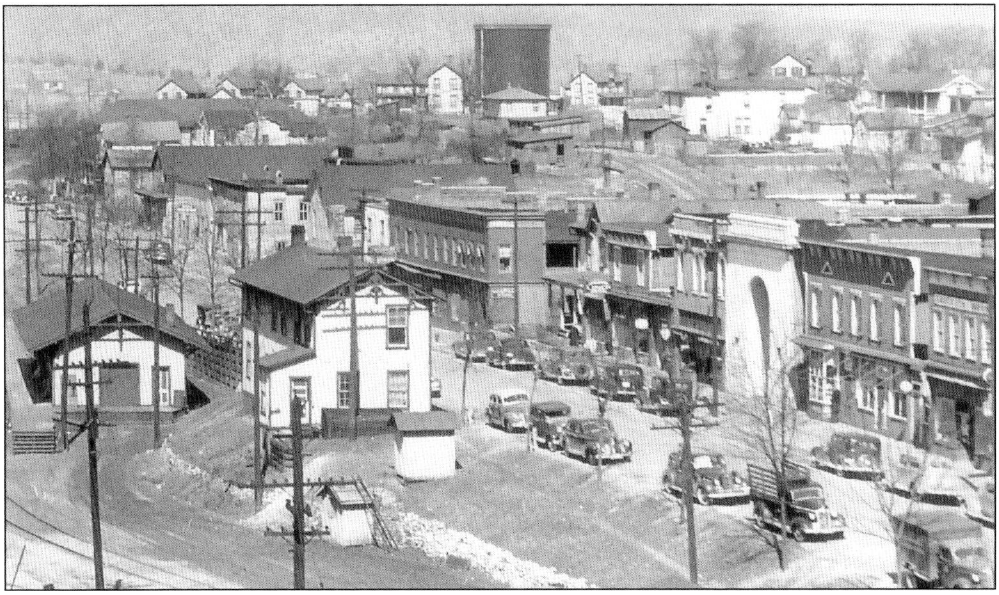

This was Shenandoah's First Street at its peak, with its activity paralleling the railroad's success. Riding on coattails was its demise when the N&W steam era ended abruptly in February 1957. Sadly, fire, another culprit even less forgiving, claimed not only the vintage Comer's Hardware, but also the century-old Eagle Hotel, murals and all. The entire county felt for the town in its hampered efforts of rejuvenation. (Virginia Tech.)

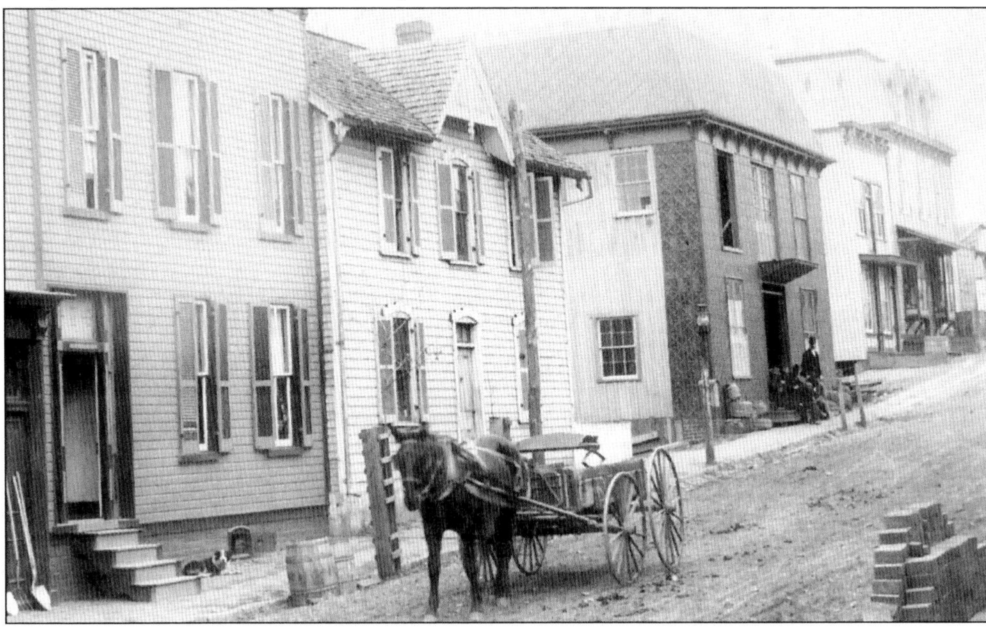

One might remark this was their grandfather's Luray in this olden view of East Main Street. A trusting horse pauses at noontime beside a hitching post complete with water barrels in this 1888 S. K. Wright photograph. At right, just beyond the kerosene lamppost, patrons gather outside the H. V. Hudson Storehouse, posing unpretentiously in their want of an event. Farther right is Read's Grand East End Bazaar store building, with Luray's Commerce Street in between. (Marleen Hansen.)

Four

Learning and Yearning

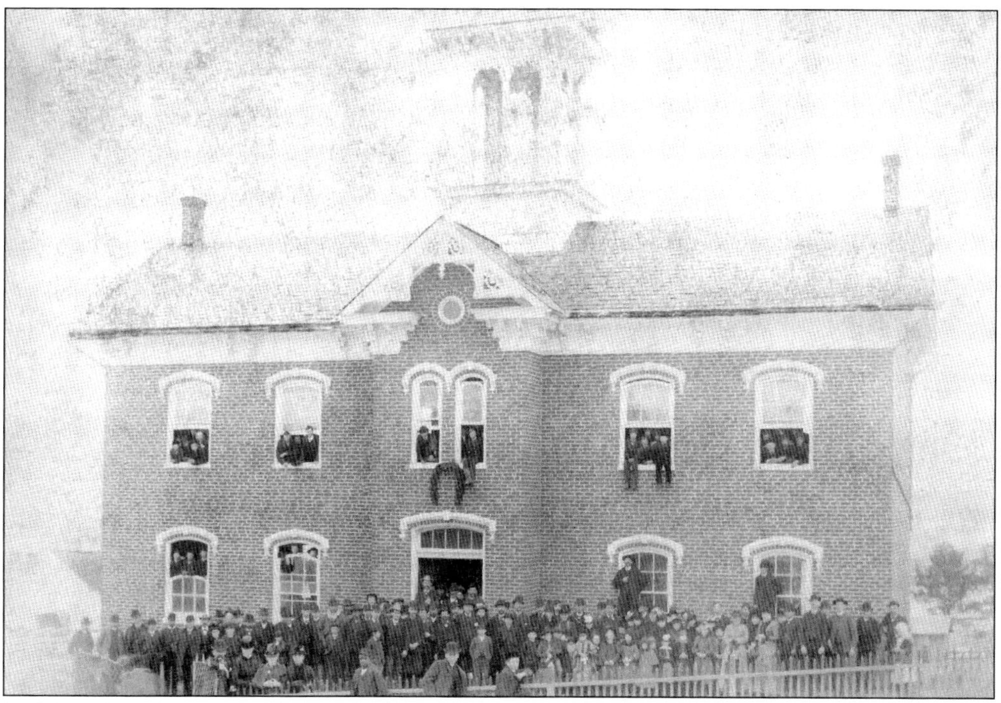

In May 1881, Harvey Coffman produced bricks, initiating construction of the long-awaited Luray Graded School. Shown in this *c.* 1885 image, the wooden fence, built two years prior and constantly vandalized, was replaced with ornate iron by 1891. By 1882, eaves trough was added, and with the building kalsomined for the fall 1886 session, the South Court Street school took on a resemblance of its current-day appearance. Pupils outside the town limits were offered board accommodations by Principal H. Sheffey Roller. (Mildred Stirewalt Coleman.)

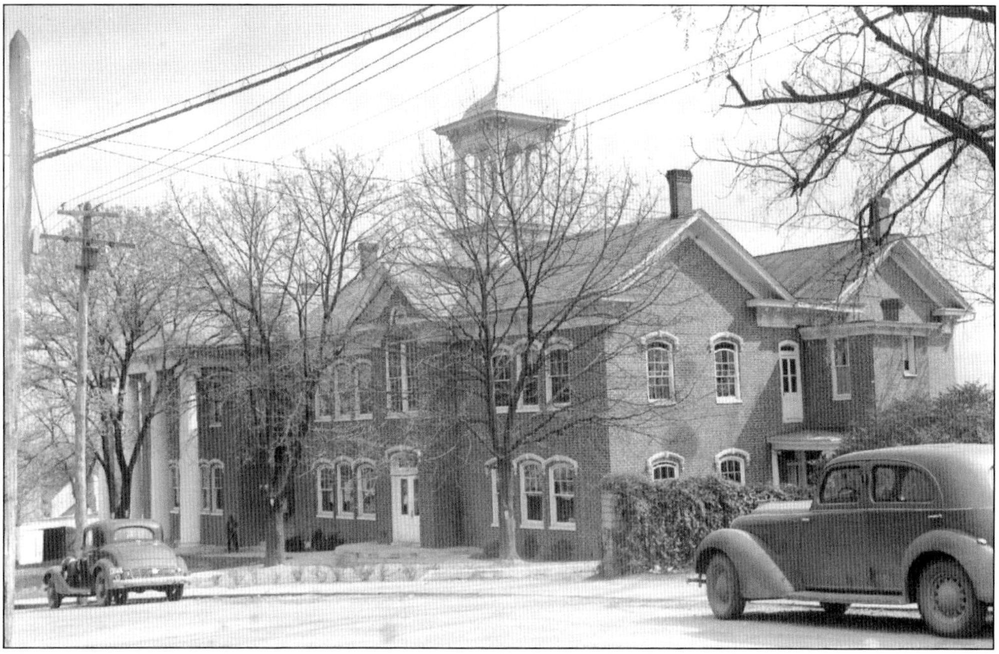

By 1906, talk of a "new" school, led largely by then-principal John H. Booton, prompted a northeast, two-story addition (now removed) that sufficed until a 1930 Luray Avenue successor was constructed. When this WPA repairs project was photographed in 1938, the building had been given to the county along with a use prerequisite. It was stated that, as a county office building, this structure "met a long-felt need." Sadly, the fate of this 125-year-old pivotal Luray landmark hangs in uncertainty. (National Archives.)

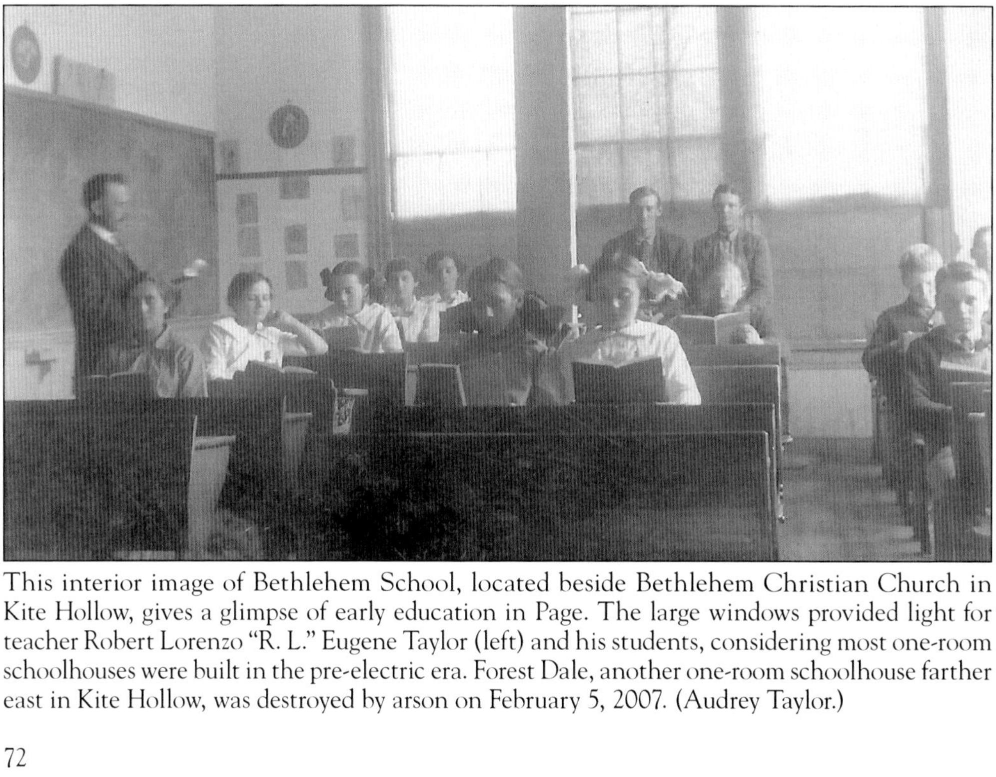

This interior image of Bethlehem School, located beside Bethlehem Christian Church in Kite Hollow, gives a glimpse of early education in Page. The large windows provided light for teacher Robert Lorenzo "R. L." Eugene Taylor (left) and his students, considering most one-room schoolhouses were built in the pre-electric era. Forest Dale, another one-room schoolhouse farther east in Kite Hollow, was destroyed by arson on February 5, 2007. (Audrey Taylor.)

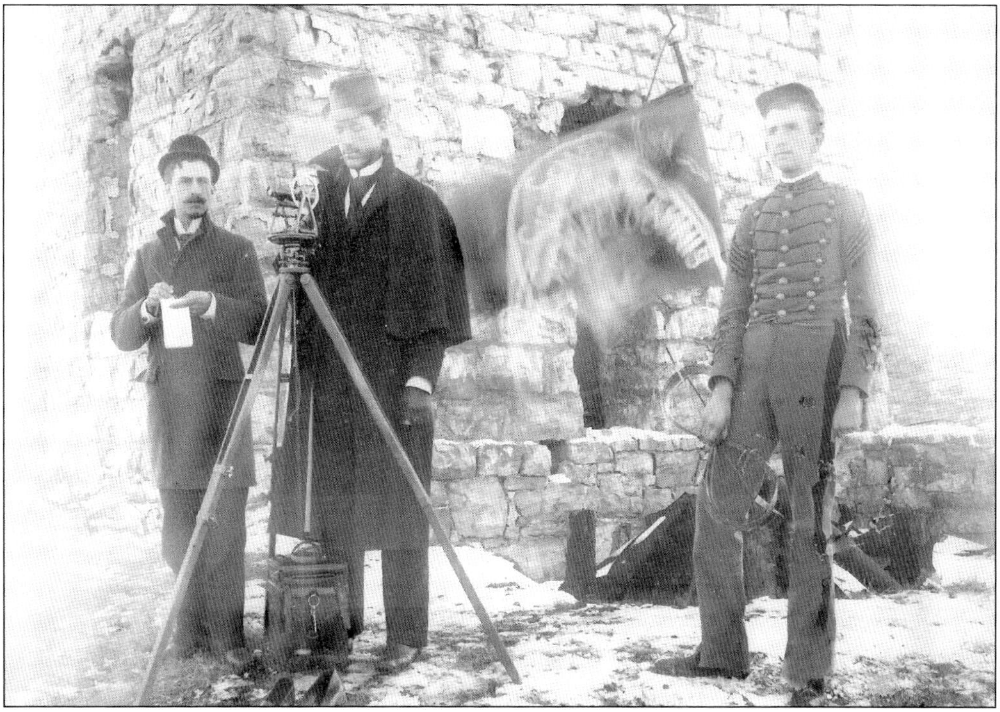

Pictured on February 16, 1894, in front of the old Luray Inn tower ruins are, from left to right, Frederick T. Amiss, J. E. Sutphin of Flint Hill, and John Booton, all of the Luray Military Academy. Headmaster Col. James H. Morrison, a Virginia Military Institute teacher whose father-in-law was VMI superintendent for 50 years, ran this school for young men on the upper floor of the S. O. Judd store building. (William and Frances Menefee.)

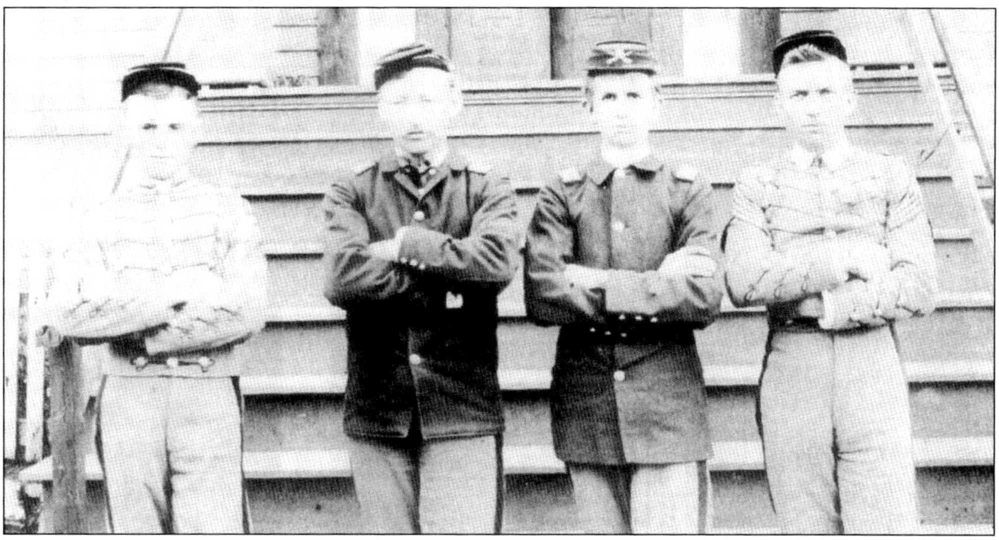

These young Luray Military Academy students—from left to right, William Stover, Horace Morrison, John Booton, and Gilbert Gander—posed outside the academy around 1893. By 1906, this local school had 40 uniformed students enrolled. The Page Valley Academy, another military school operating in Stanley at the dawn of the 20th century, was headed by Rev. B. B. White, onetime principal of the Luray Graded School. (*PN&C.*)

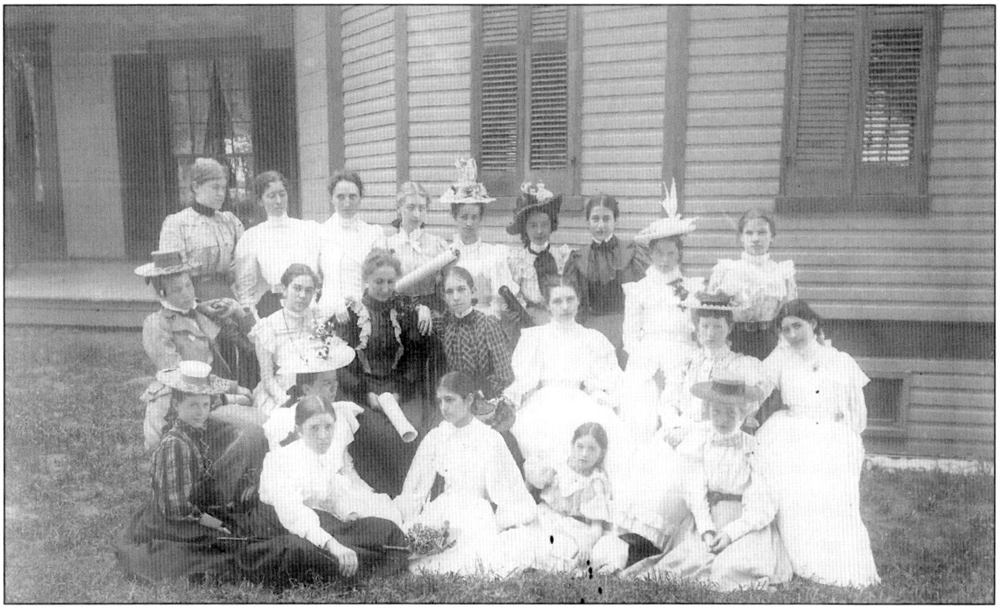

The Luray Female Institute opened in September 1889, with instruction in Latin, telegraphy, stenography, Bible, art, and music. The school gave a Christmas 1896 benefit for the Whosoever Farm orphanage of Luray's East End. Rev. H. M. Wharton, owning the orphanage, purchased the institute in 1895 and changed the name to Luray College. It had its best year when 108 students attended the 1897–1898 session. Here Mary Caroline Weaver's 1898 music class poses on the west lawn facing South Court Street. (William and Frances Menefee.)

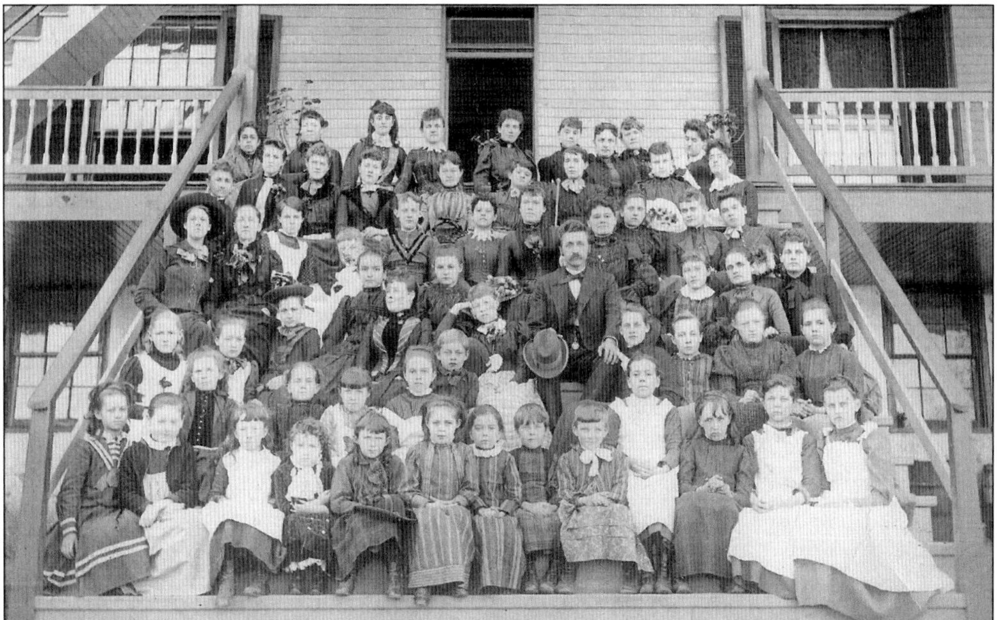

Prof. M. M. Hargrove (center), a University of Virginia graduate, was aided by a corps of scholarly Christian teachers at the Luray Female Institute. Their duties included having a close association with the young ladies beyond school hours as moral witnesses. A Luray Female Seminary previously operated around 1870 with Andrew Broaddus as principal. (William and Frances Menefee.)

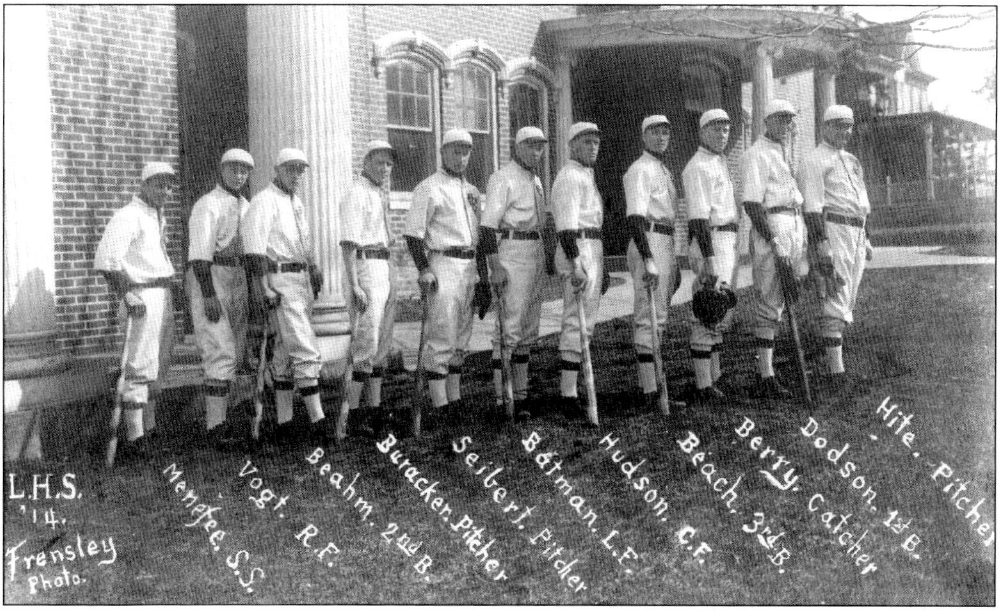

Max S. Frensley photographed the formally posed Luray High School Baseball Team in front of the school in 1914. From left to right are M. J. "Peachy" Menefee, William Vogt, Wharton Beahm, William Buracker, Leon Seibert, James Batman, J. Ober Hudson, Carroll Beach, "Dutch" Berry, Carroll Dodson, and Hugh Hite. Wallace Laws was absent when the picture was taken. (Dorothy Ann Beach Seal.)

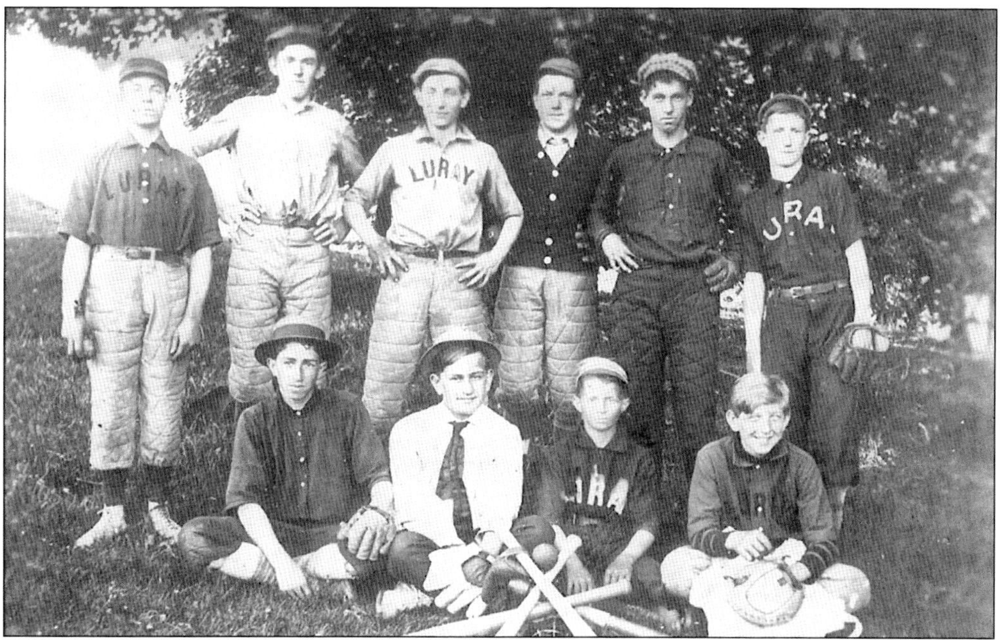

Frensley also captured this less formal 1903 Luray team. Seated with bats is manager M. J. "Peachy" Menefee. Games were then played on the "local diamond," a field that would later become home to Luray's Singing Tower. On June 18, 1887, a game between Luray Inn's Painters and Plumbers was played on the "commons," west of town. The Painters won by a score of 11-3. (William and Frances Menefee.)

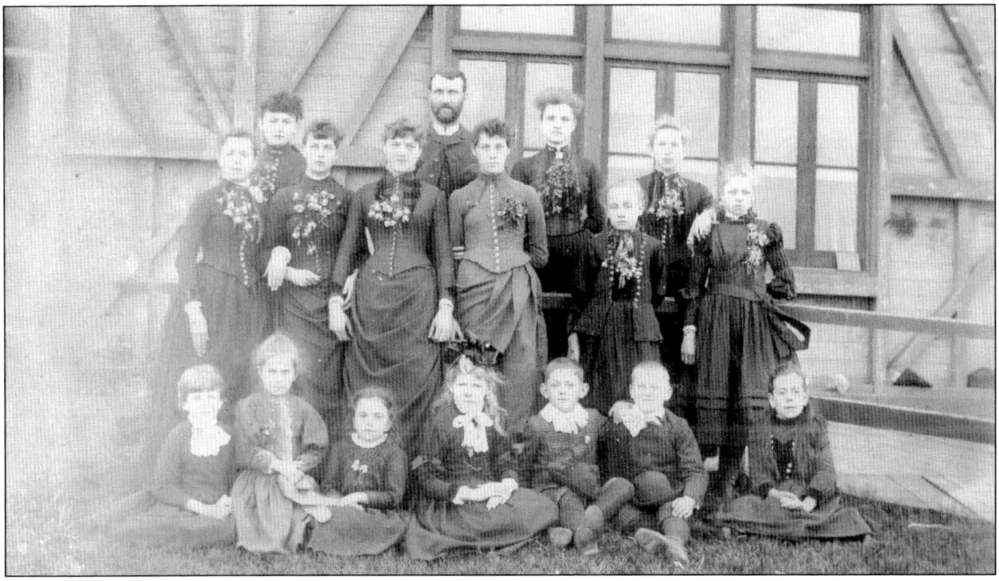

The 1890–1891 class of Read's Select School in Luray poses for photographer S. K. Wright. From left to right are (seated) Bertie Read, Olive Hudson, Gertrude Hudson, Alice Weaver, Ned Weaver, Wharton Read, and Mabel Hudson; (standing) Mattie Dovel, Blanche Jet, unidentified, Ada Read, John H. Read, unidentified, teacher ? Loving, Mamie Hudson, Mary Dovel, and Victoria Read. John Read previously operated the 1880s Grand East End Bazaar on Main Street. (William and Frances Menefee.)

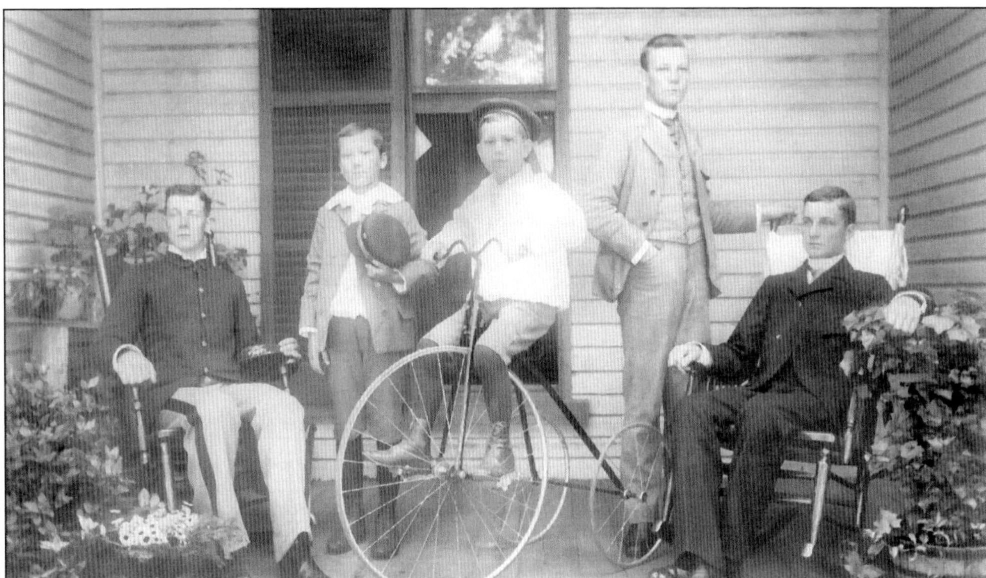

At its height of popularity, Luray's Von Bora College on North Deford Avenue had a faculty of 10, offered four-year courses, and enrolled near 100 pupils. Unfortunately, this all-girls school closed in 1894, a victim of economic hardship. Rev. John Stirewalt's efforts to establish a school for boys here faltered also. In this summer 1894 image are, from left to right, Jacob Stirewalt (in Luray Military Academy uniform), Vernon Stirewalt, Ezra Stirewalt (on velocipede), Arthur Stirewalt, and John Stirewalt. (Dan Vaughn.)

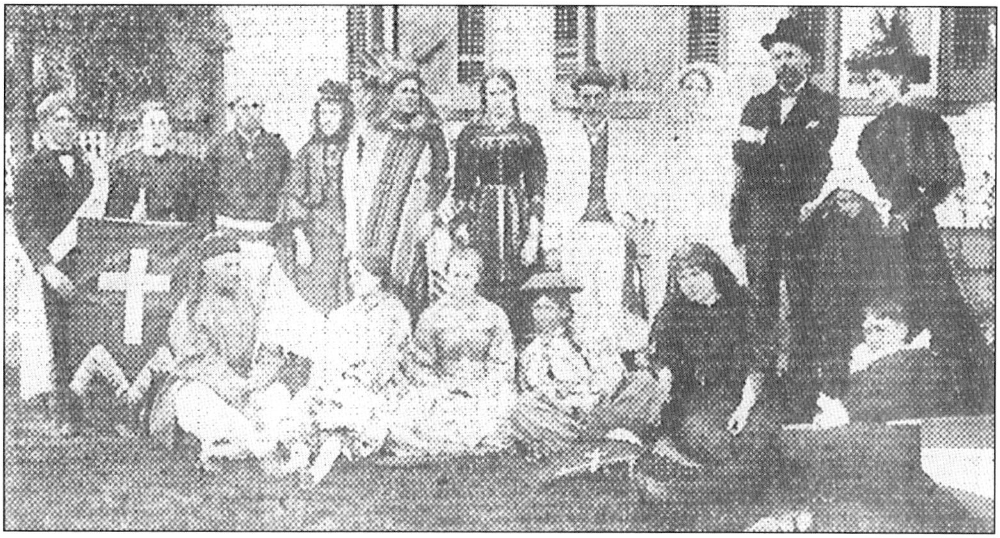

Valley View Seminary students in Stanley posed in full costume around 1907 for a play given to benefit Marksville Baptist Church. The school opened in 1896 under the ministry of Elder Tolbert S. Dalton. From left to right are (first row) John Graves, Lottie Volandt, Cora Varner, Evert Koontz, Maude MacSpeiden, and W. M. Grim; (second row) R. D. Koontz, Lena Beidler, William Brumback, Vinda Koontz, Charles Judy, Minnie Phillips, Joseph Kiblinger, Lillie Graves, Charles Foote, unidentified, and teacher Inez Quisenberry. (*PN&C.*)

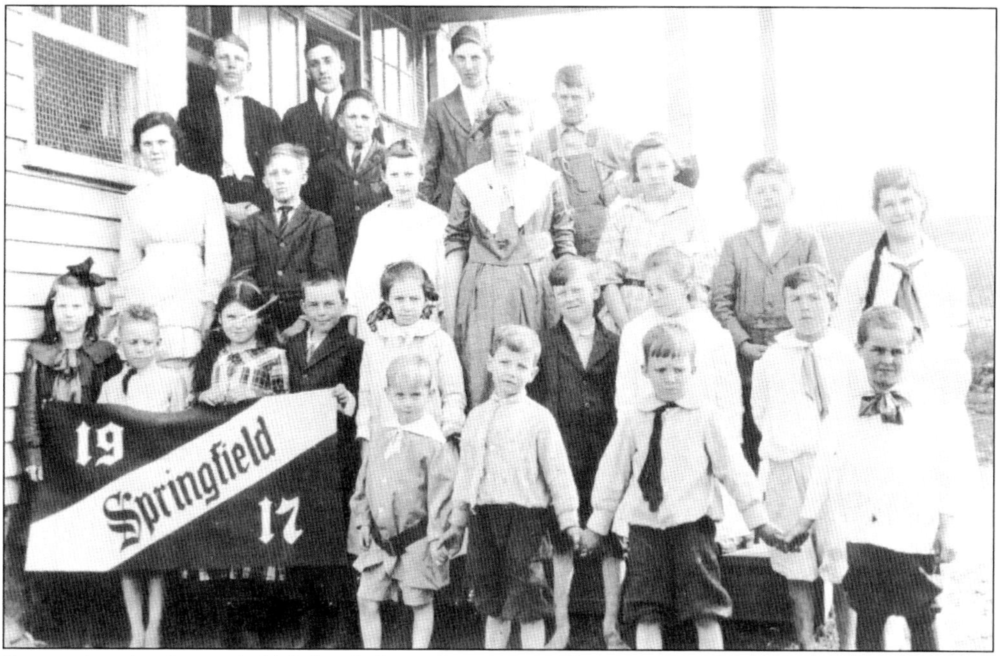

Pictured is the Springfield School class of 1917. From left to right are (first row) Walter Baker, James W. Baker, Fred Baker, and Virgil Shenk; (second row) Maude Myers, Frank Fox, Kathleen Kibler, Leo Shenk, Julia Zirkle, Bennie Sedwick, Josephine Cave, and Haywood Nichols; (third row) Lena Wood, Ezra Fox, Nellie Burrill, Katye Zirkle, Margaret Zirkle, Elma Kibler, and Essie Zirkle; (fourth row) Lynn Zirkle, Leo Hoak (teacher), Basil Fox, Ralph Kemp, and Ashbourn Kibler. (Dan Vaughn.)

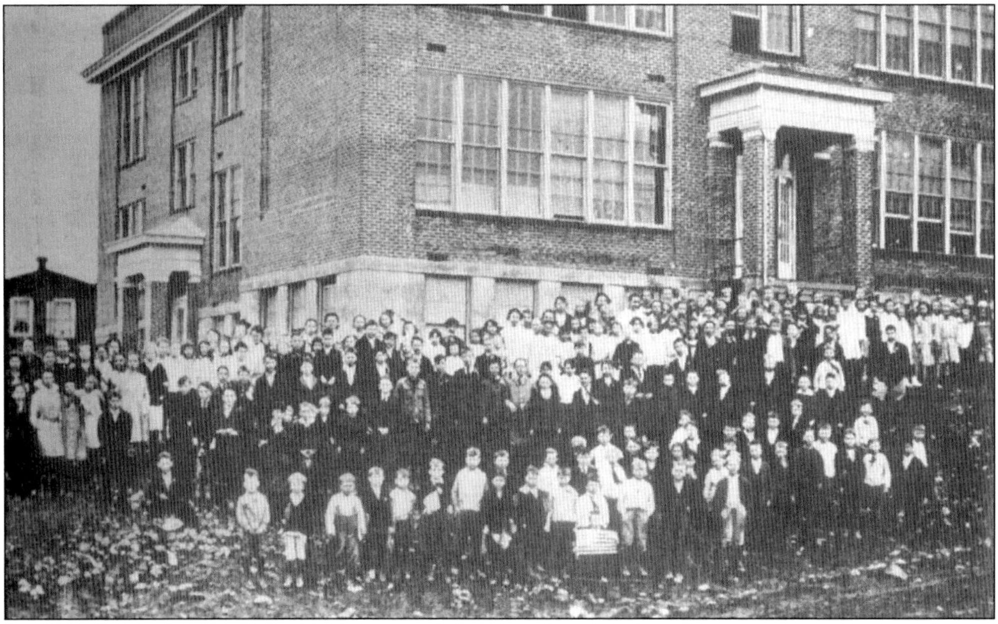

The Shenandoah School student body was photographed in front of their new two-story, brick schoolhouse in 1918. R. T. Kingree's kiln furnished the brick for the 1917 structure. It dwarfed the previous 1884 school with its subsequent humble, wooden-framed addition, as seen at far left. The structure's south-side twin, built in 1928 and still standing, filled a void when this building burned in 1934. (*PN&C.*)

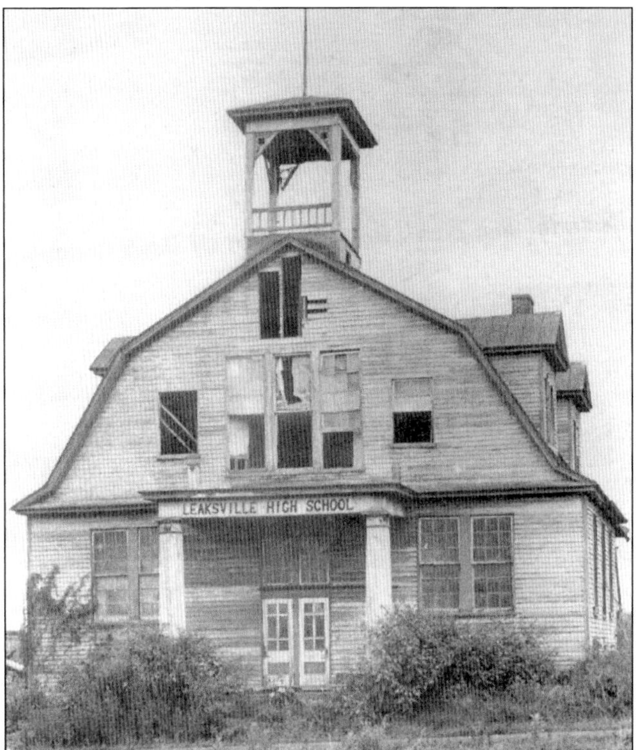

Even though it was called Leaksville High School, this gambrel-roofed structure, built around 1893, only housed grades one through seven. Ralph O. Rothgeb painted the school's name in 1916. When last used in 1948, it contained four classrooms and an auditorium on the second floor. Located on the south end of Leaksville Cemetery, the school was torn down in 1975. (*PN&C.*)

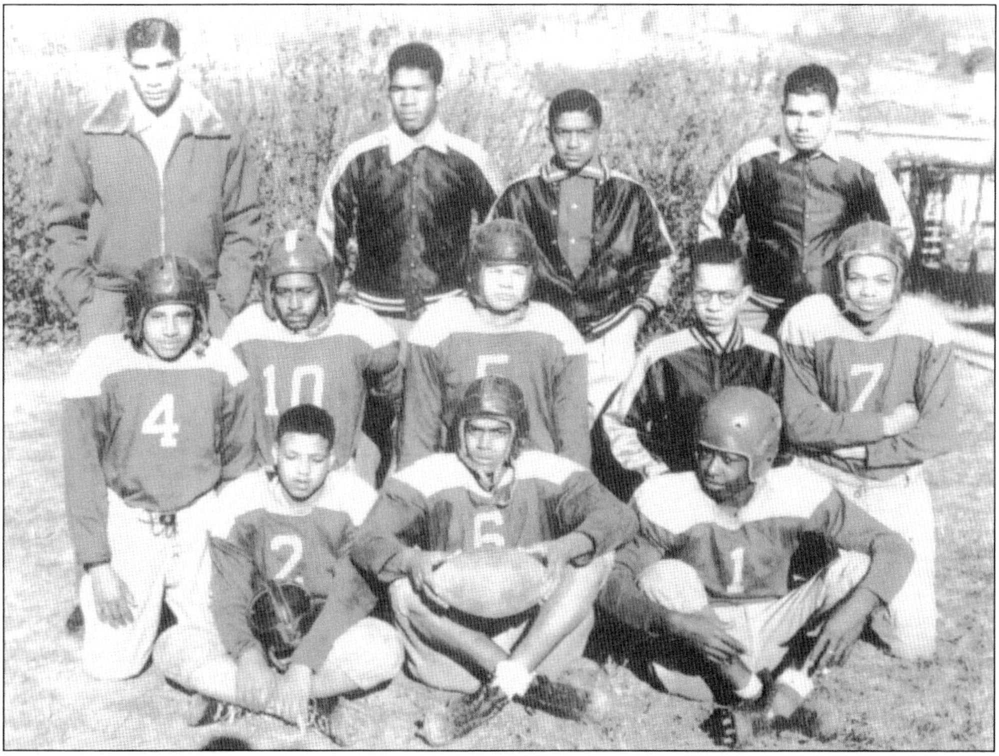

The Luray District Andrew Jackson football team posed in the early 1950s. The school, named after the prominent West Main merchant, functioned until integration took place in 1964. From left to right are (first row) Gerald Veney, Wayne Bundy, and Walter Mitchell; (second row) Clyde Williams, James Parks, Dunbar Haines, Melvin Tutt, and Jessie Porter; (third row) Stanley Brown, Derwood Frye, James Brown, and Maurice Johnson. (*PN&C*.)

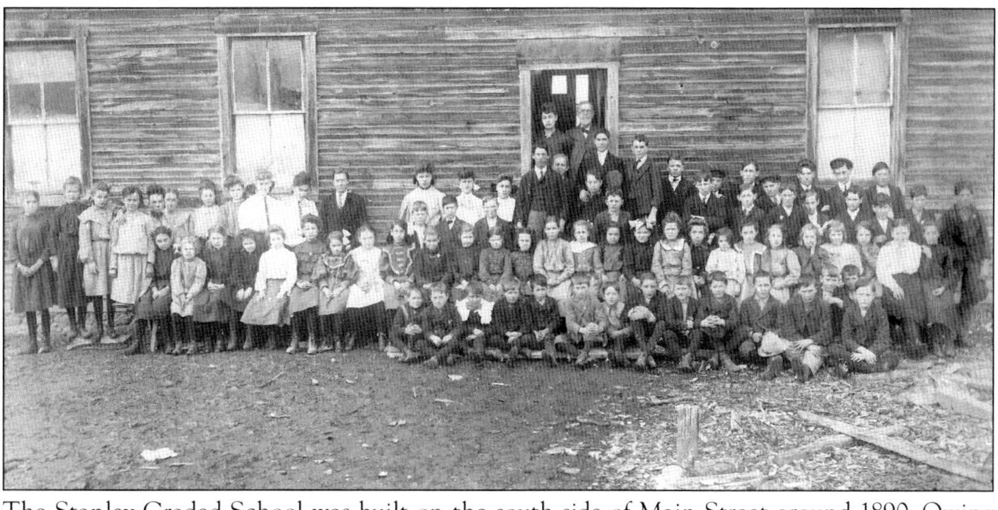

The Stanley Graded School was built on the south side of Main Street around 1890. Owing to the number of students seen here, it was a welcomed addition to the town over Marksville District's smaller Oak Shade School located just west. Later I. Casper Bradley used the building as a funeral home in Stanley. In the doorway of this *c.* 1910 image are Professor Hodge and his assistant Alberta Jett. (Town of Stanley.)

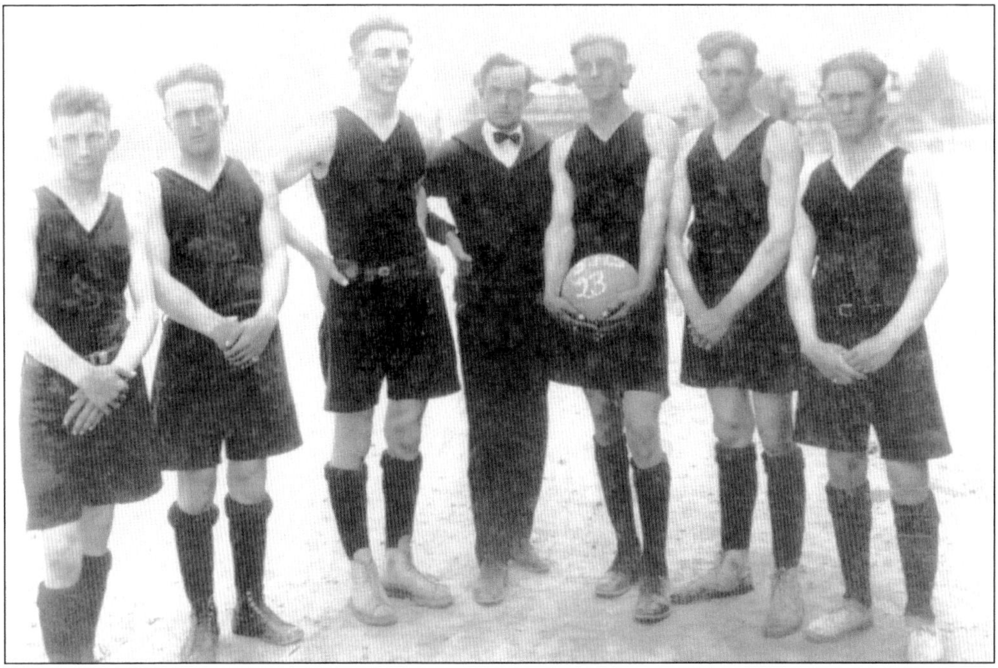

The Stanley High School boys' basketball team posed for their team portrait in 1923. From left to right are Carlos Gochenour, Shirley Kiblinger, Curtis Foltz, Principal Floyd Koontz, Leslie Foltz, Edward Long, and Nelson Koontz. The players' shoes hardly seem appropriate compared to today's standard. (Dan Vaughn.)

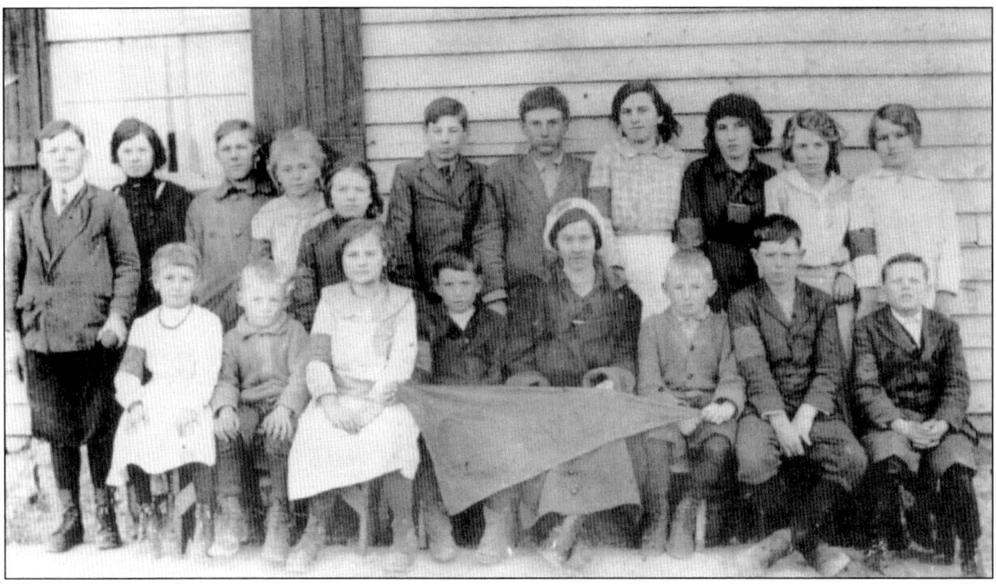

Located west of Luray, these Cave School students proudly sport their school's name complete with banner and arm bands in this 1916 image. From left to right are (first row) Virginia Dofflemyer, Oscar Brubaker, Flossie Foltz, Jennings Shenk, teacher Grace McHaney, Rufus Brubaker, H. A. William Miller, and Malcolm Shenk; (second row) Roscoe Barham, Meta Shenk, Ordway Rickard, Alice Brubaker, Reva Shenk, Otis Rickard, Frank Kibler, Gladys Brubaker, Carrie Nichols, Ressie Brubaker, and Genevieve Dofflemyer. (*PN&C*.)

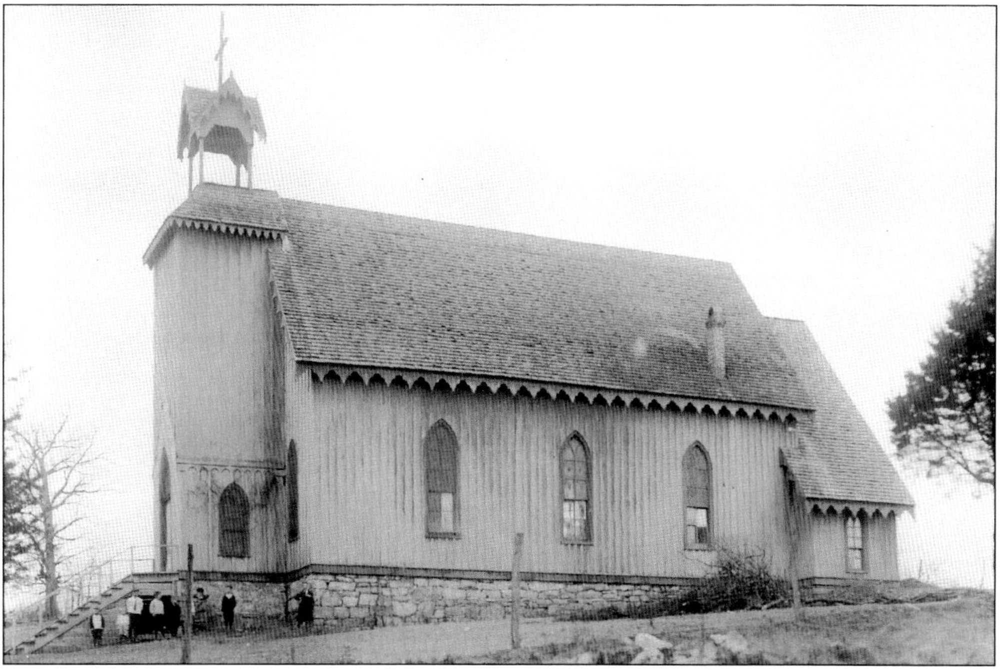

On February 10, 1872, construction began on the balloon-framed Christ Episcopal Church on Luray's West Main Street. A decade would pass before its completion in 1882. A bell from an unknown donor arrived in 1885 with the stipulation it be installed by February 5. Rector Murray went to work at once. These young children took time out from play to pose for photographer Max Frensley. A new church was erected on Amiss Avenue in 1915. (Christ Episcopal Church.)

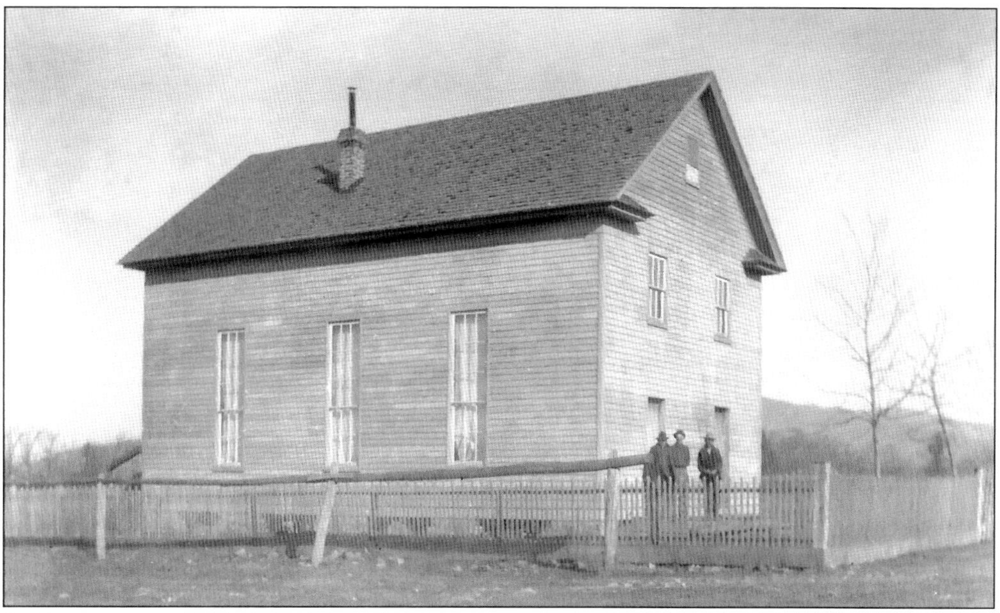

Sadly, over time, the details of many local images were lost to obscurity. That is the case with this 1890s glass-plate positive of this church in the Massanutten section of Page. Its starkness conveys a simpler era. And though its name and denomination are possibly all forgotten, the message of Truth meant to be spoken here remains forever. (*PN&C.*)

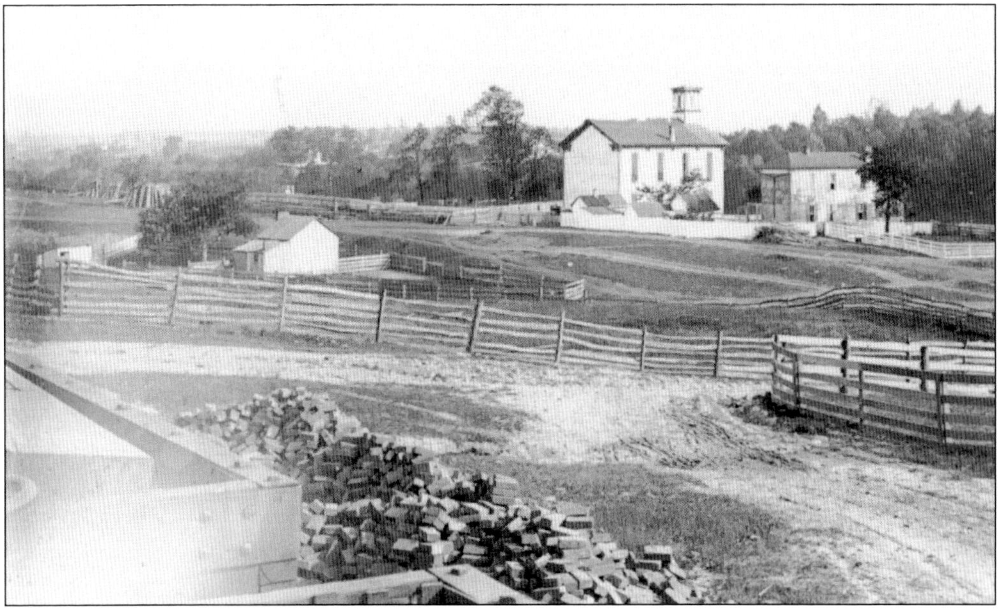

John Fields built Shenandoah's first Methodist church in 1870. Facing the river, it was located at the northern end of the Methodist cemetery. As it neared completion, the 1870 flood washed it away, with its bell tolling eerily as it floated down the river. This 1880 image documents the second structure. The parsonage, at right, was removed in 1954 for a Maryland Avenue expansion. (Virginia Tech.)

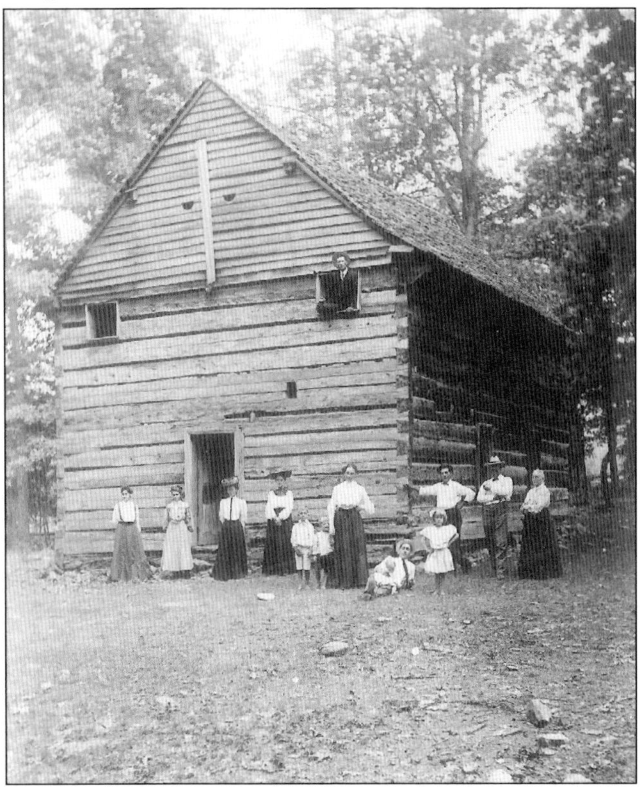

Stoneberger Lutheran Church was built southwest of Stanley near Honey Run in 1795. In front of the hewn-log structure, from left to right, are Maye Lucas Stirewalt, Ida Printz, Mamie Hershberger, Minnie Lucas, Anna and Ed Lucas (on ground), with their four children, Hubert Lucas, David and Susan Hershberger, and Vernon Stirewalt (in window). Contained within the wall's cornerstone when dismantled in 1920 was a brass-clasped German Bible, a book of manuscript, and a 1795 half-dollar, all folded in a sheet of hammered lead. (Mildred Stirewalt Coleman.)

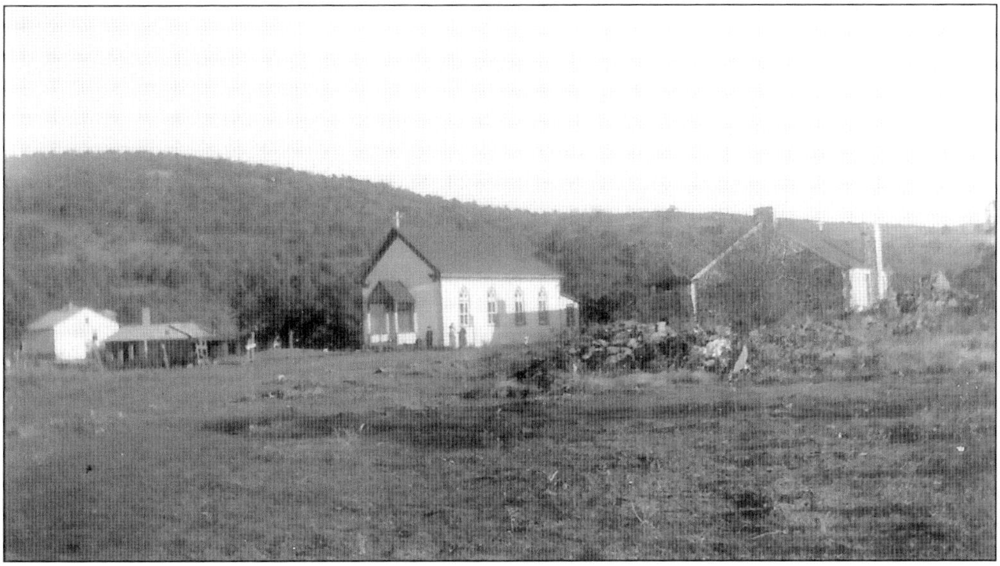

On the western edge of the Shenandoah National Park, Tanner's Ridge Episcopal Mission was one of 30 mission fields of the Archdeaconry of the Blue Ridge. Under the direction of two mission builders, this frame building, which was located near Markham, Virginia, was dismantled and reassembled in 1937, providing a church here. (St. George's Episcopal.)

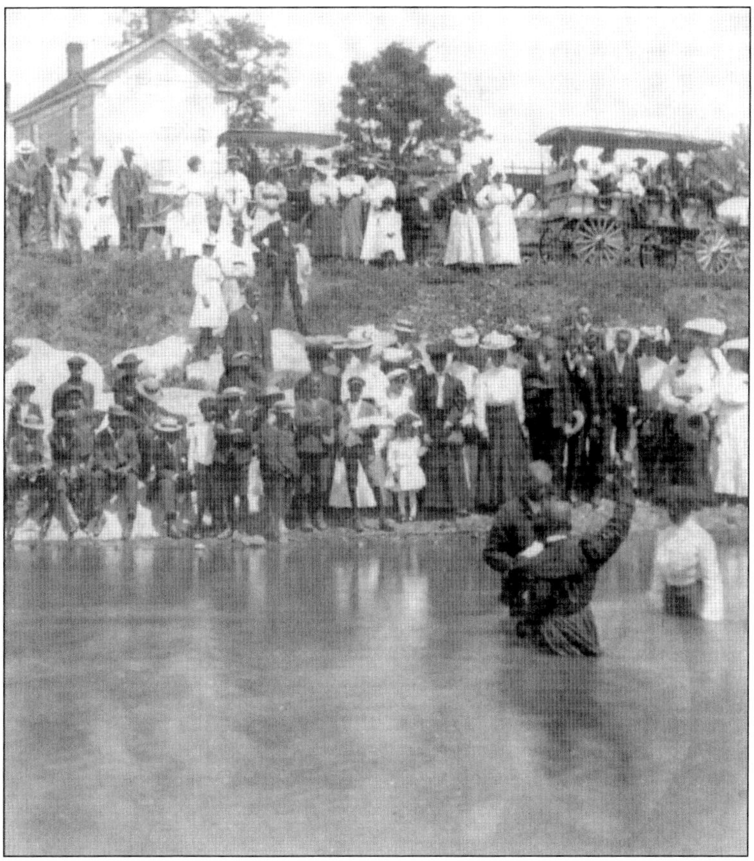

Rev. James Woodson, pastor of Bethel Baptist Church in West Luray, often baptized members in the Hawksbill Creek, as seen here. The church was organized in 1884. Looking north, photographer Wallace Rhodes documented this c. 1915 event. The creek's location was later moved about 100 yards east, when a new Route 340 road was constructed in the 1930s. At top left is the old J. B. Hudson residence, and at top right is the N&W's Hawksbill Crossing trestle. (*PN&C.*)

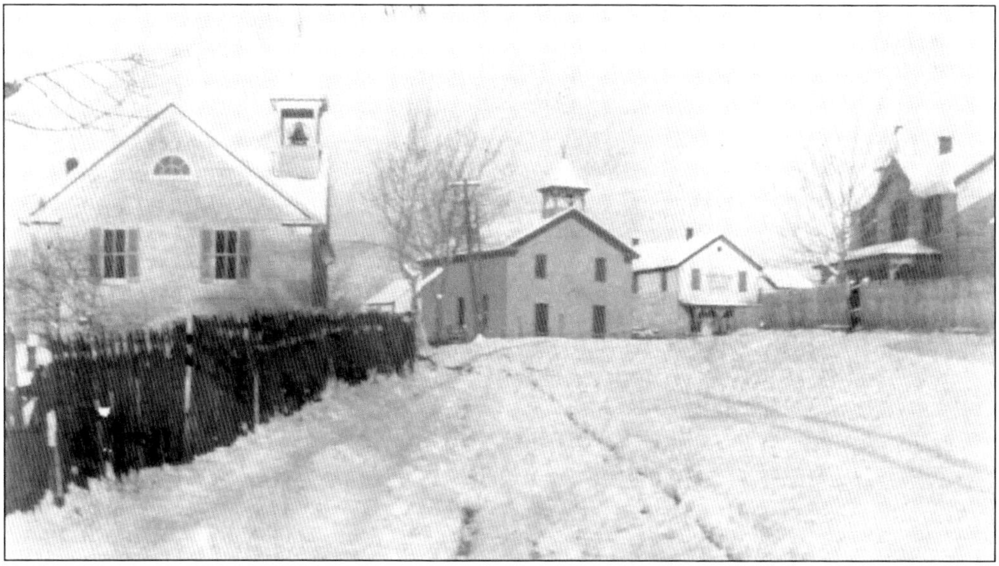

Standing at left is the Rileyville Church of the Brethren in this 1910s wintry view of West Main Street. Rileyville Baptist Church, at center, a New School Baptist organized on January 25, 1885, had L. R. Milbourne as its first pastor. The first 10 individuals to join, interestingly, were all women. Farther right is the A. B. Hockman General Merchandise Store. Hockman would issue in-store trade tokens to promote sales. (Carol Seely.)

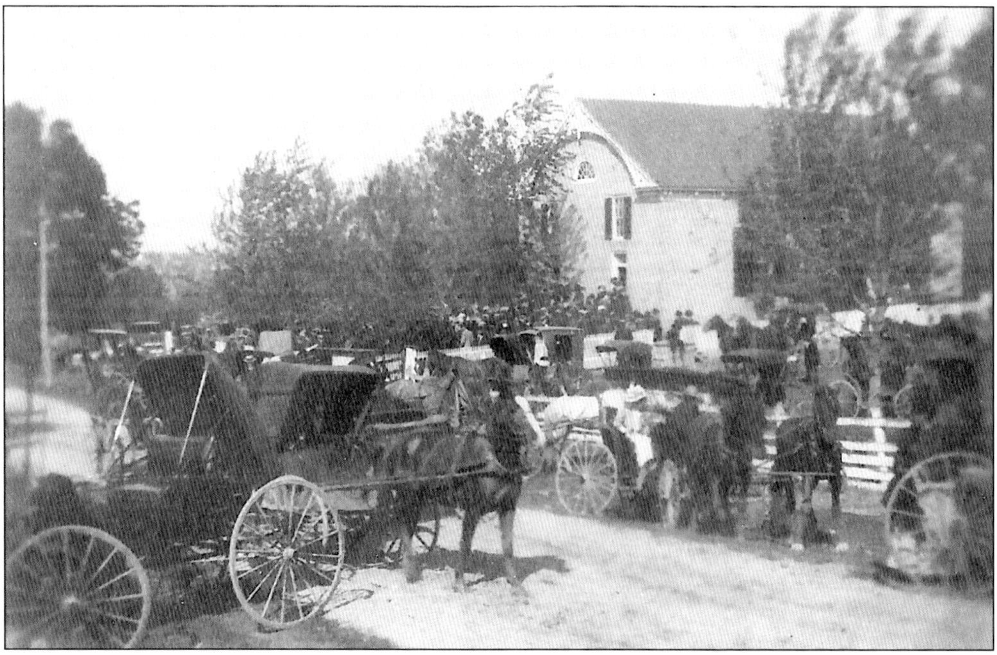

Carriages gather for this May 10, 1908, Union Meeting at Mill Creek Baptist Church in Hamburg. In preparation for the services, women whitewashed the fences, with Hamburg's Luray Lime Company providing the main ingredient. Elder John Koontz founded the church, Page County's oldest, around the time of the American Revolution. The existing church (shown) was built in 1889 for $650 to replace the congregation's former meeting place, the nearby Mauck Meeting House. (Bob Graves.)

Five

The Rail's Arrival

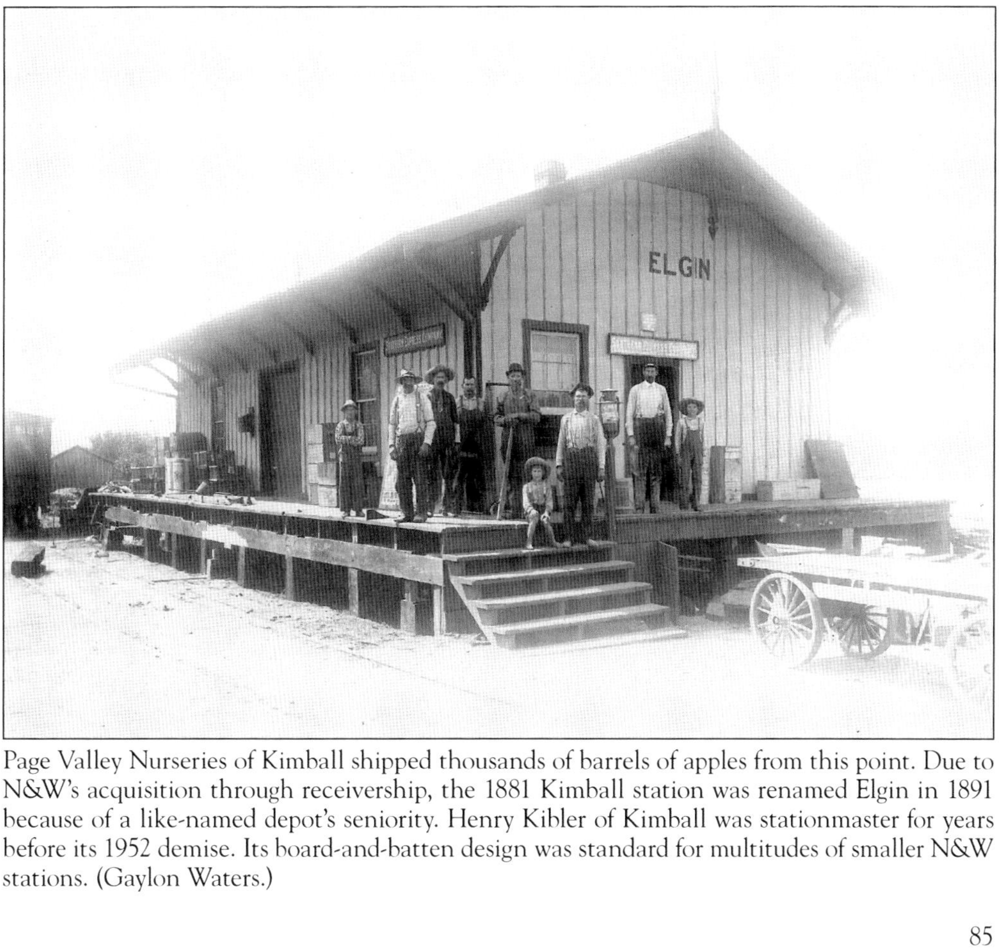

Page Valley Nurseries of Kimball shipped thousands of barrels of apples from this point. Due to N&W's acquisition through receivership, the 1881 Kimball station was renamed Elgin in 1891 because of a like-named depot's seniority. Henry Kibler of Kimball was stationmaster for years before its 1952 demise. Its board-and-batten design was standard for multitudes of smaller N&W stations. (Gaylon Waters.)

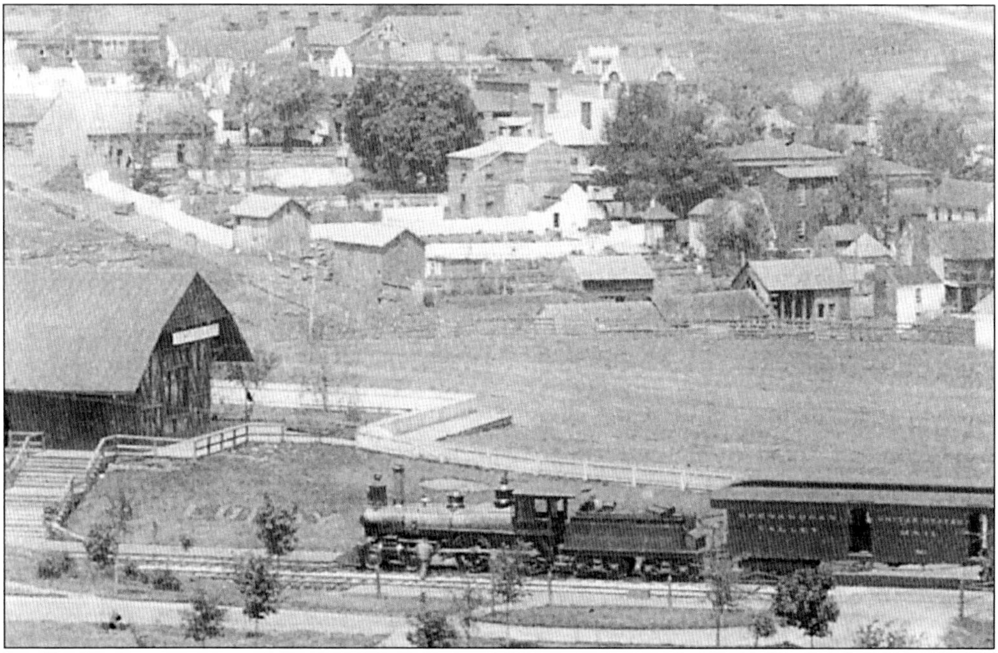

A rail worker inspects the drive linkage of this idle 4-4-0 SVRR steam locomotive. Just behind the wood-filled tender is a railway post office mail rail car, operating in conjunction with the U.S. Postal Service. Interestingly, the word "Luray" is whitewashed on the bank between the Luray Inn's Excursion House Restaurant and the southbound train. (Warren and Penny Smith.)

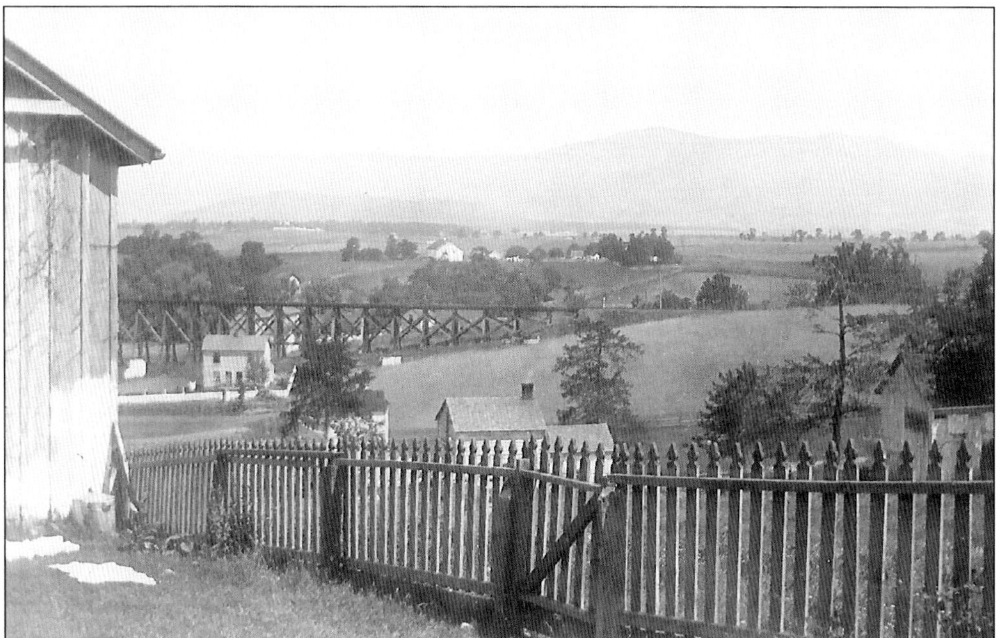

This 1896 wooden trestle at Luray's Hawksbill Creek Overpass was just one of dozens in Page. Ultimately, the primitive beginnings would be replaced with steel throughout the 1900s. Perhaps the South Court Street whitewashing job, at left, was interrupted to photograph the mountain scene in this July 1900 image. (Dan Vaughn.)

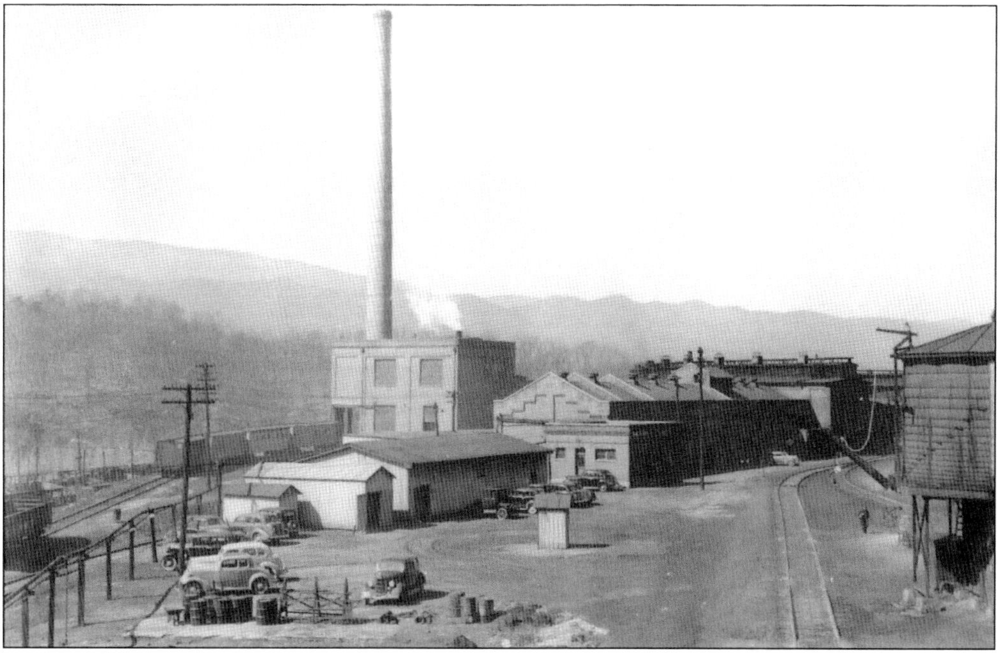

In November 1916, fire destroyed Shenandoah's machine shops, including the divisional roundhouse. This was a blow to the World War I–period work needing to be accomplished here. By 1919, new shops and an enlarged roundhouse were rebuilt. Within two years of this 1941 view, the 250-foot smokestack had been banded, repaired, and painted. (Virginia Tech.)

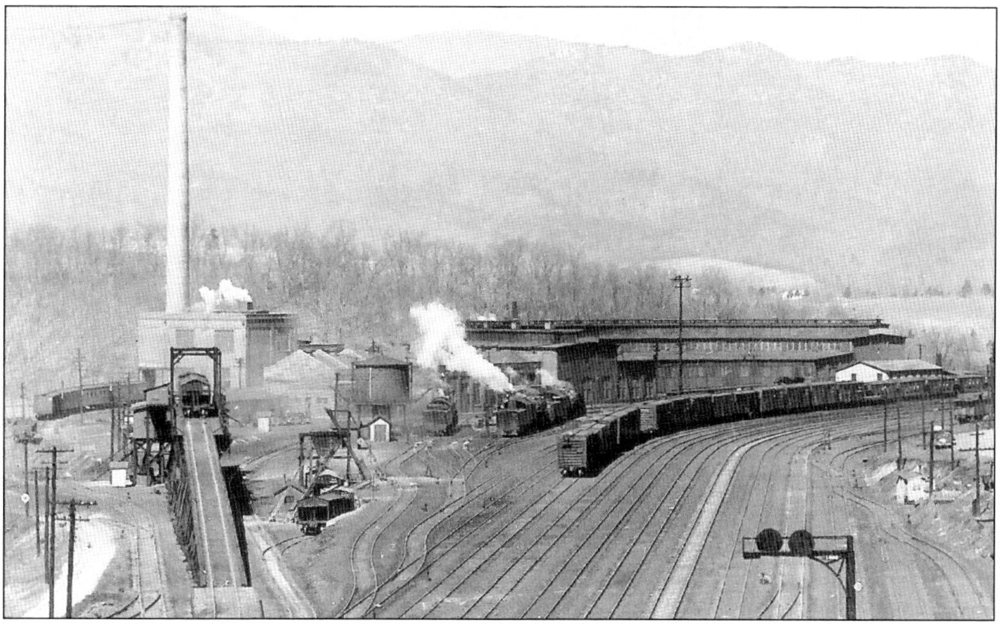

N&W spent a fortune here—rail yard, machine shops, roundhouse, turntable, lubritorium, coal tipple, dual-operable water tank (one of only three on the line), passenger and freight stations, and the divisional offices. When the GP series diesels arrived in January 1957, one month premature to steam's demise, it gave an odd flair to the yard with the two operating simultaneously. The Shenandoah workforce knew how detrimental the "tenderless" newcomer would be. (Virginia Tech.)

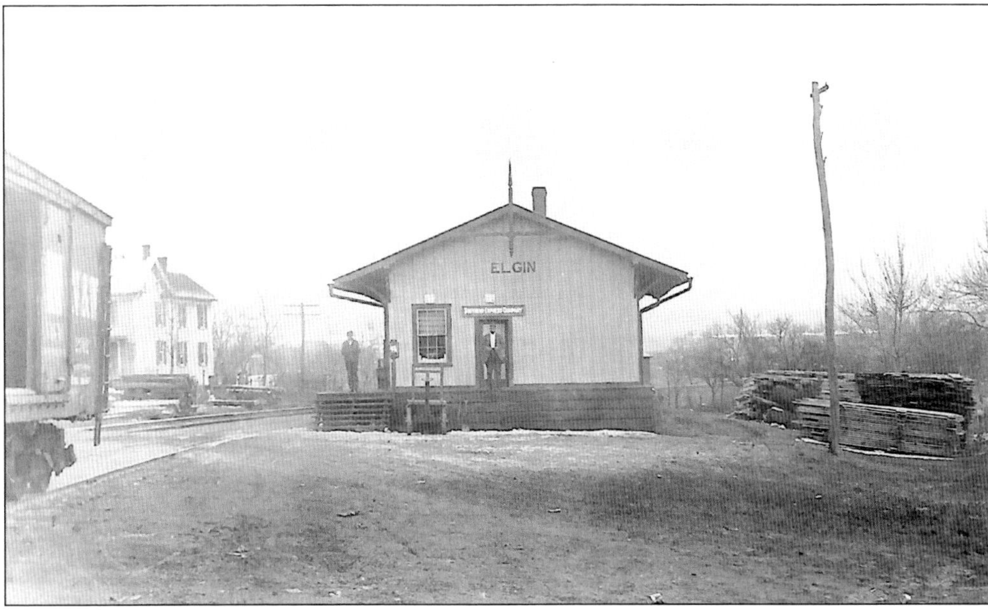

This view of Elgin Depot in Kimball gives a glimpse of the rural activity in this 1910s setting. Lumber stacked on site was quite possibly for the station's scheduled expansion, needed to accommodate N&W's growing freight business. By now, electricity had trickled to the community. A lone boxcar rests on the line's inner-rail sidetrack, while the town's post office sits out of view, directly behind the station. (David Moyer.)

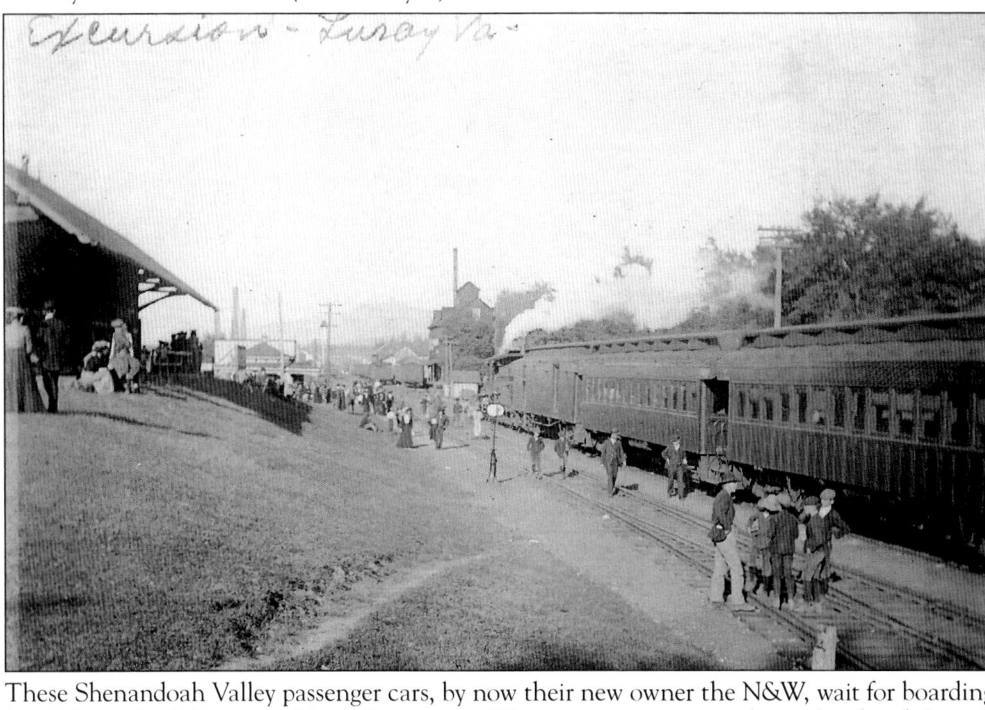

These Shenandoah Valley passenger cars, by now their new owner the N&W, wait for boarding beside Luray Inn's Excursion House Restaurant. The restaurant, commonly confused with Luray's 1907 depot, satisfied overflow crowds from Luray Inn. In April 1885, a new Pullman Palace Buffet Sleeping Car, SVRR's Road No. 437, was aptly named "Luray." (Mildred Stirewalt Coleman.)

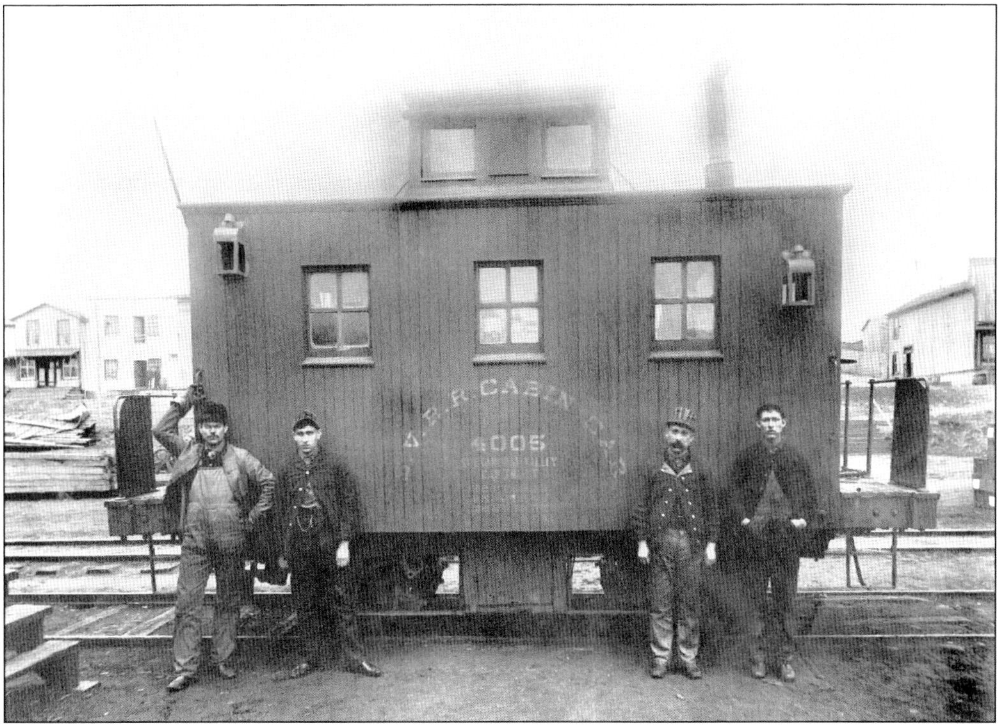

This SVRR caboose sits idle in Shenandoah Yard in 1887. Through receivership, N&W acquired the vintage four-wheeled version that was its standard till about 1915. Up until the 1980s, U.S. law required a caboose on every freight train. It was then outmoded by an electronic component called FRED, or Flashing Rear-end Device, that monitors train activity, all but eliminating its need. (Virginia Tech.)

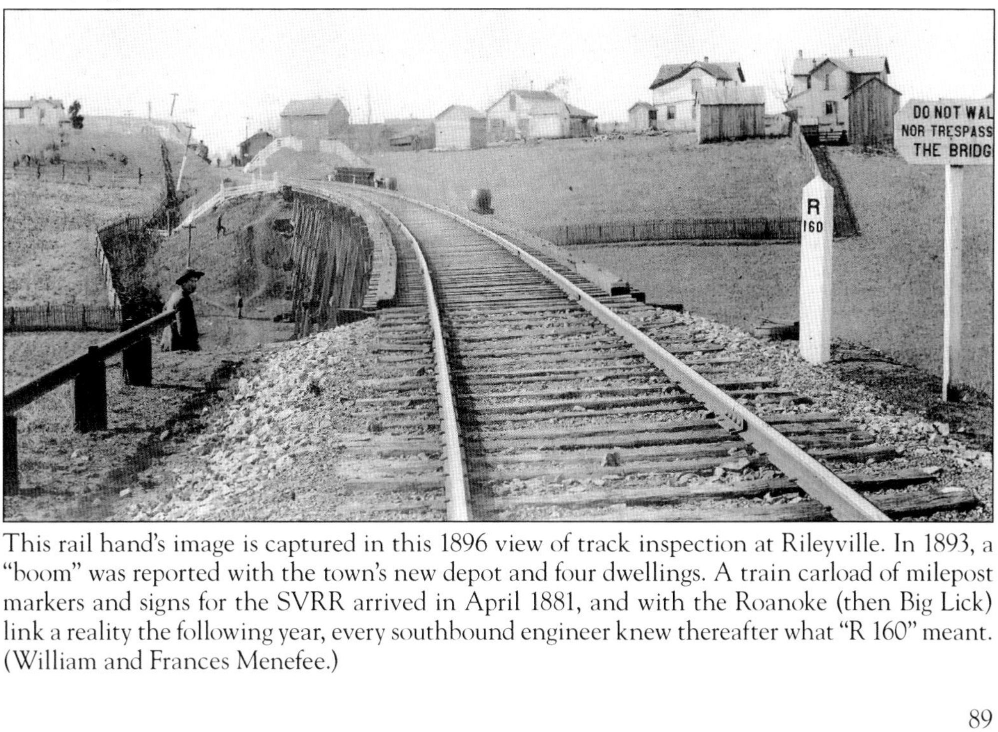

This rail hand's image is captured in this 1896 view of track inspection at Rileyville. In 1893, a "boom" was reported with the town's new depot and four dwellings. A train carload of milepost markers and signs for the SVRR arrived in April 1881, and with the Roanoke (then Big Lick) link a reality the following year, every southbound engineer knew thereafter what "R 160" meant. (William and Frances Menefee.)

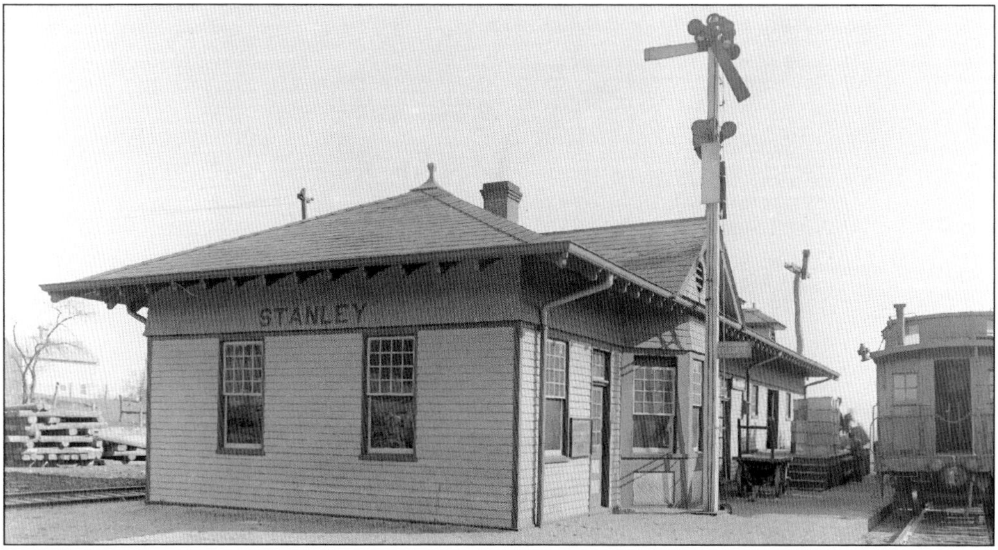

Over 6,000 passenger tickets sold in fiscal year 1881–1882 by T. O. Graves, Marksville Station's (present-day Stanley) first depot agent. By 1972, Stanley's depot was all but abandoned, except that N&W retained ownership. The town solicited the purchase to no avail. This longest-lived of three Stanley stations, and a fire survivor, closed on March 24, 1972, being razed later that year. Stanley's depot sign, its most identifiable keepsake, was donated to the town by this author. (Virginia Tech.)

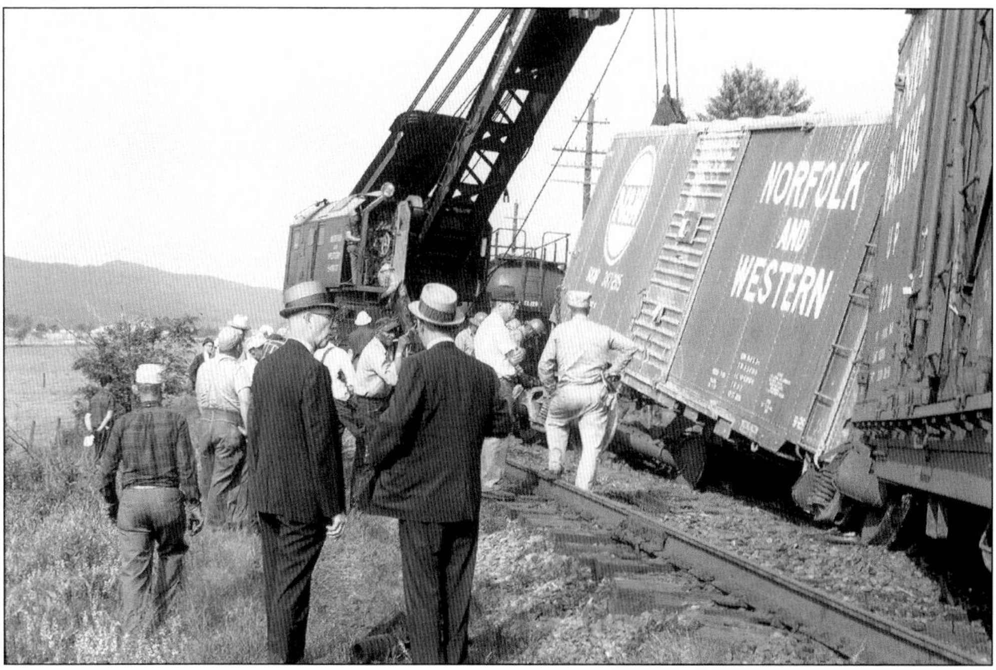

Fine met coarse when these two unidentified businessmen conversed in front of N&W's No. 540037, 250-ton derrick rail crane. It had been sent from Roanoke to remedy this June 10, 1967, northbound derailment of a dozen cars across Stanley's Main Street. Gondolas gouged, boxcars remained "listing," and trucks (rail wheel assemblies) littered the intersection. There were no injuries, and its mention continues to this day. (Town of Stanley.)

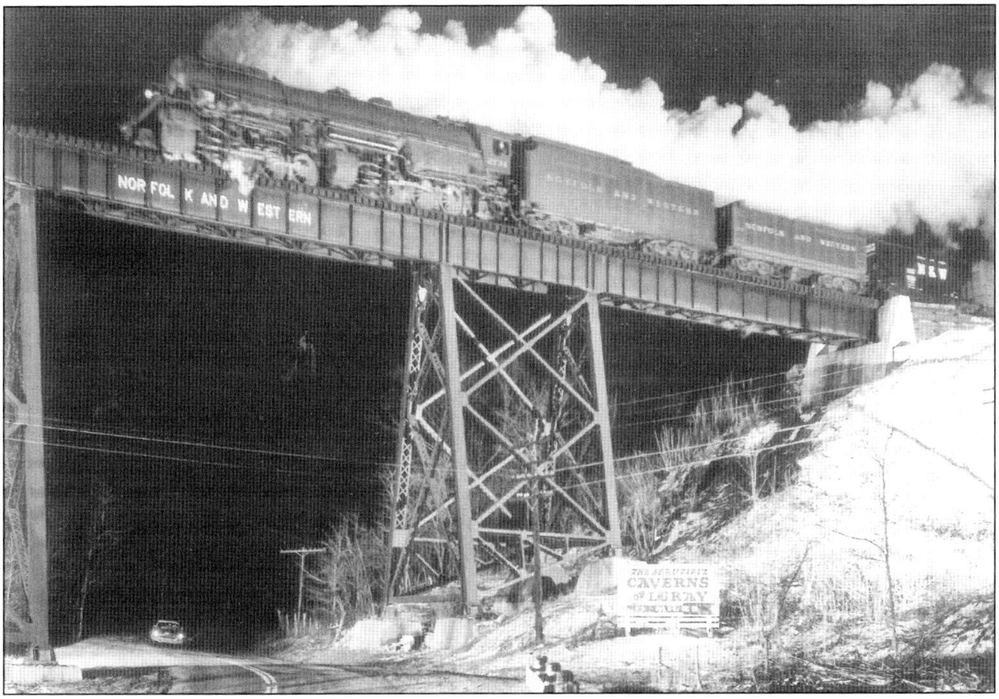

N&W's class Y6a R/N 2174, a 2-8-8-2 Mallet makes a commanding appearance as it crosses Trestle No. 633 heading north. Plenty of steam is available since this mixed-freight has both a tender and an auxiliary water car. A sign advertising Luray Caverns directs U.S. Route 340 traffic through the trestle between Overall and Compton, Virginia. O. Winston Link, famous for his illuminated nocturnal photography, used his 1952 Buick for comparison in this March 1956 scene. (O. Winston Link Museum.)

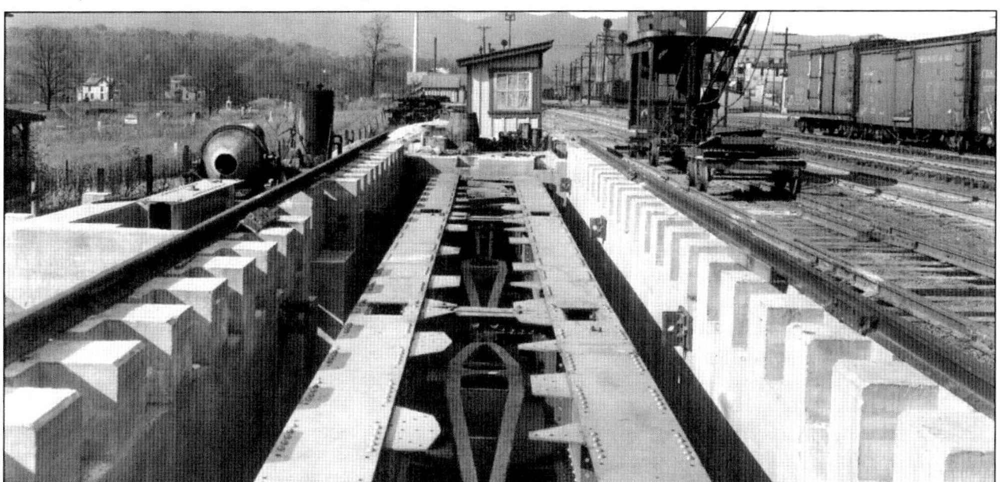

Freight transport was big business for N&W. By 1910, it was operating 10 times the number of freight cars than passenger. These track scales, pictured in 1929 south of Shenandoah's Maryland Avenue, were installed to handle the enormous tonnage of raw materials extracted from Blue Ridge's western slopes. Spur rails linked the Garrison, Kemble, and Smith Ore Banks, as well as Big Gem's Furnace No. 1 and Fox Mountain Mine's Furnace No. 2, to Shenandoah Yard. (Virginia Tech.)

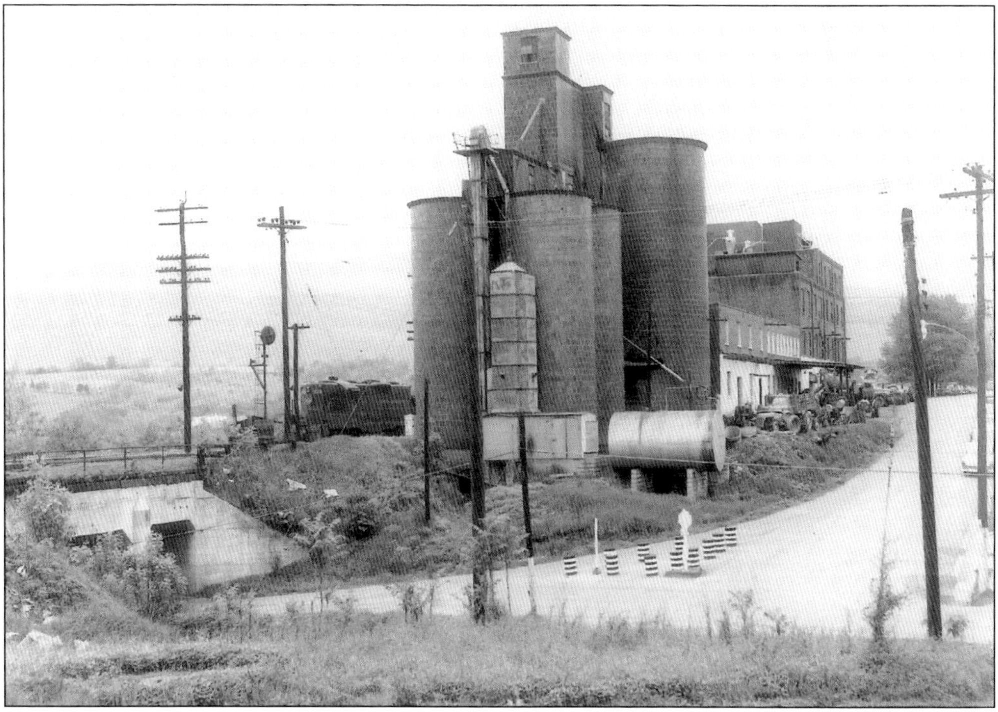

May 9, 1960, marked N&W's final day of revenue for steam operations. Shenandoah was still lamenting over their conversion to diesel power. In this 1959 image, a General Motors EMD GP9, No. 679, peers out from behind an East Point Mills grain tower. In October 1960, one of the ceramic towers burst, spilling 6,800 bushels of wheat. Miller R. Randolph Koontz dealt with the blow. (Allan Rinaca.)

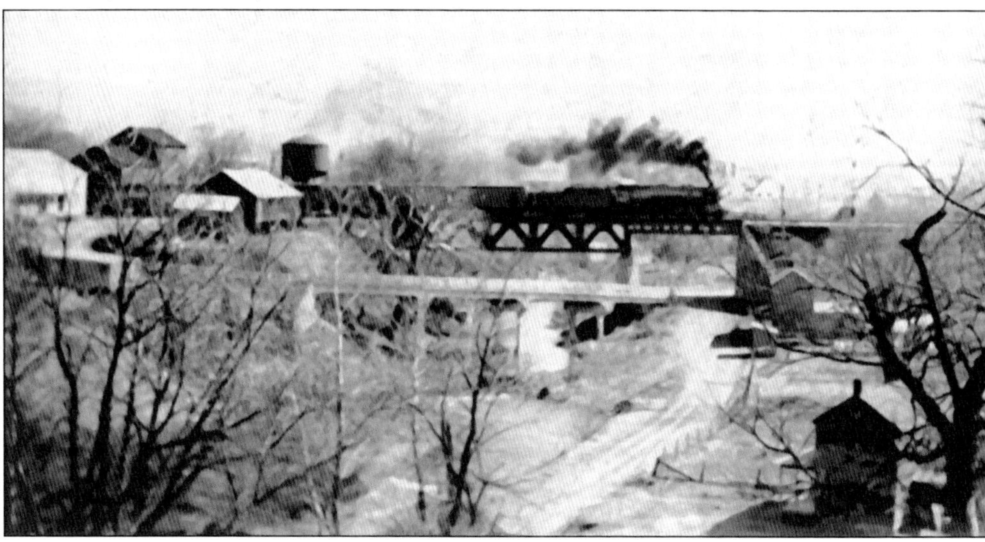

Page Cooperative Farm Bureau (left), the oldest in Virginia, had a close relationship with the railroad in handling bulk agricultural shipments. A southbound freight thunders just above the newly constructed Route 340 bridge in this early-1930s photograph. The bridge was of great convenience, but the growing U.S. road system was delivering a crushing blow to the rail industry. (Robert K. Schlatzer Jr.)

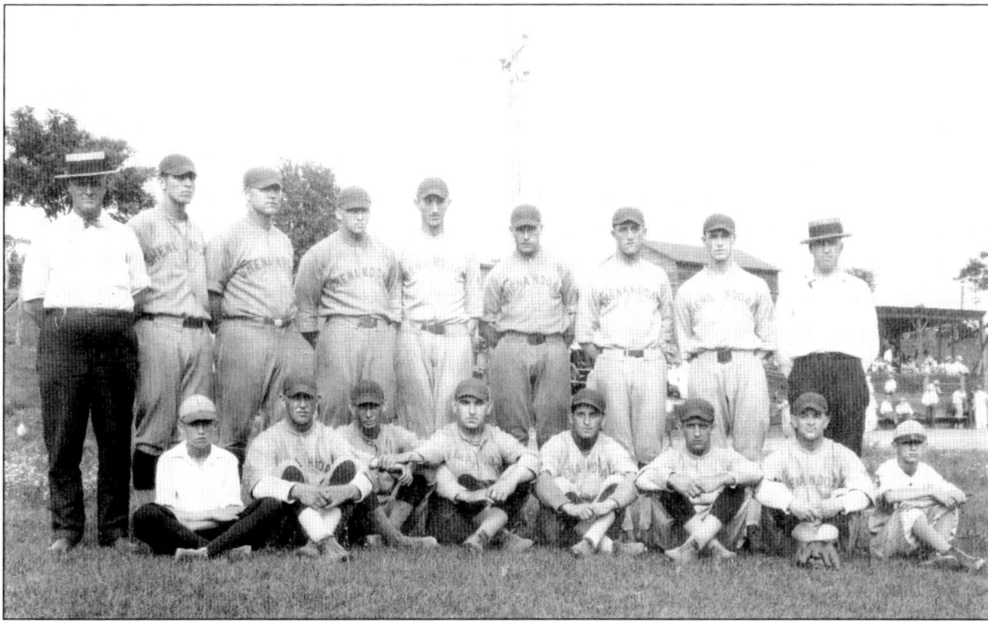

Shenandoah Shops N&W baseball team posed for this 1927–1928 season portrait. Pictured from left to right are (first row) Freelyn "Hip" Stanley (bat boy), T. R. Morris, Bill Manning, George Bear, Jack Monger, Betts Breeden, Jack Elliot, and James Frazier (bat boy); (second row) F. L. Wysong (supervisor), J. W. Coon Jr., Babe Adams, Evans Cook, J. E. "Sis" Whitehead, L. T. Lefler, Harry Dean, Cloral McDaniel, and coach W. C. Whitmire. Home games were played on the 1910s field just north of Shenandoah Power Plant. (Laura Rosazza.)

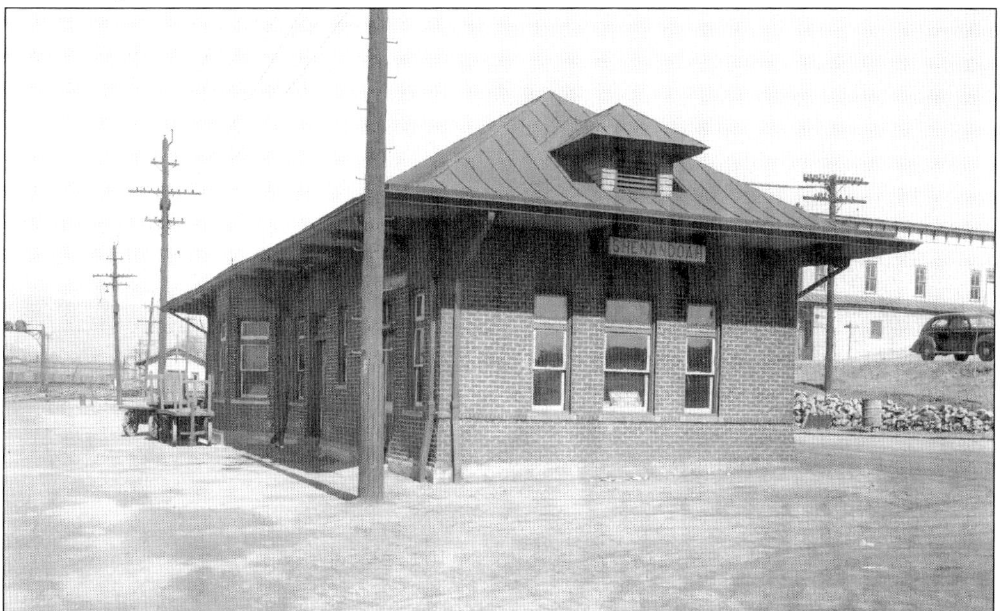

This 1910s brick Shenandoah Passenger Station replaced an undersized original 1880s wooden structure. Passenger service at the mid-divisional depot, pictured here in March 1941, was discontinued around 1960. The 1956 creation of the Eisenhower Interstate Highway System had greatly changed modes of transportation. (Virginia Tech.)

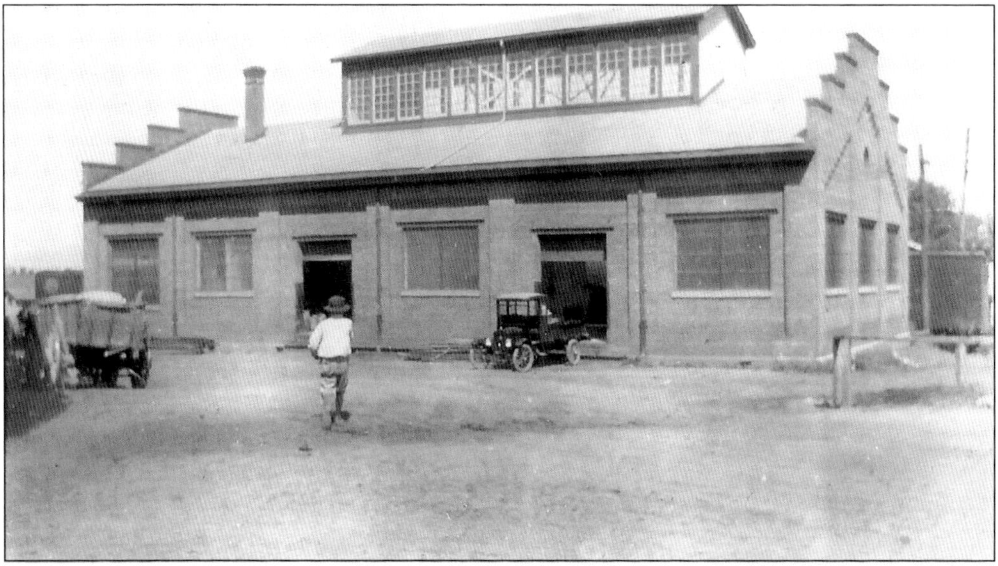

Built as an upgrade by N&W around 1910, Luray's Freight Depot handled the railroad's increasing demands. In 1881, E. H. Davenport was Luray's first freight agent for the newly constructed SVRR. Then the depot consisted of a tapestry of wooden buildings for the various freight, including livestock pens. The structure shown was torn down in December 1988. (Naomi Inskeep.)

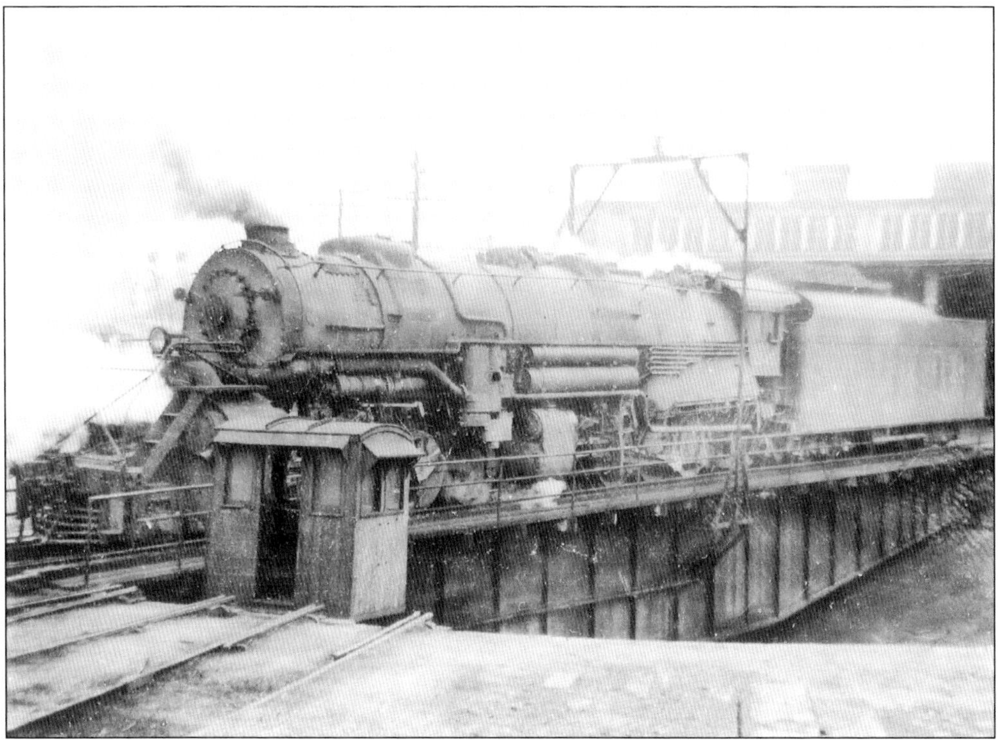

The operator's shanty, revolving with this 115-foot turntable in Shenandoah Yard, was kept busy supplying the 21-stall roundhouse with work like this 2-8-8-2 Mallet with tender. The Shenandoah workforce would surpass 500 men at the divisional workshops in the 1920s. The turntable remains buried on site. (Norfolk and Western Historical Society.)

Train traffic was held up for days when this N&W freight wrecked just north of Compton Trestle on October 15, 1942. The *Page News and Courier* reported the story in a Saturday, October 17 "extra." The October 1942 flood, the worst since 1870, was to blame for the derailment. Because of the wreck's severity, mail was brought to this point and exchanged between trains. (Mary Ann Painter.)

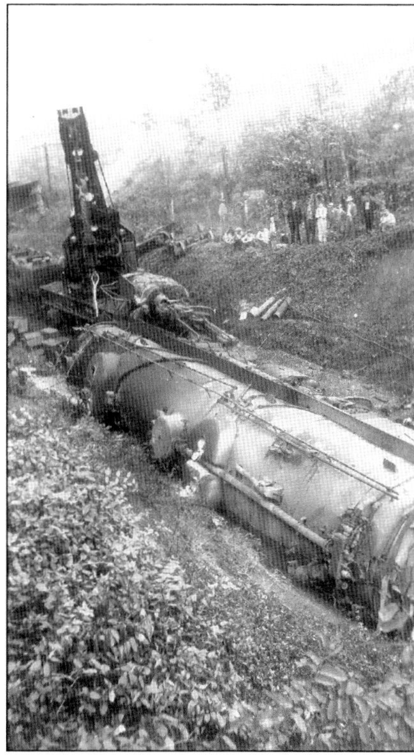

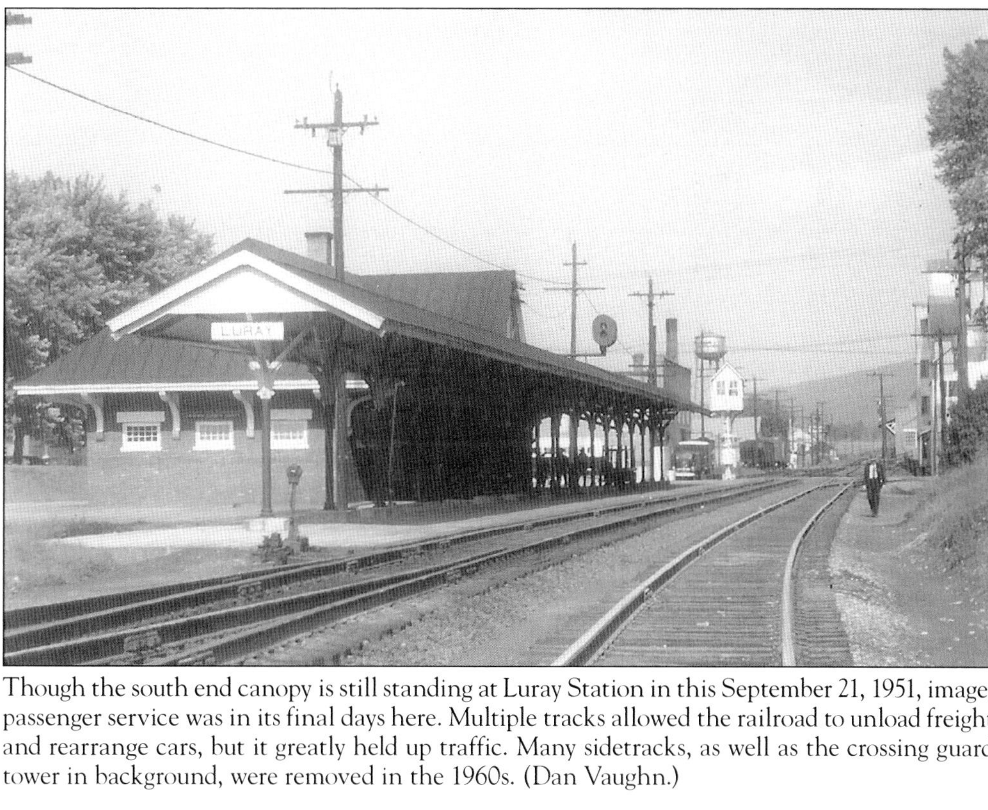

Though the south end canopy is still standing at Luray Station in this September 21, 1951, image, passenger service was in its final days here. Multiple tracks allowed the railroad to unload freight and rearrange cars, but it greatly held up traffic. Many sidetracks, as well as the crossing guard tower in background, were removed in the 1960s. (Dan Vaughn.)

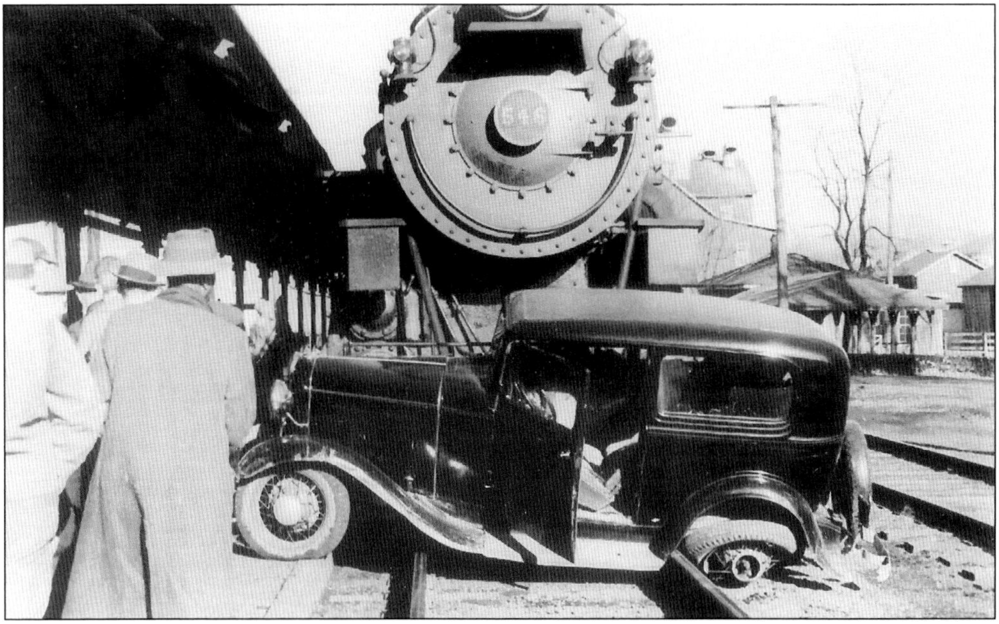

On December 10, 1937, N&W train No. 13 impales on the drawhead a car driven by Hubert Fox, accompanied by his daughter, A. Marie Miller of Dry Run. He had run past Luray's Campbell Street crossing guardsman, D. D. Armstrong, only to stop on the tracks and into the path of locomotive No. 546. Automobiles represented not only competition for the railroad, but sometimes hazards as well. (Page Public Library.)

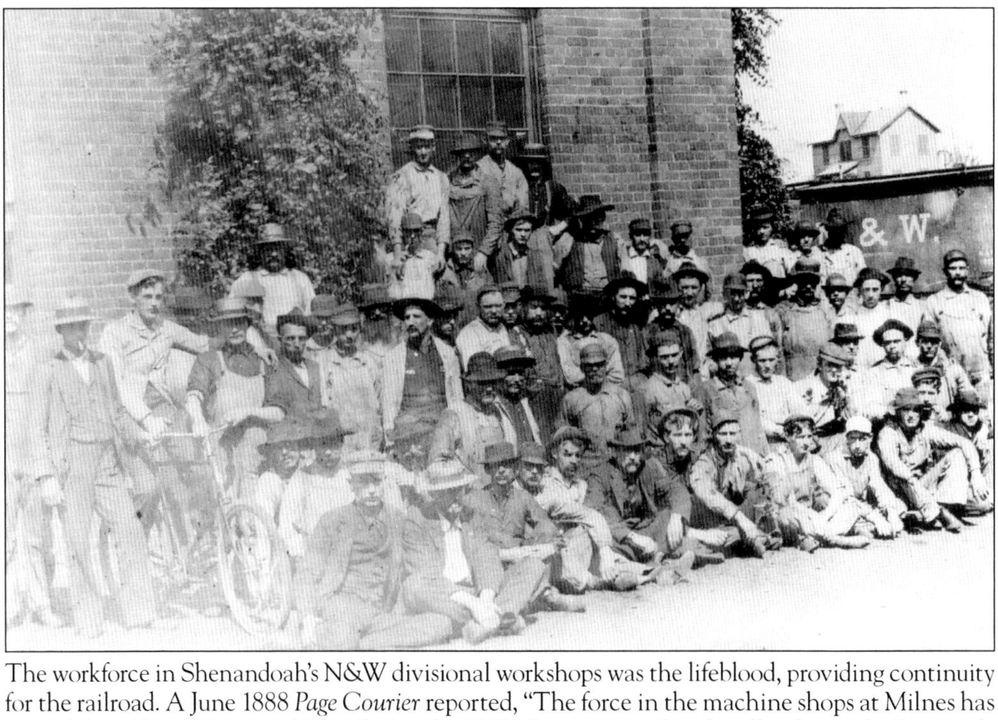

The workforce in Shenandoah's N&W divisional workshops was the lifeblood, providing continuity for the railroad. A June 1888 *Page Courier* reported, "The force in the machine shops at Milnes has recently been largely increased." But during the 1890s depression, railroads suffered severely. Seemingly a hat was prerequisite for employment, as seen in this 1935 photograph. (Virginia Tech.)

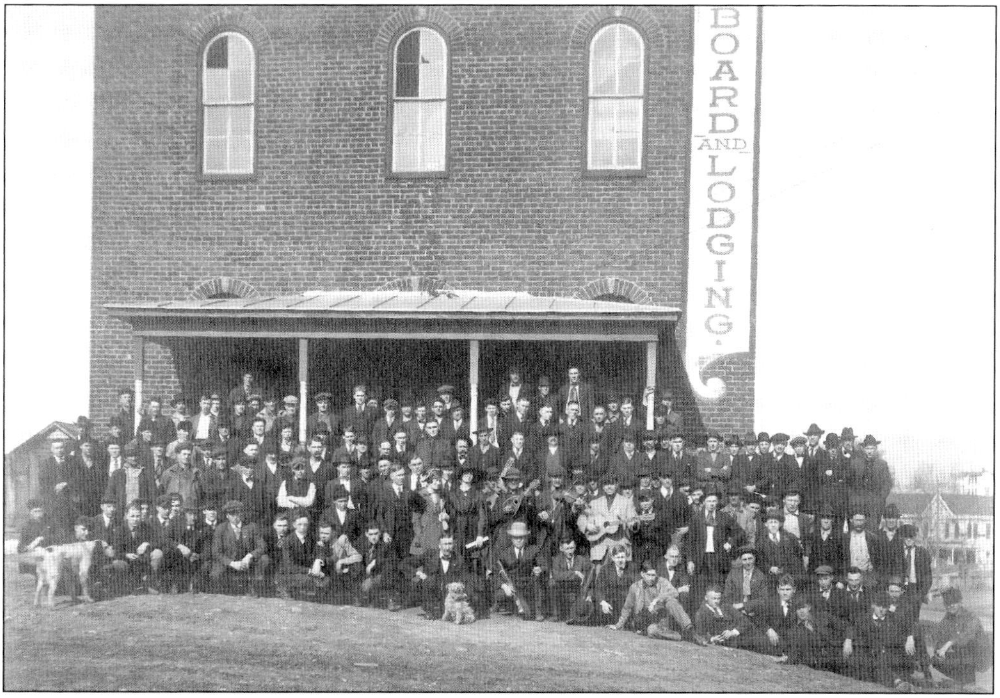

N&W Railroad strikers posed in Shenandoah in front of the old brick hotel on Pennsylvania Avenue and Second Street in 1922. Uncertainty was commonplace with so many variables affecting the economic climate of the railroad. In January 1885, one-half of the workforce in the Milnes railroad shops was discharged, and the events of the 1930s Depression spoke for themselves. (Mildred Stirewalt Coleman.)

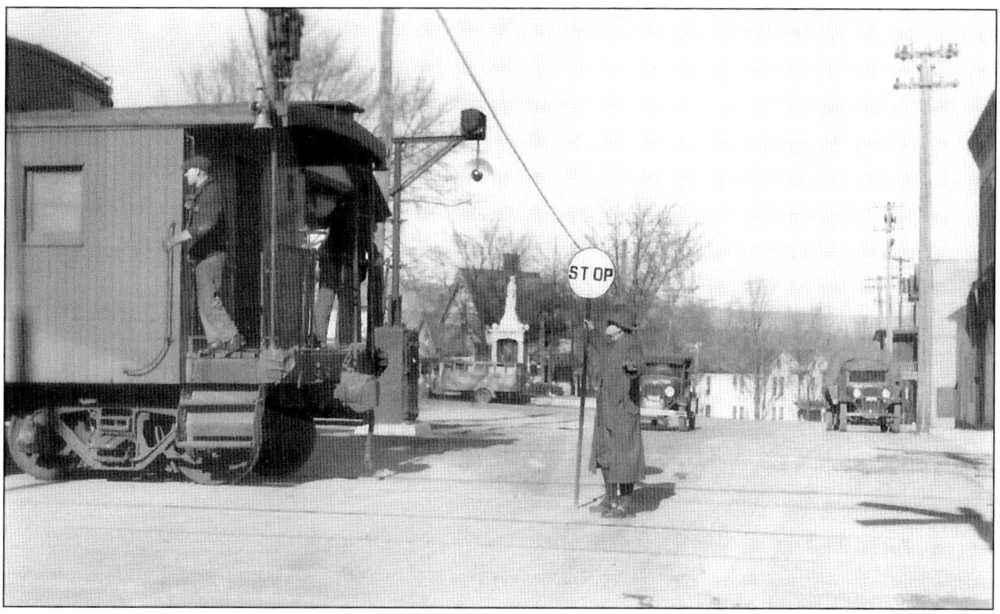

Before the use of automatic grade-crossing equipment and because a mishap could often be tragic, the railroad had watchmen placed at its busier intersections. Here Hughes Campbell of Luray stops the early morning Campbell Street traffic on February 8, 1938. (Page Public Library.)

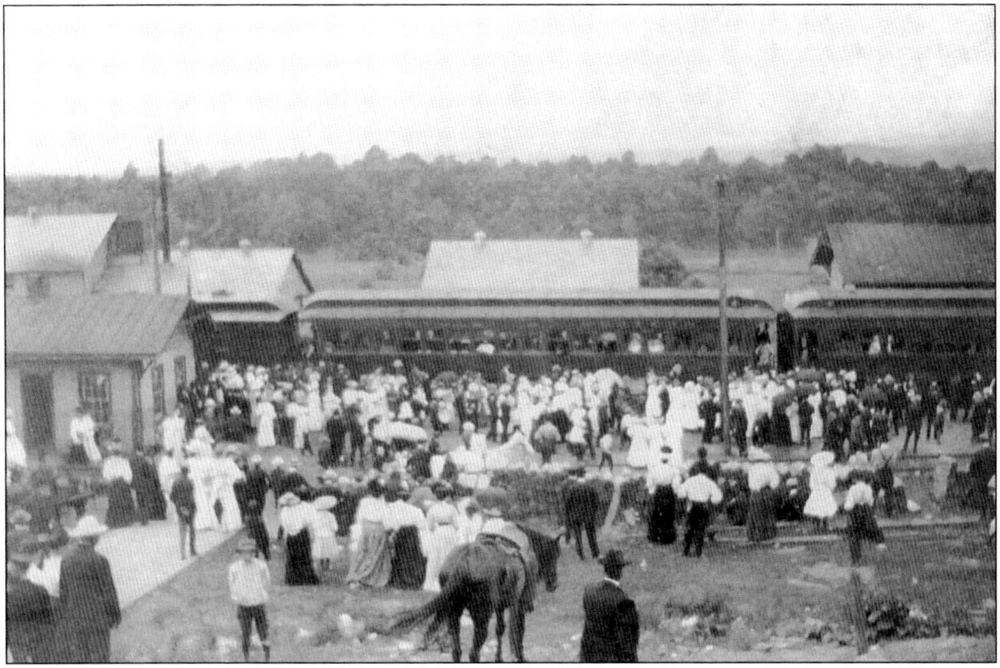

In 1905, this group met beside the 1880s Shenandoah Depot for an excursion to Pen-Mar, a summer resort north of Hagerstown. Family and friends wait in the foreground as the locals prepare to board for this $2 round-trip venture. Quite a crowd also went from Stanley, and the event was popular until the 1930s Depression. (Charles Stevens.)

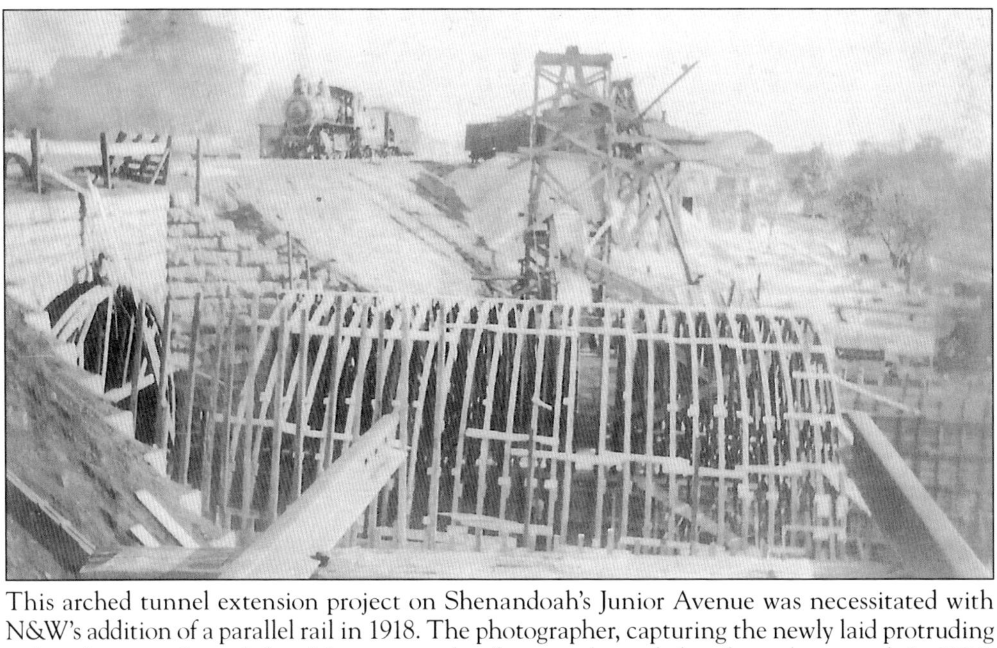

This arched tunnel extension project on Shenandoah's Junior Avenue was necessitated with N&W's addition of a parallel rail in 1918. The photographer, capturing the newly laid protruding rails at bottom, showed the elaborate wooden framework needed to form the tunnel. In 1906, N&W constructed the stone archway over Luray's South Court Street extended between Warren Frank's and Frank Stover's farm, thus dispensing with its wooden trestle. (Jim Brown.)

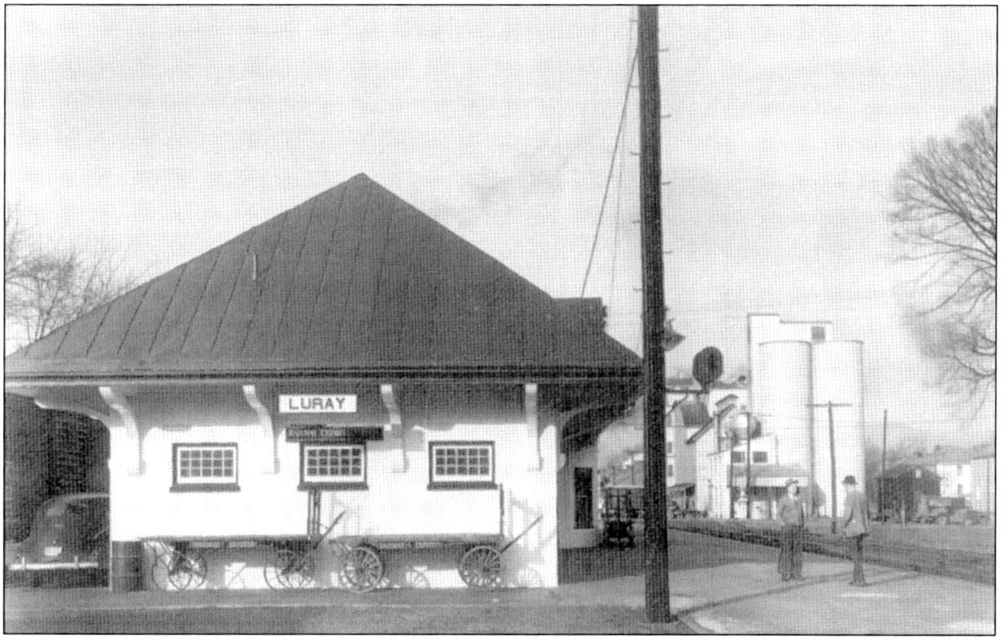

Luray Depot's stationmaster, Bill Leach (left), converses with an unidentified citizen. When the Town of Luray was afforded the opportunity for ownership of the depot, it leaped, and now its century-old refurbishment has given it a second lease on life. (Curtis Harrell.)

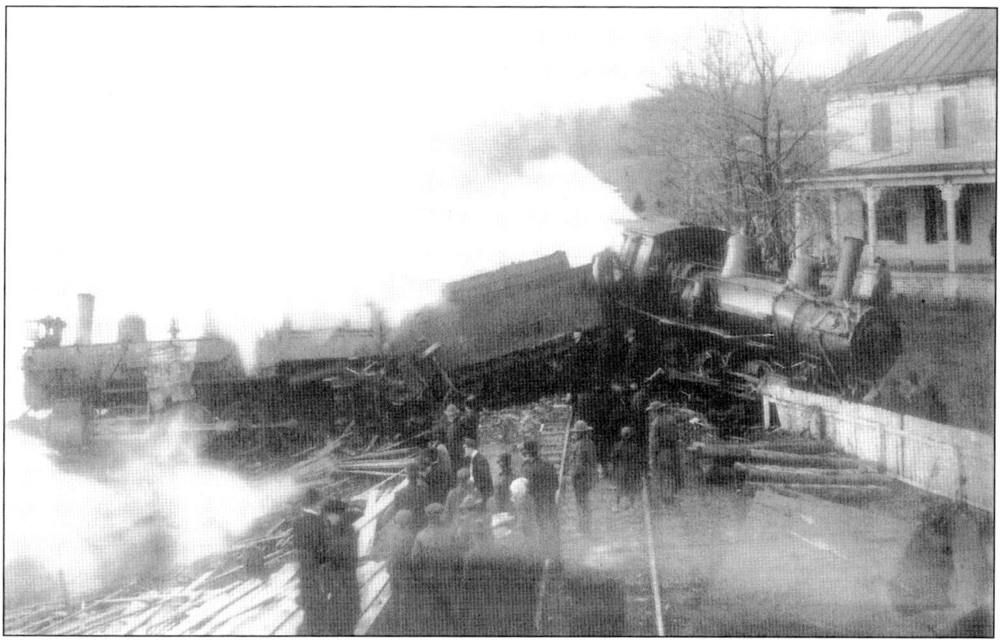

Steam fills the mid-morning sky, somewhat obscuring the view of this December 23, 1906, rear-end collision of two freights. The wreck occurred at Ann Hudson's, near the old brickyard immediately south of Luray's Hawksbill Creek Overpass, when a double-headed, northbound freight slammed into a train taking on water at Luray's tank. The scene was photographed by hundreds of Kodaks, and the wreck was costly, but no one was seriously injured. The dwelling, Prospect House, was built in 1810 by John Whitting, an original trustee of Luray's establishment. (Kenneth Morris.)

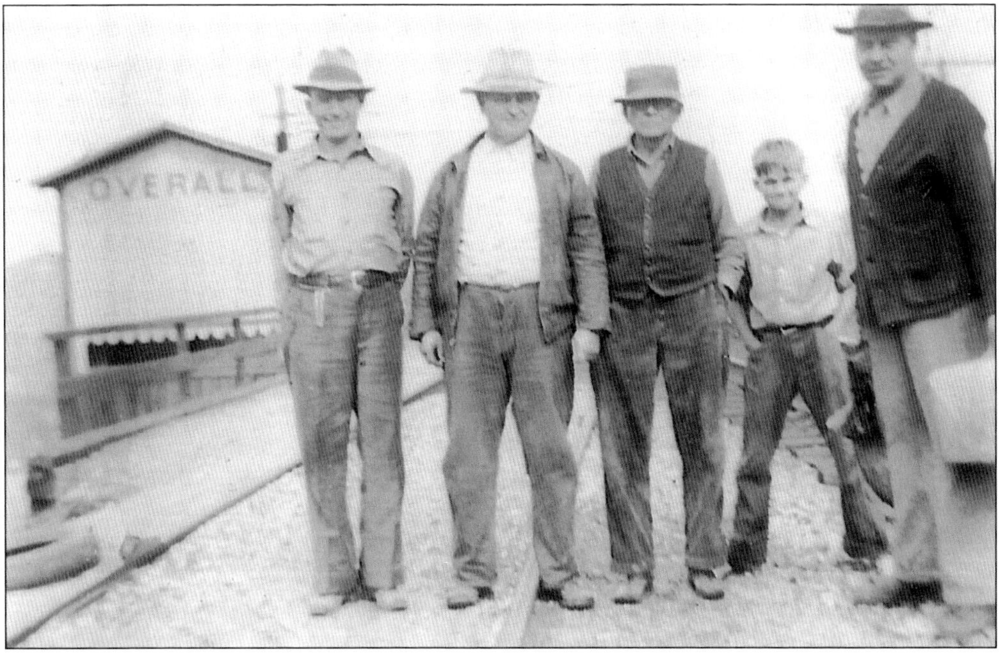

This rare glimpse of Overall Station also includes, from left to right, Raymond Triplett, Clarence Fristoe, Henry Hodges, James Triplett, and Overall merchant A. L. Rinker. On July 14, 1880, Martin Beidler of Marksville shipped the first cattle from Page County over the SVRR from this point. Though the rail didn't extend farther southward at the time and wouldn't connect at Luray until March 1881, its potential was already being realized. (Dorothy Atwood.)

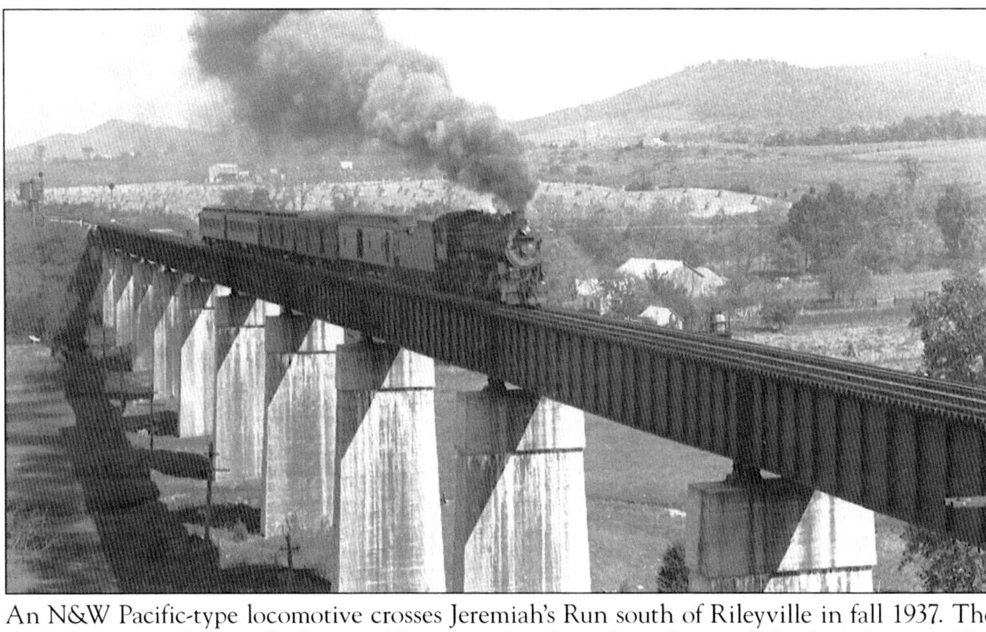

An N&W Pacific-type locomotive crosses Jeremiah's Run south of Rileyville in fall 1937. The grade increases substantially for train No. 14 as it heads southward toward Vaughn's Summit. The bridge received extra support when Virginia Bridge and Iron Company erected the 1,218-foot plate girder. Shortly after its 1931 completion, its trademark brace was added to a shifting pier. Rileyville's 50,000-gallon water tank, filled from the run, is at extreme left. (Howard W. Ameling.)

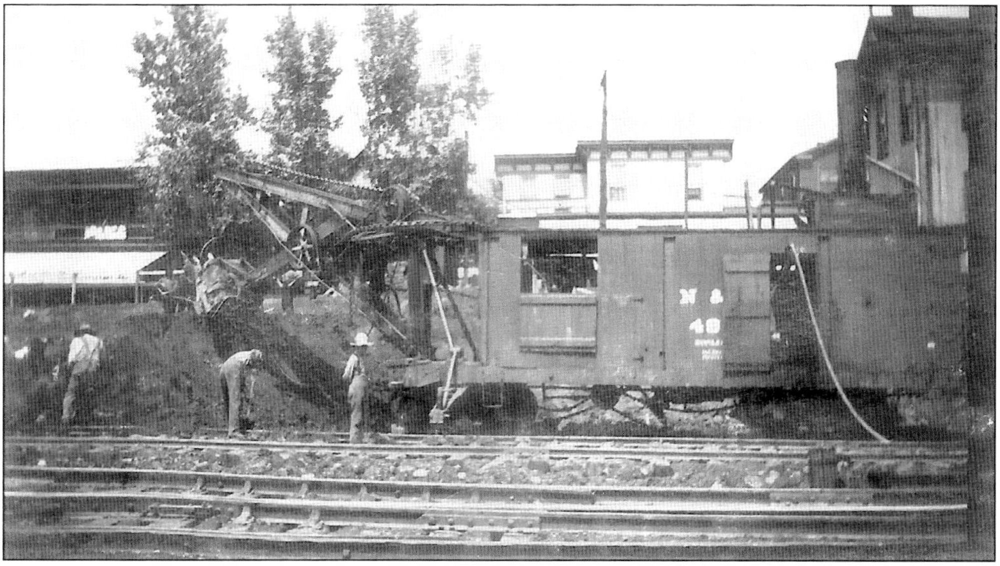

An N&W Shenandoah Yard rail shovel is at work in this 1918 view. Shenandoah Shops' worker Patrick Henry Rinaca (in white hat) oversees the project, as Maintenance of Way workers add manual labor. The former Strickler's Hardware, at left, and the railroad's divisional offices, at right, bordered Shenandoah's First Street. (Jim Brown.)

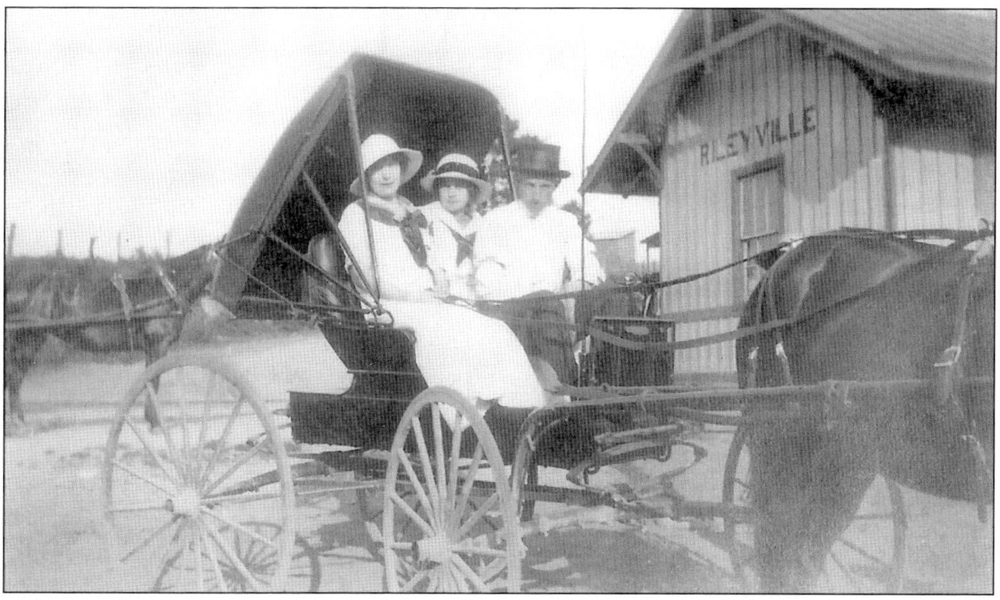

Hubert Strickler, with two female companions, paused at Rileyville Depot in the 1910s. In 1903, the Bonanza Mines, located two and one half miles south of Rileyville at Blue Ridge's western base, transported ore here for rail shipment. One could basically judge the economy by its rail passenger numbers. Roughly 2,000 passengers would travel through this local station each year. (Robert Modisett.)

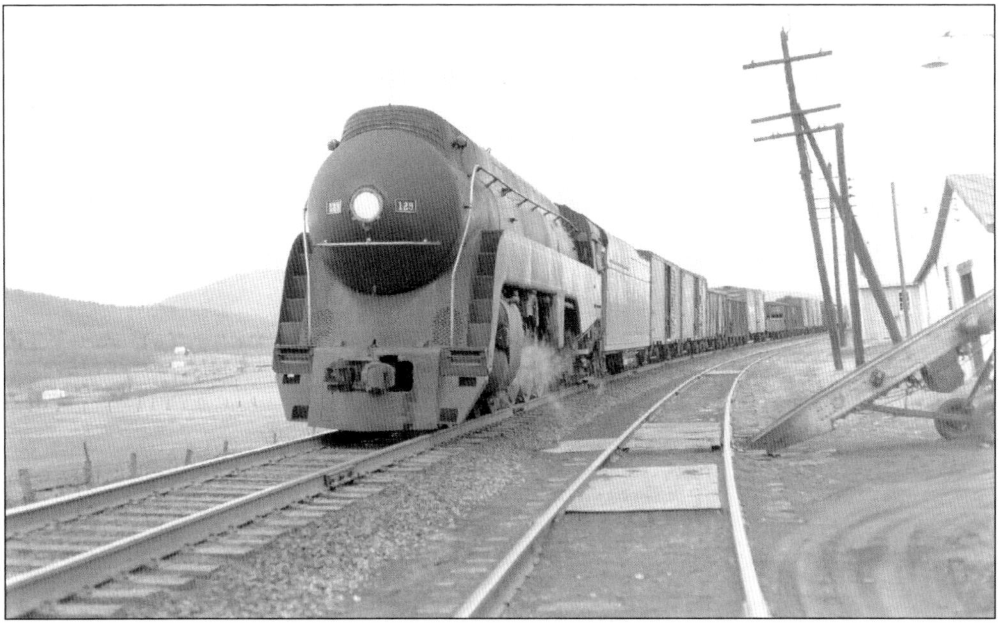

Pictured on its final Stanley stop is N&W's K2a class No. 129. The first diesel-electric had already run through Page on January 3, 1957. Previously, the world's largest train locomotive, N&W's TE-1 No. 2300 "Jawn Henry"—a coal-burning, steam-turbine-electric weighing 1,172,000 pounds and measuring over 160 feet in length—passed here on May 21, 1954. It was N&W's last design effort to save steam, but to no avail. Steam was no more. (*PN&C*.)

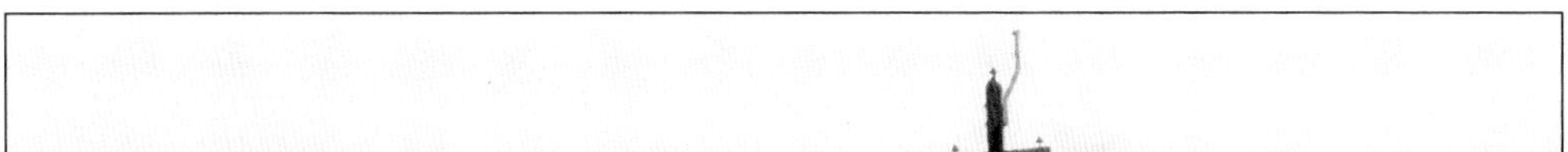

Northbound for the last time, engineer S. A. Basore crosses County Line Trestle at Overall Pass on February 19, 1957. Gone is the steam engine, for diesels have replaced the old. Also gone is the "clickity-clack" of rail joints since continuous ("ribbon") rail was laid throughout the later 1980s. Talk also exists of eliminating the train's whistle, a call to attention to all boys at heart to "stop, look and listen." (*PN&C*.)

Six

THE GOLDEN RULE

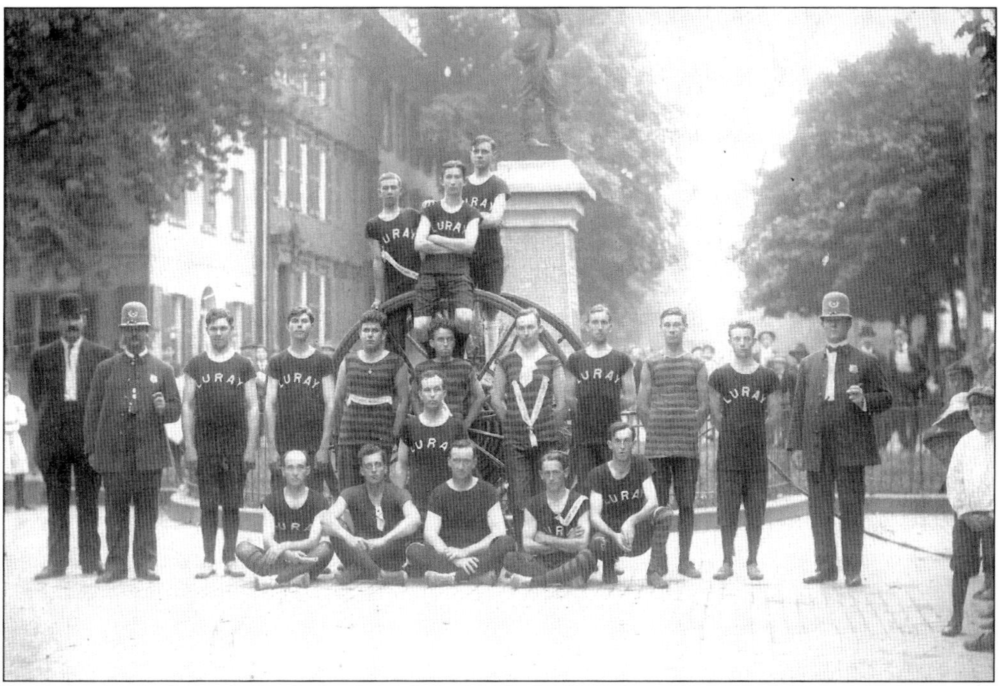

The Luray Reel Team, competing in Alexandria on August 24, 1910, posed on Prince Street for the Jameson Studio in front of the Confederate statue. From left to right, the members are (seated) E. L. Rothgeb, Virginus Berry, Will Wright (kneeling), Leith Renalds, J. T. Campbell, and Elmer Moyer; (standing) Ed Fox, Ernest Menefee, Sam Ritchie, Albert Chapman, Orville Aylor, Harry Grove, Luther Beach, and Vernon Menefee; (on reel) Amos Bradley, Bernard Dyche, and Bob Beach. Luray set a world record in Lexington in 1929. With reel teams disbanding shortly thereafter, the record still stands. (Page Public Library.)

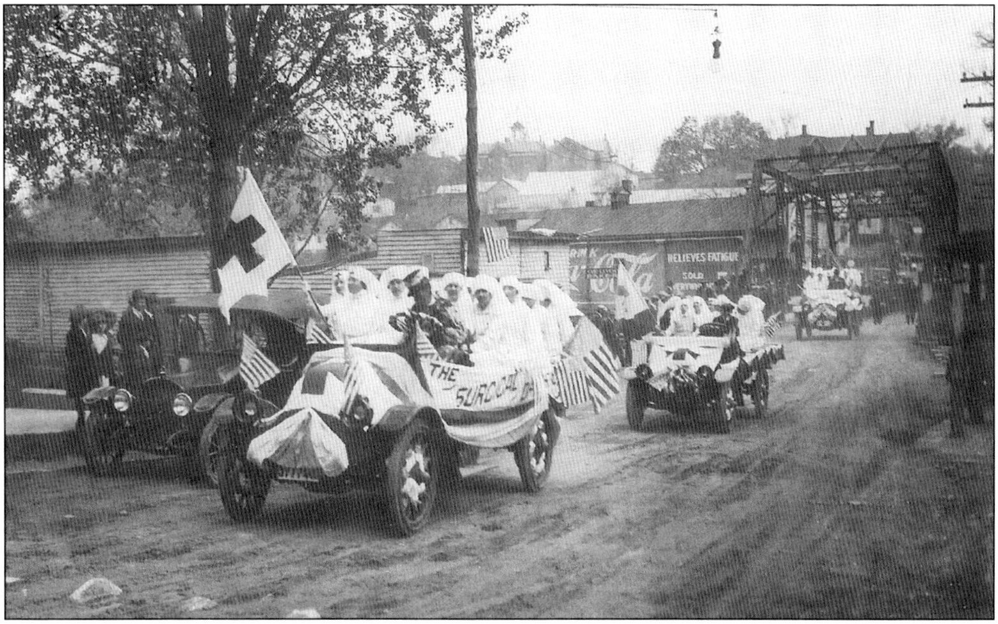

Local members of the Red Cross Nurse Corps ride in a rally parade crossing Luray's West Main Street iron bridge on July 28, 1917. In this World War I–era image, the old Casino Theatre has become a billboard advertising Coca-Cola. A primitive streetlight would illuminate the stepping-stone crosswalk, at bottom, later that evening. (Alice Moyer.)

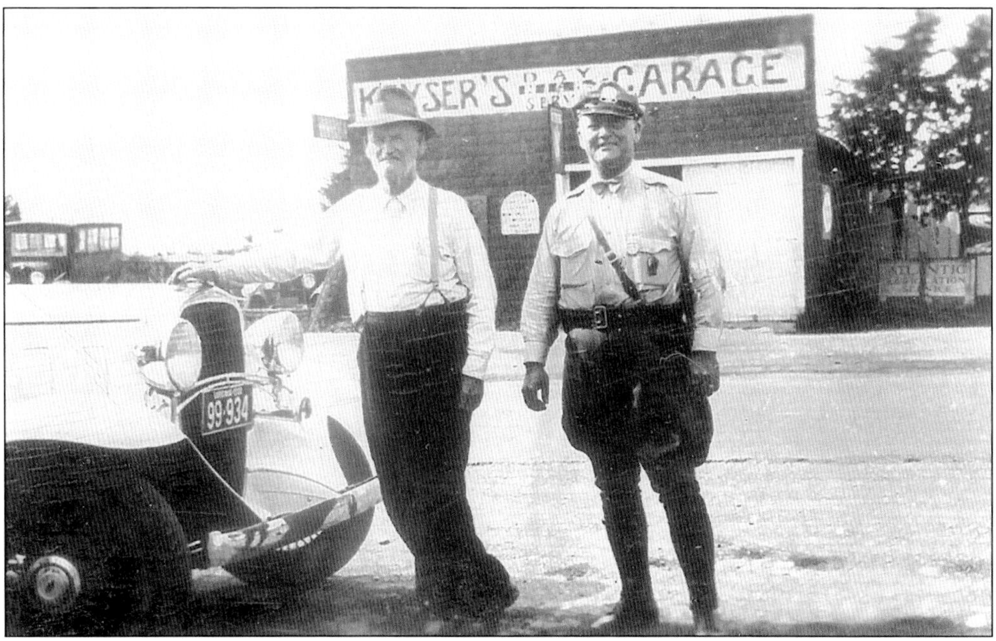

Leon Keyser (right), Page County's lone Virginia state patrolman, poses with his father, Thomas Keyser, in front of Keyser's Garage in 1932. The business, run by Leon's brother Melvin, was located on Lee Highway west of Luray in what was then known as "Tom's Town." It was named after the senior Keyser. (Lillian Keyser Fox.)

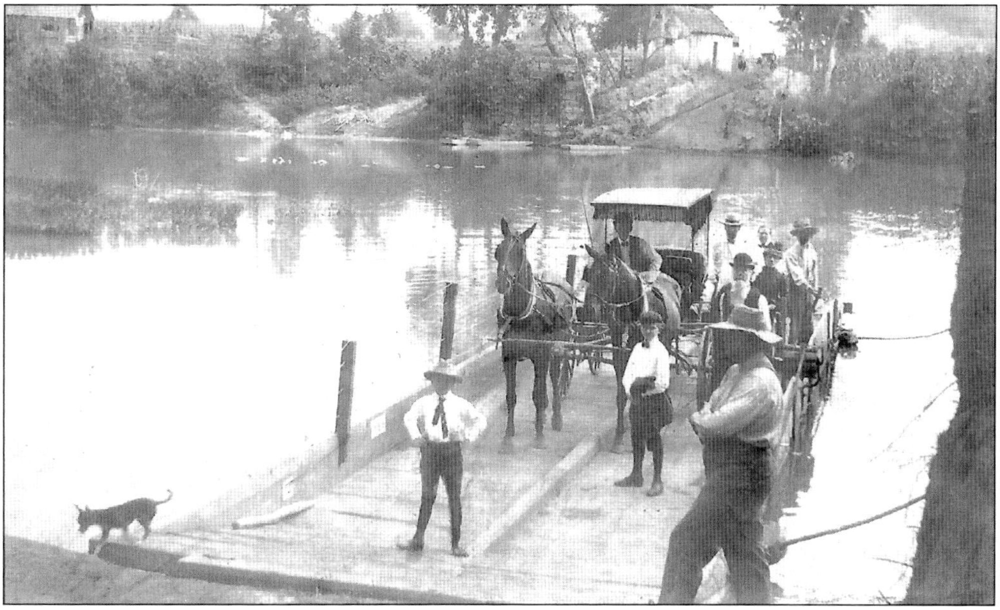

In 1886, the board of supervisors voted against appropriating funds to rebuild the White House Bridge, gone since the 1870 flood. White House Ferry (shown) was a pay ferry, and when the bridge was ultimately rebuilt in the 1910s, it unfortunately put John Henkel and John Platt, the last operators, out of commission. Gil Zirkle's coach, Fast Line, crossed here, making the three-hour trip to Luray on the New Market–Sperryville Turnpike up to three times daily with passengers, mail, and express. (Wayne Gray.)

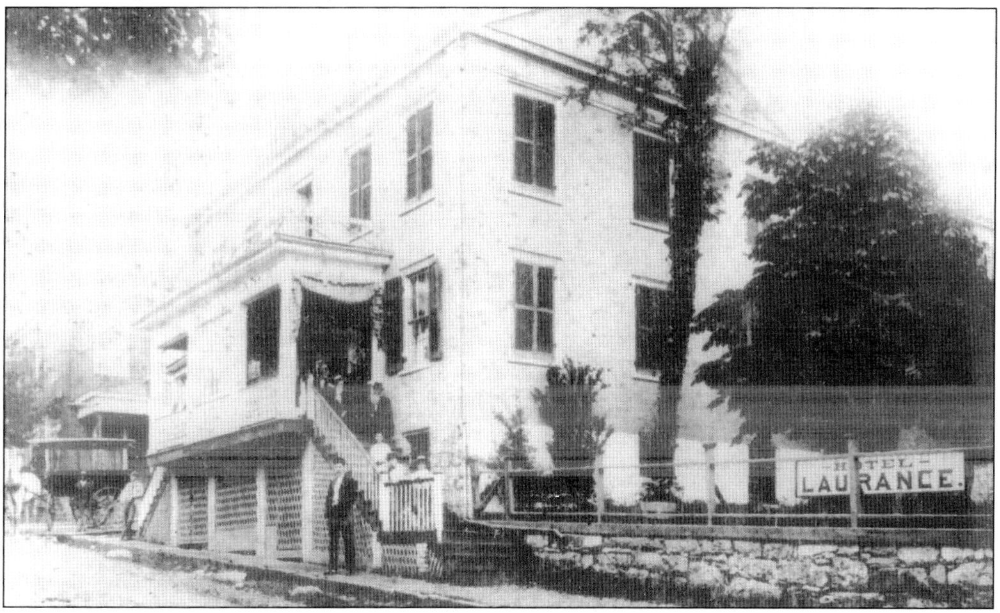

This 1890s view shows the Hotel Laurance omnibus (left), which used to meet all trains. The hotel's porch, like others on Main Street Luray, was removed in the 1930s. Emanuel Grove, father to the initial Grove and Brother owners, John and Charles Grove, conducted a general merchandise store on the Court Street side from 1833 to 1856. The Luray Post Office, once operating in the R. L. McKim Building at far left, five locations later, has called South Broad Street home since 1938. (*PN&C*.)

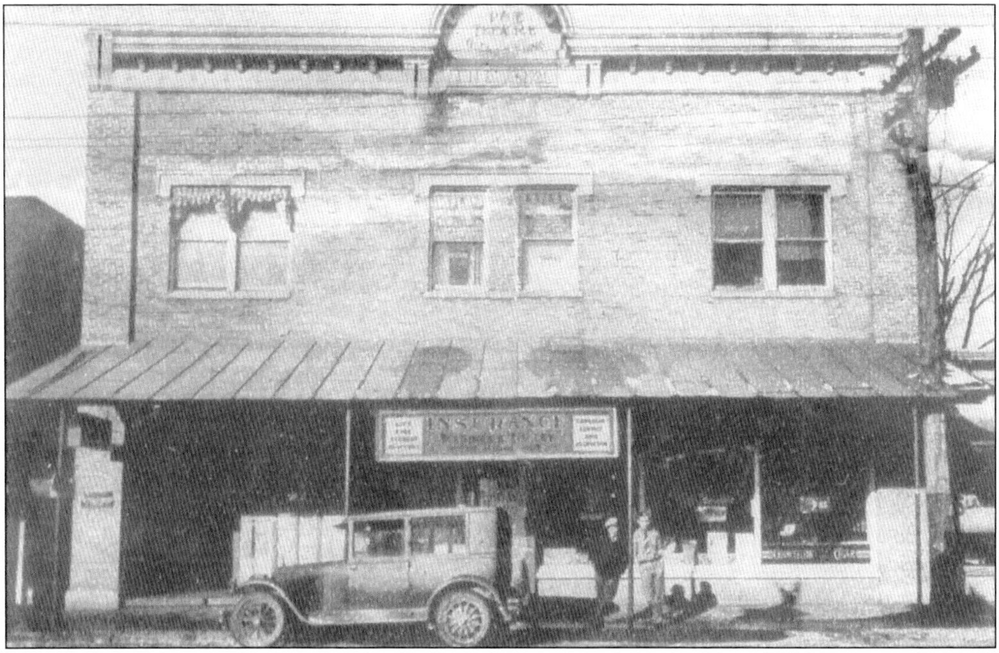

Built by I. N. Dovel and originally opening as the Page Theatre under proprietor D. F. Aleshire, this movie house would be renamed Bridge Theatre when an East Main Street relocation took prominence. Cecil B. Demille's *Something to Think About* was shown on its June 29, 1921, opening night. After operating for over 30 years, it closed in 1953. (*Richmond Times-Dispatch*.)

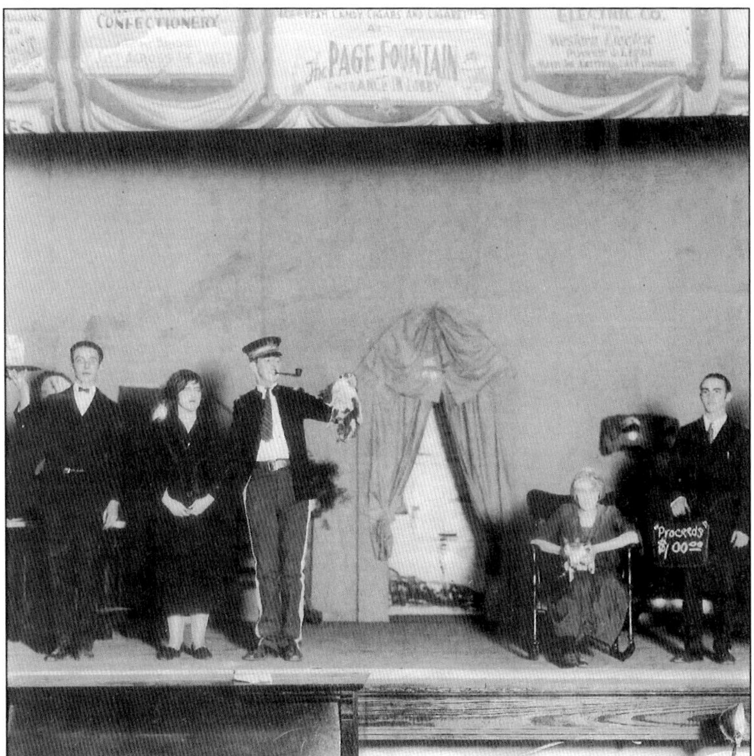

Luray's first all-talking movie, Amos and Andy's *Check and Double Check*, played in the Page Theatre on January 20, 1931. Moving picture parlors had come to Luray and Shenandoah as early as 1907, and movie houses opened in Stanley, Rileyville, and Stony Man. In this benefit stage performance, Robert Harnsberger (far left) and Carl A. Kauffman (far right) are among the cast. The drawn curtain advertises local merchants, including the theater's own Page Fountain. (Rod Graves.)

Valley Marble Works, more commonly known as Bradley Brothers, originally located in Kimball in 1890 before moving to Luray. This rare image documents the primitive beginnings of this forerunner to Bradley's Funeral Home. "With stock to make monuments, tombstones, tablets & cetera in American and Italian Marble," they advertised their work to be "delivered anywhere on the line of the Shenandoah Valley Railroad." (Nancy Racer.)

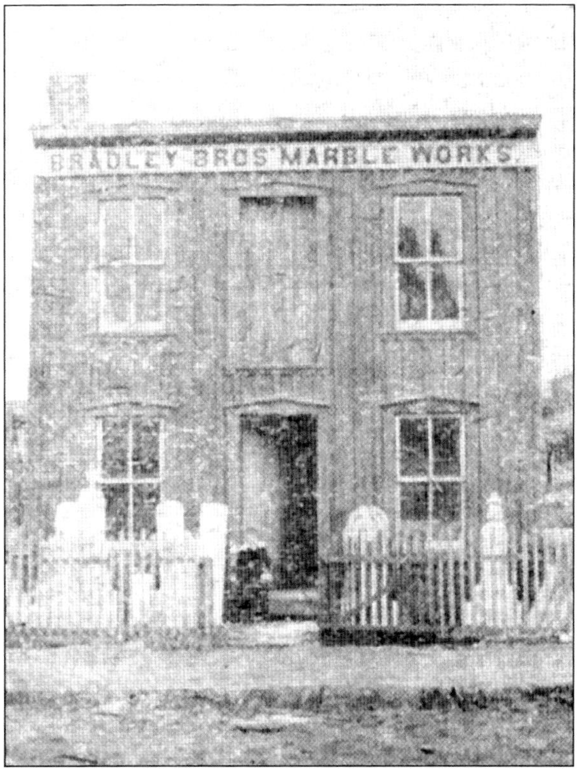

I. Casper Bradley and his brother, J. Sam, established Bradley's Funeral Home in 1892. Originally located on East Main Street, it was moved to West Main from 1921 to 1956 before returning east, when a new facility was built on the property of the home of the late John Woodward, a former undertaker himself. Bradley's employee, David S. Fox, poses in front of Luray's Grove and Brother Store in 1909. (*PN&C*.)

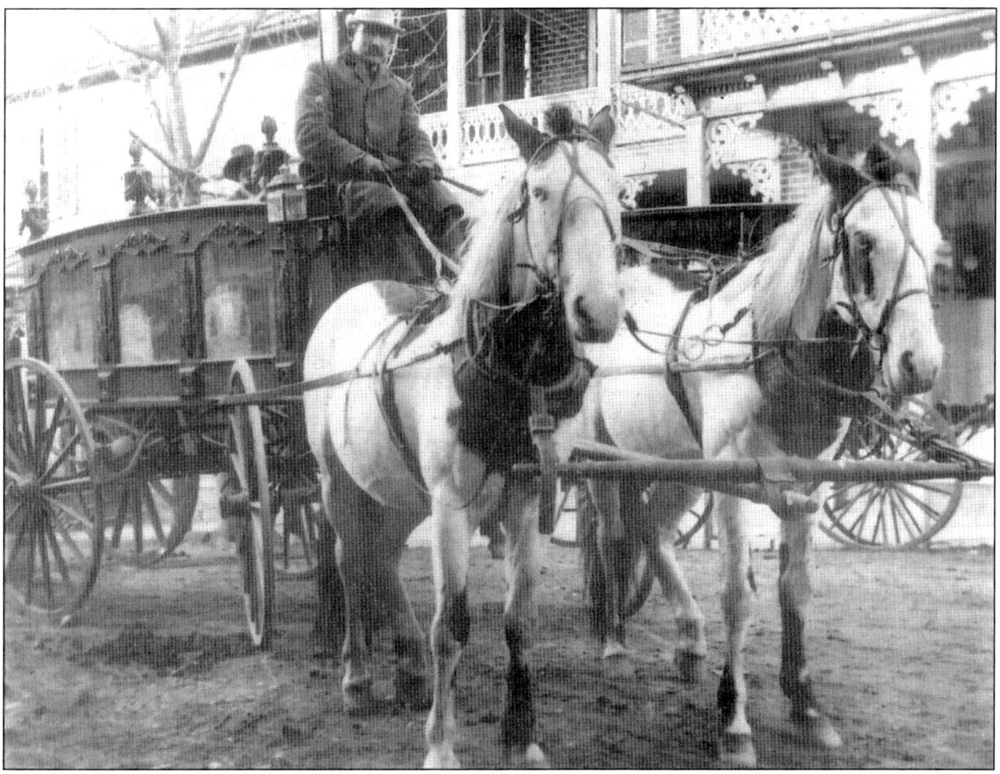

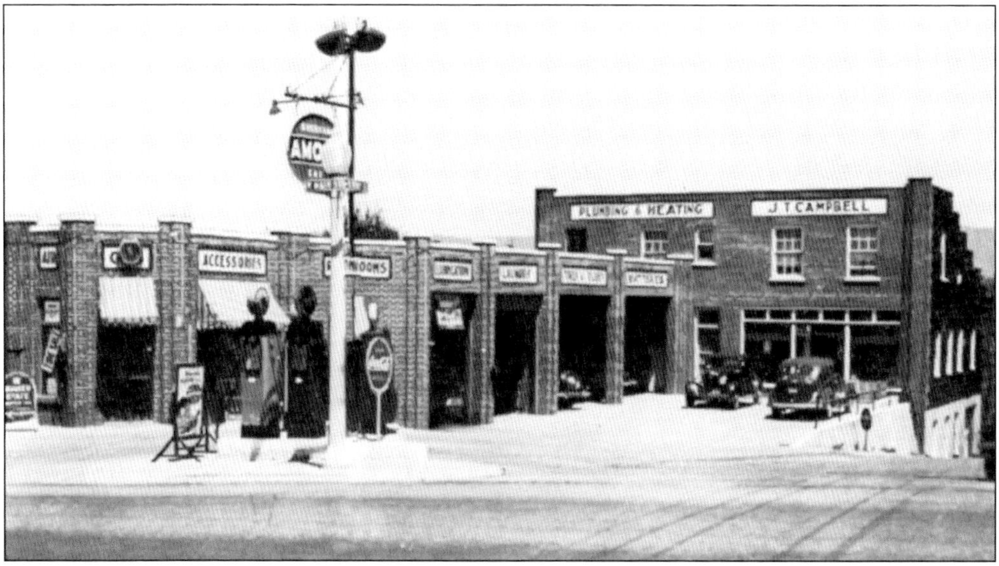

In 1937, Joseph T. Campbell tore down the old Harry Fravel watch and jewelry store on the corner of West Main and North Court Streets to construct this up-to-date service station. Building an extension onto his established plumbing and heating business, Campbell's son, Paul, ran the station. Luray's "auto row" evolved thereafter, immediately west of here. (Dan Vaughn.)

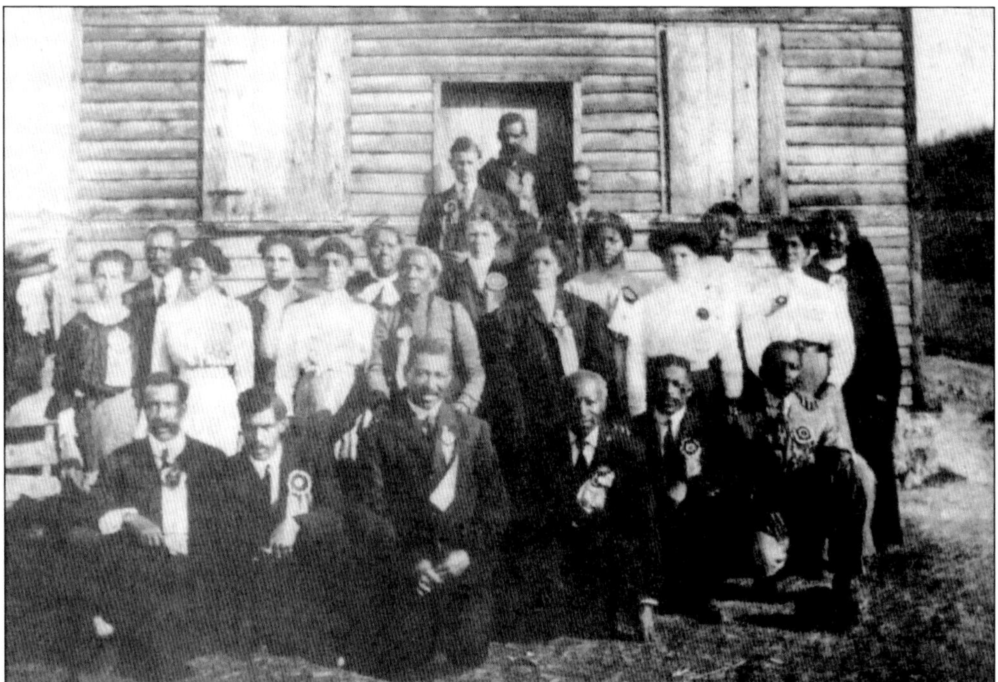

Blainesville, named in honor of two-time presidential candidate and former U.S. congressman James G. Blaine, was home to the Young Men's Sick Benefit (members shown here). In 1940, the Page County Court approved the sale of Blainesville's one-room schoolhouse to the YMSB for $45. Women were also involved in the Christian-like services that the group, organized to help those in need, performed. (Dan Vaughn.)

With the Stony Man Post Office discontinued on March 31, 1905, C. B. Dyche delivered this 26-mile route from Luray. A former resident remembers most fondly, "Horse needed no guiding, knew the route, and all the stops. Mr. Dyche carried a bugle in his cart and would give a blast before he arrived. You could run out to the road, climb on the fence and yell, 'Give us a toot on your bugle Mr. Dyche.' He was always good to the kids," recalled J. R. Mims Jr., a former resident who now lives in Richmond. (Mildred Stirewalt Coleman.)

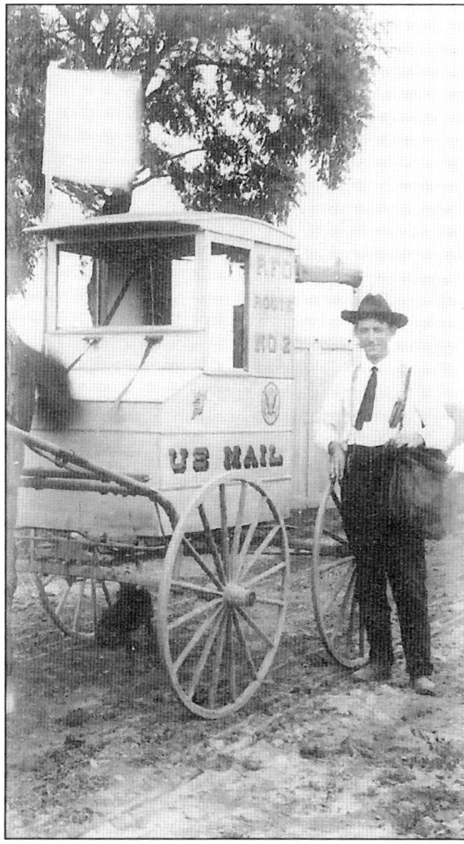

This 1957 Pinkerton Studios photograph show Luray's new right-hand-drive U.S. Mail truck used to extend delivery. On the left is postmaster Caroll Beach, with city carrier William Burner at right. Interestingly, when a Luray post office was also established in Pendleton County, West Virginia, in 1901, it was so decried because of confusion that a move to abolish it caused its discontinuance by 1902. (*PN&C.*)

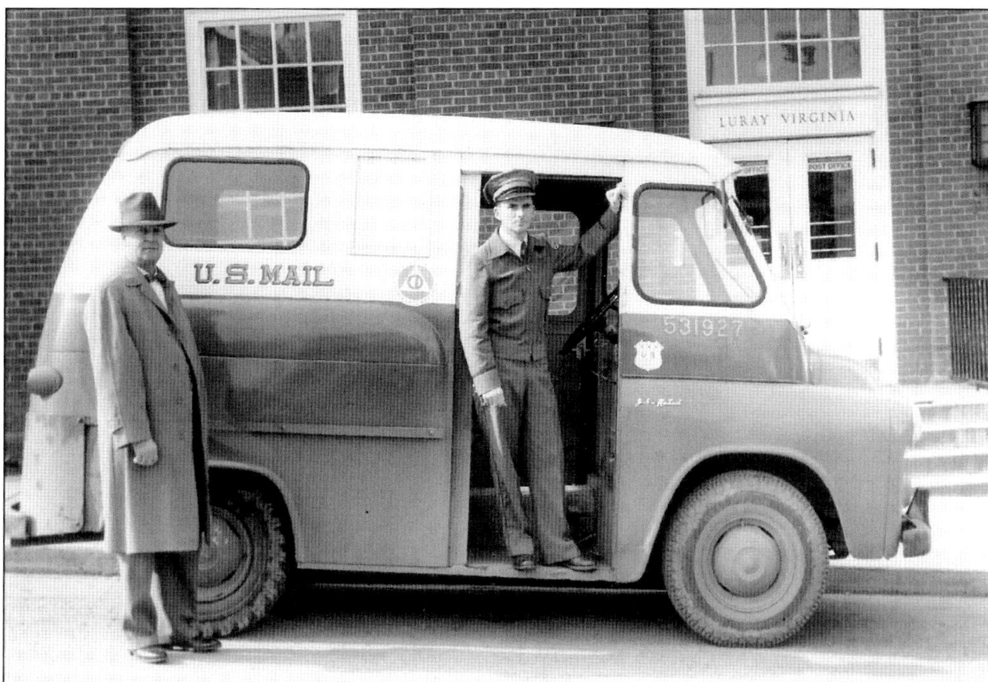

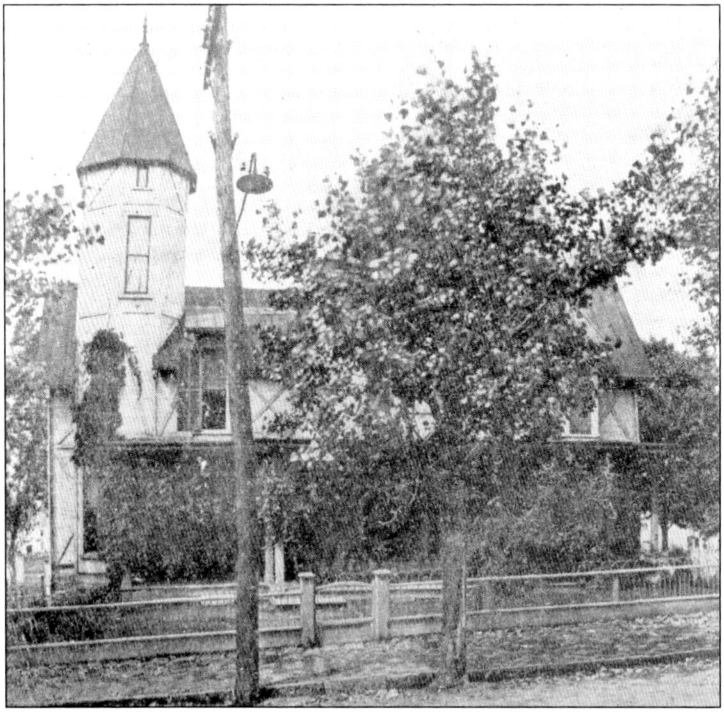

This quaint, fairy tale–like English Tudor, built in the 1880s during the rail's arrival, is secluded among its own landscape. Proprietor J. N. Chapman operated this tourist home, the Province, when pictured in 1910. A Luray Caverns visitor lodging here complimented that it was a "perfectly grand place." Located on Luray's East Main Street, the structure still stands, though the turret has been lowered one story. (Dan Vaughn.)

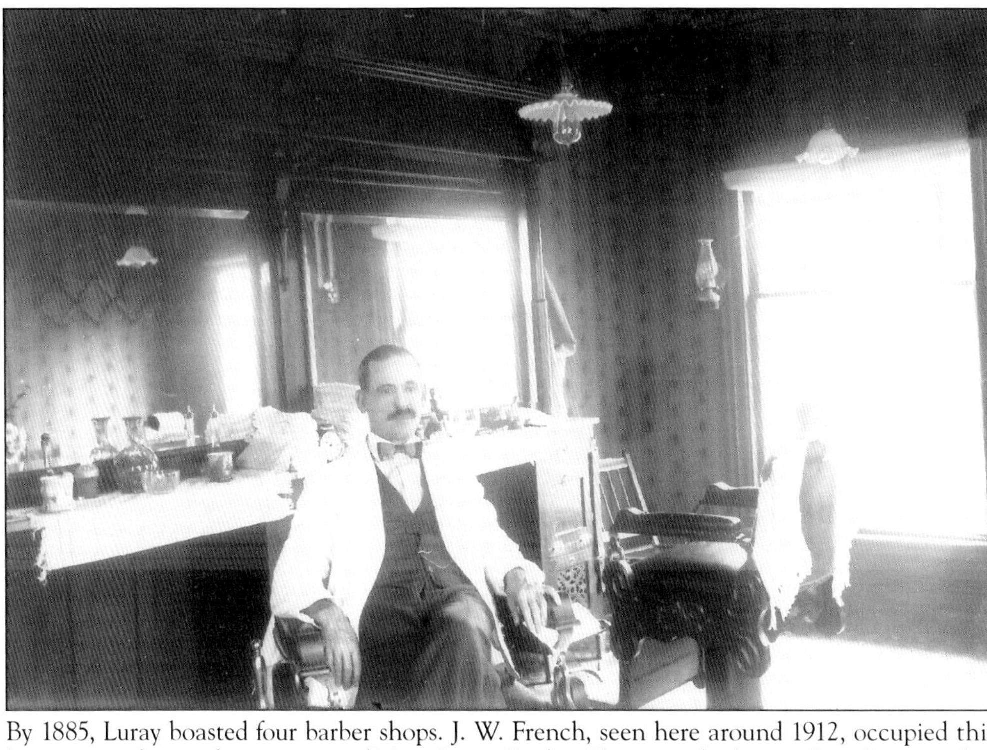

By 1885, Luray boasted four barber shops. J. W. French, seen here around 1912, occupied this location on the northeast corner of Main Street Bridge. Electricity had arrived in the town, but a lone kerosene lantern still lingers on the tonsorial parlor's front wall. Charles G. Parks once operated his Ye Olde Barber Shop here as well, around 1910. (*PN&C*.)

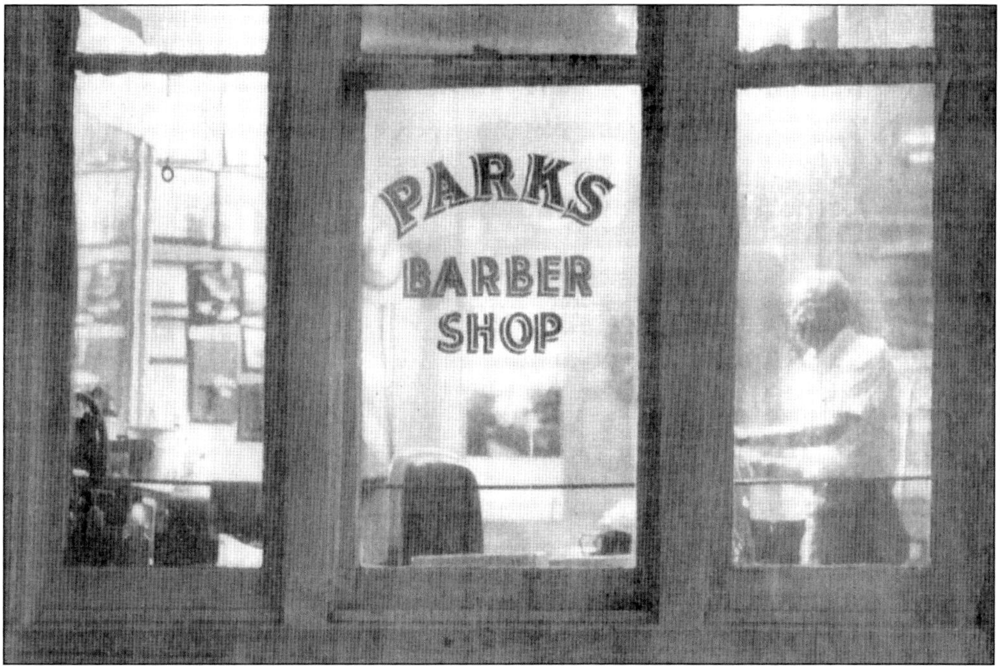

Charles G. Parks, cutting hair for over 50 years, began in 1906 at John H. Slater's barbershop in the old D. F. Kagey Building on Bank Street in Luray. Ultimately, in 1928, he moved to the then-vacated Page Valley National Bank Building. In the 1930s, sons Jim and Charles Jr. came alongside, all barbering simultaneously. Pictured here in 1984 is Jim Parks in the old bank building. (Dan Vaughn.)

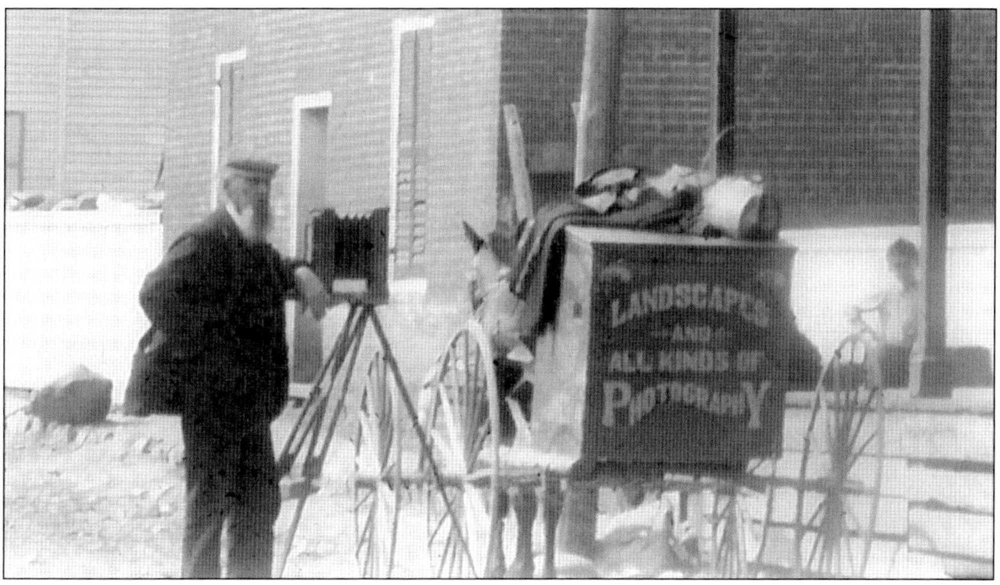

Confederate veteran Silas K. Wright documented his own image in Sperryville in this 1900s promotion of his profession. This well-known Luray photographer preserved a rich pictorial history of Page County for the present generation. Located on Luray's South Broad Street and operating as both the Sunbeam Galleries and Excelsior Studios, he was at the center of activity in this emerging tourist community. (*PN&C.*)

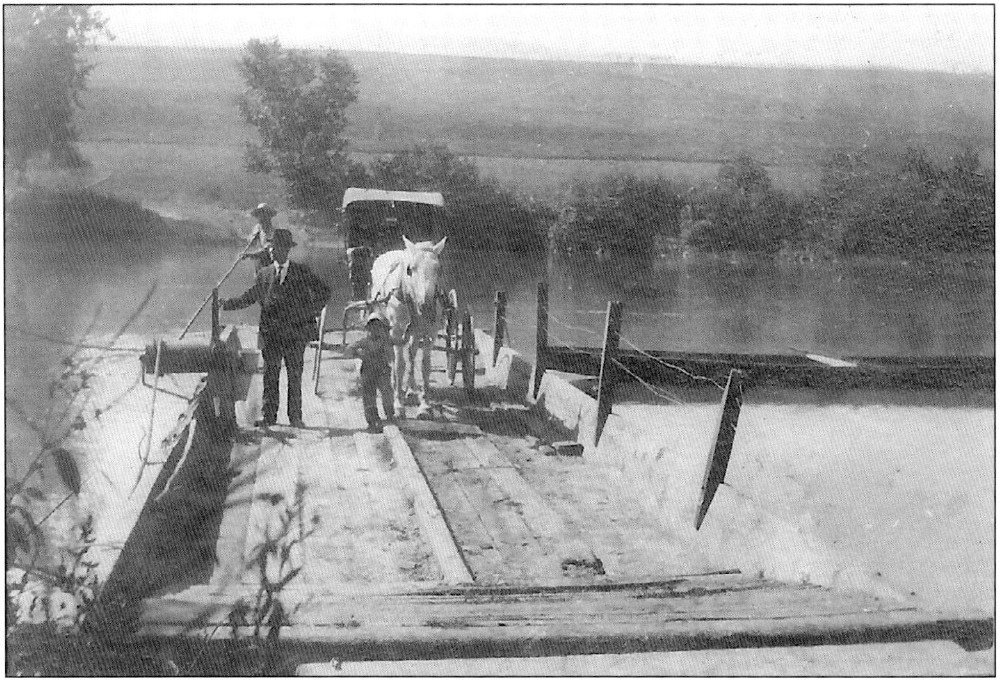

Bridge construction not only came at an enormous cost, but equally there had to be a need. Ferries such as Will Ruffner's, shown here with Lester Ruffner and son Malcolm below Luray's Shenandoah River hydroelectric dam, were plentiful throughout Page. Will's brother, Jake, operated above the dam. Fording was done mostly by mechanical device, while others were self-initiated by "push poles." Occasionally, a frightened team continued off the ferry's end, plunging into the river. (Nancy Lee Shifflett.)

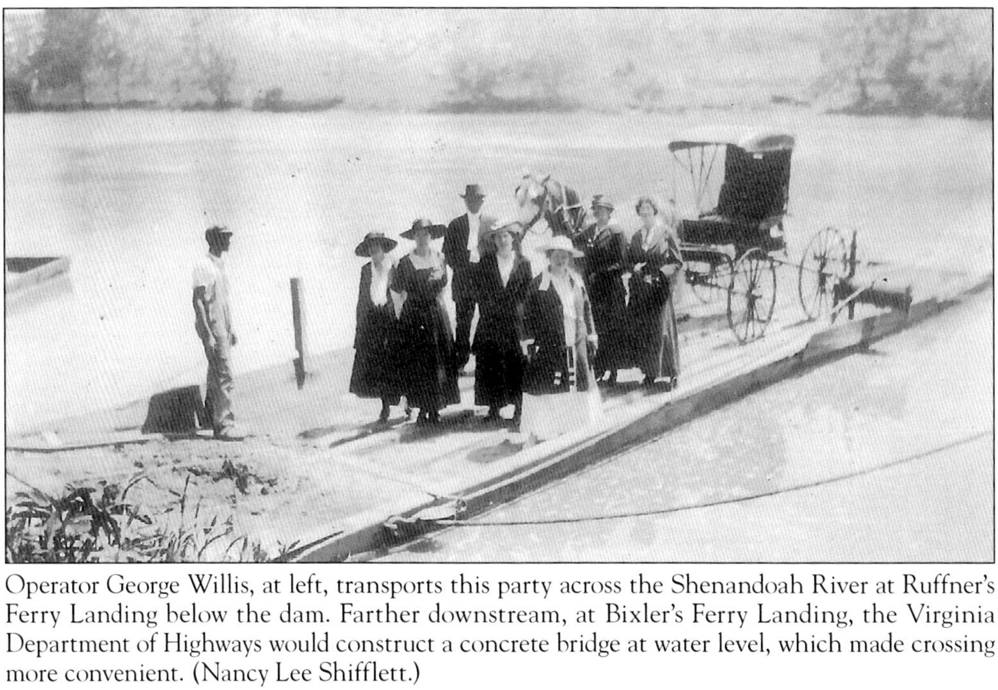

Operator George Willis, at left, transports this party across the Shenandoah River at Ruffner's Ferry Landing below the dam. Farther downstream, at Bixler's Ferry Landing, the Virginia Department of Highways would construct a concrete bridge at water level, which made crossing more convenient. (Nancy Lee Shifflett.)

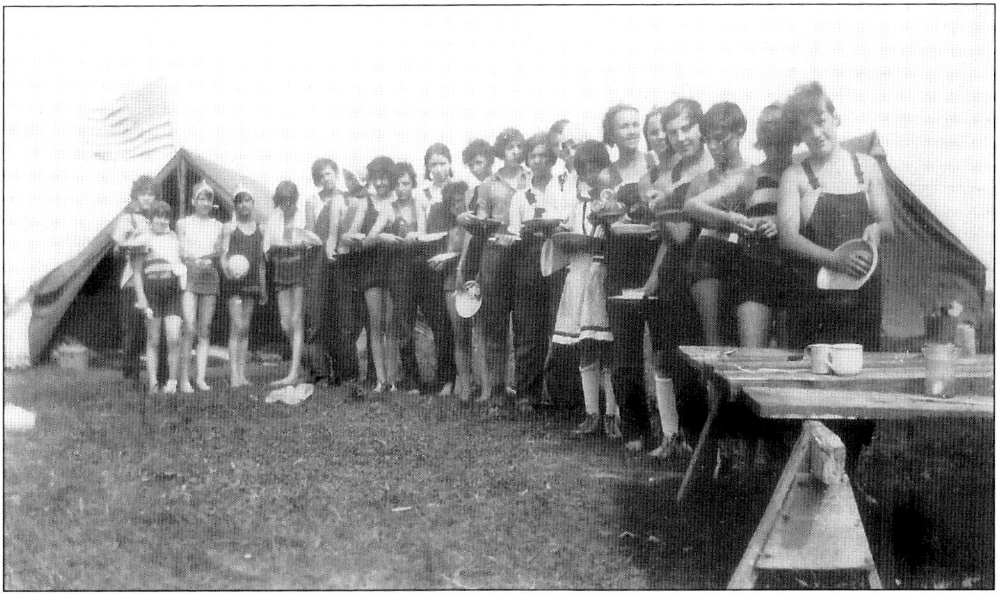

These local Girl Scouts from Luray's Troop No. 1 camped at Kauffman's Mill. Included among others in the August 1932 image are Ada Jean Rankin, Io Miller, Lavillon Morrison, Leta Mildred Frank, Ophelia Printz, Virginia Barrett, Jean Berry, and Anna Hershberger. Chaperones were Pearl Berry and Catherine Booton. Originally named Girl Guides when organized by Juliette Low in Savannah, Georgia, on March 12, 1912, the last of its 18 original troop members, Mrs. Marian Corbin Aslakson, visited Luray Caverns in 1984. (Dan Vaughn.)

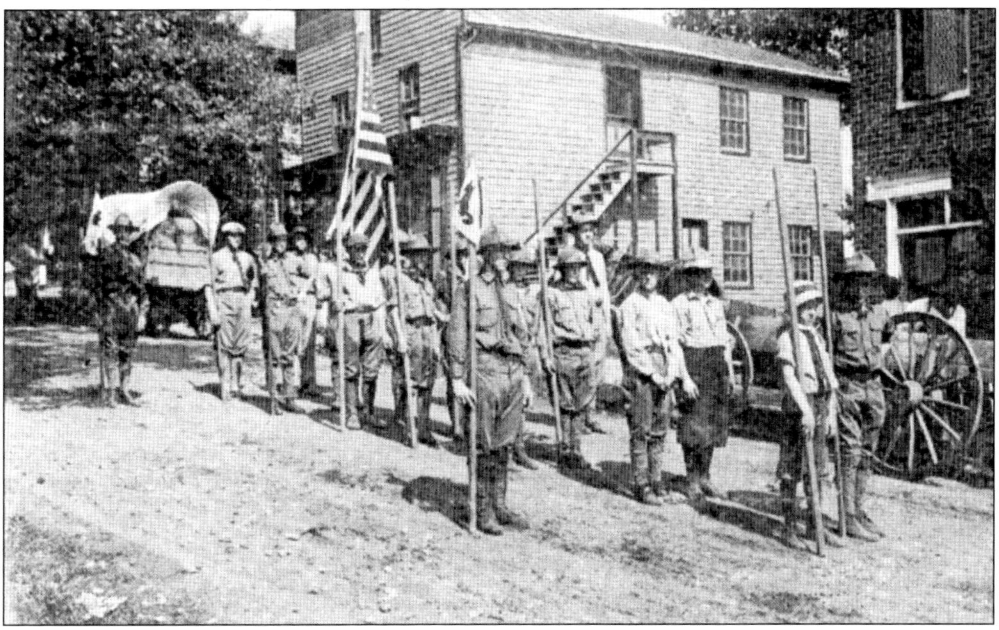

Variations of Boy Scouts existed around 1900, but it was William Boyce who founded what is known today as the Boy Scouts of America, on February 8, 1910. Arthur Grove, main partner of Grove and Brother, was Luray's first scoutmaster. Rev. C. J. Gibson followed in his steps when, in this 1914 parade, the Boy Scouts marched east near the corner of Hawksbill and West Main Streets. (Dan Vaughn.)

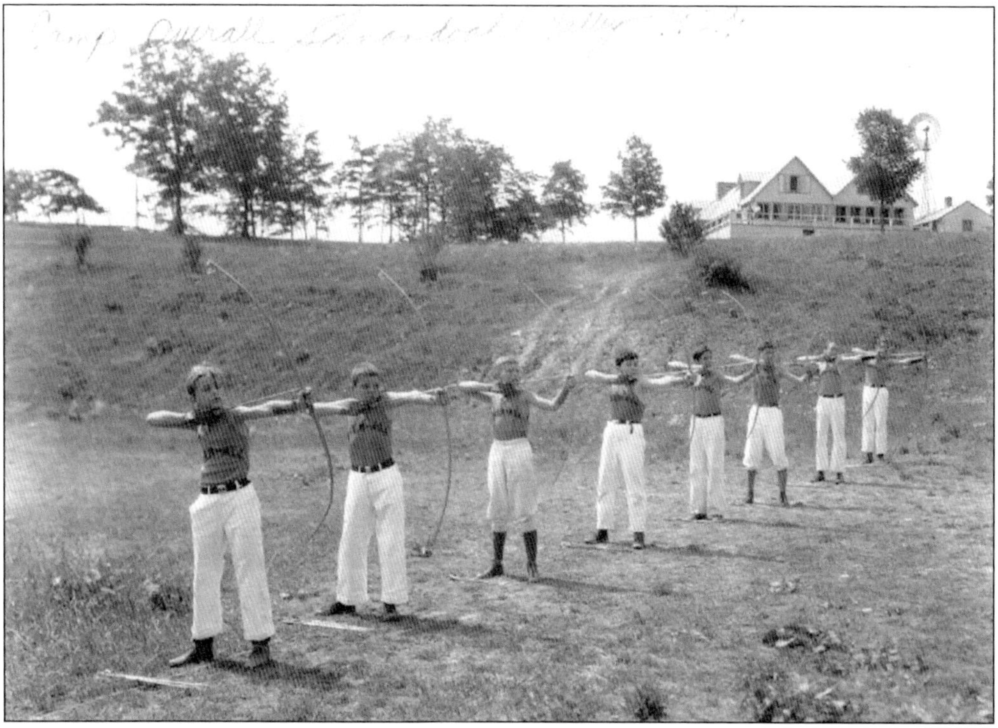

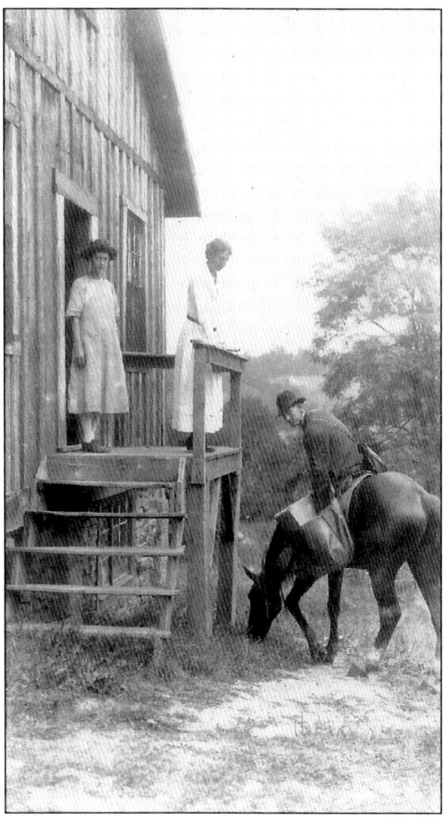

These young boys take aim as they prepare to hit the mark in archery class at Camp Overall. The camp, located at the extreme northern end of Page County along the Shenandoah River, also offered tennis, horseback riding, baseball, and basketball. Camp Skymont, a girl's version of the same, also operated here. The camp's lodge is seen at top right in this 1929 view. (Virginia Tech.)

This 1920s image records the length some carriers went in delivering mail. These Tanner's Ridge ladies wait outside the Grace House for their hand-delivery as the horse takes advantage of the moment. When the Rural Free Delivery (RFD) went into effect in Page in 1902, it ultimately caused over two dozen Page County post offices to be discontinued. (St. George's Episcopal.)

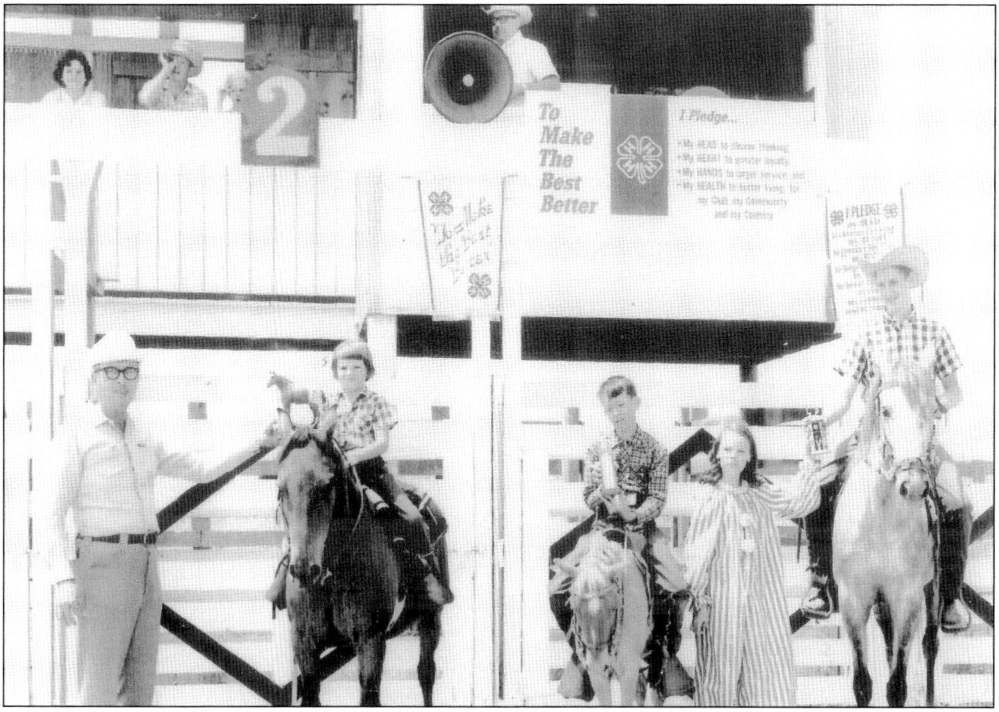

By 1954, there were eleven 4-H Clubs in Page, with over 450 members. Overseeing this 1966 event, are, at top from left to right, Joy Payne, Glendon Vaughn, Hazel Waters, and Sam "Sporty" Griffith. Assistant ringmaster Cletus Waters, bottom left, presents the Horse and Pony Pee-wee Class award to Sheila Payne, while "clown" Sharon Sampsell presents the Western Division winners Robbie Sampsell and David Moyer (far right) their trophies. (Sharon Sampsell.)

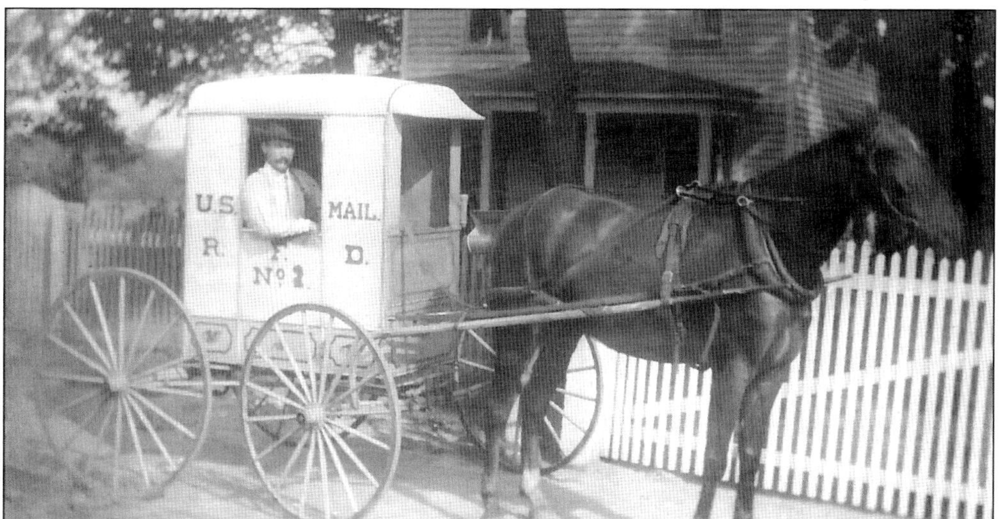

Talk of free delivery had surfaced in Page as early as 1891. Here appointed mail carrier John Graves poses around 1905 in his mail wagon, used in the Alma area west of Stanley. Though many of the small post offices were short-lived, and though some were just outright political favors if nothing more, the RFD officiated in the naming of multitudes of communities, not only in Page, but throughout the country. (Bob Graves.)

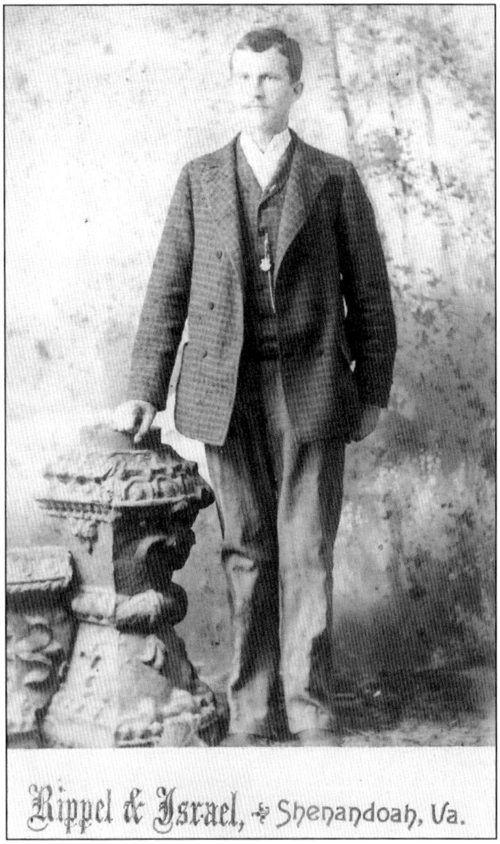

This unidentified gentleman poses inside Shenandoah's Rippel and Israel Photographic Studio. The September 21, 1894, issue of the *Shenandoah Argus*, a local Shenandoah newspaper, advertised the First Street business. The Star Studio and Gem Studio, also operating in the town, were just a few of the county's photographic galleries documenting the era in Page. (Dan Vaughn.)

The Shenandoah Police Department, jail, and town offices all occupied this building at various times. From left to right in this 1952 photograph are Ben Stanley Jr., Noah Clem, Owen Comer, Hedley Morris, Charlie Morrison, Jimmy Purdham (behind), Walter "Sonny" Thompson, Billy Ringle, Roy Wade Laconia Jr., Mayor Jim Orye (behind), "Puffy" Mowbray, and John Page Foltz in his Pontiac. In 1938, the Shenandoah Volunteer Fire Department, another one-time tenant, had the siren mounted. (Allan Rinaca.)

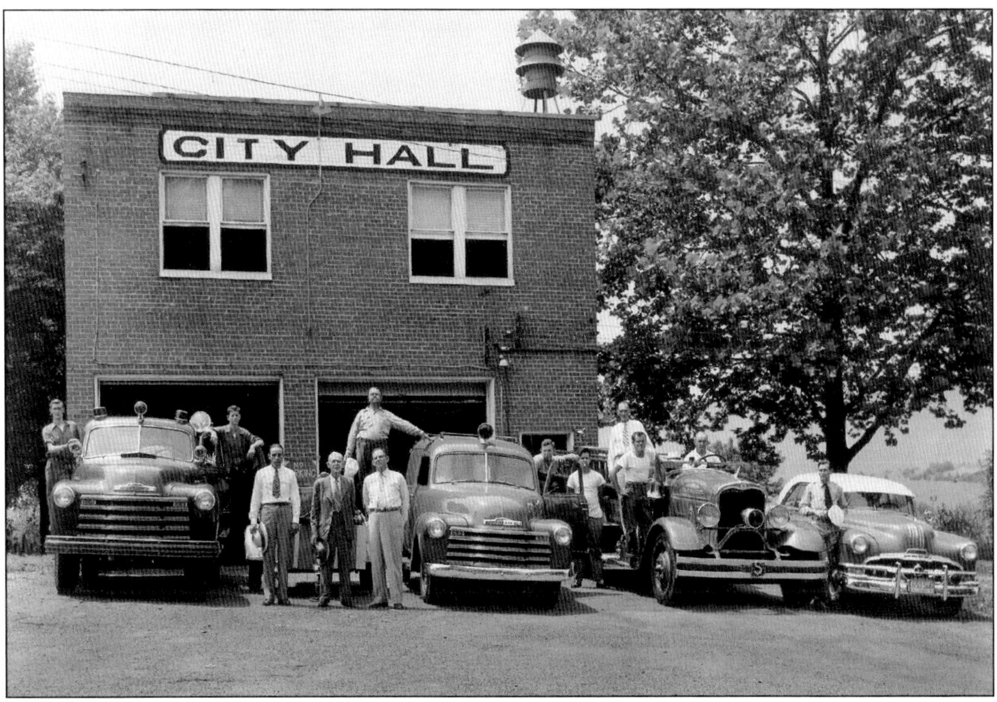

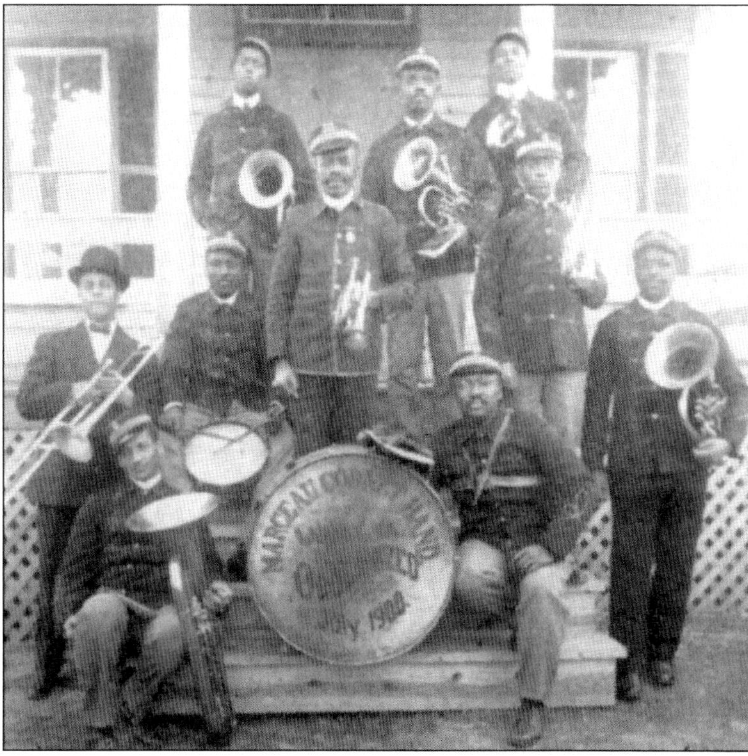

The Marceau Cornet Band organized in July 1900. Members included, from left to right, (first row) Tom Dougans, Gen. U. S. Grant Frye, and (standing at right with horn) Charley Beasley; (second row) unidentified, Dan Jefferies, leader John H. Slater, and Harry Henderson; (third row) Clifford Cyrus, Harry Fisher, and Henry Black. This picture was taken in front of the Odd Fellows Hall on West Main Street in Luray. (*PN&C.*)

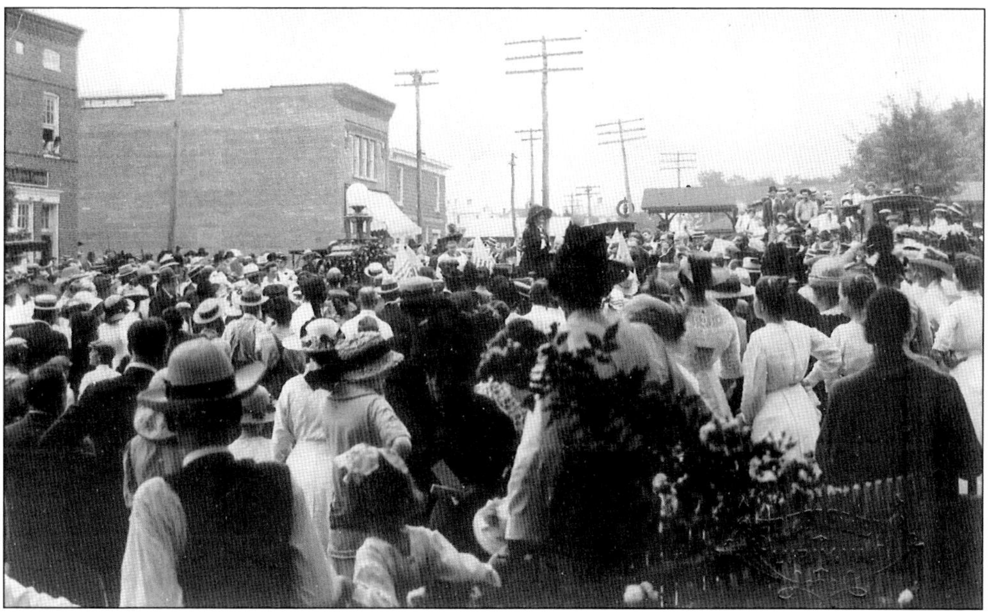

A large crowd was on hand for this July 30, 1913, dedication of Luray's town drinking fountain, seen left of center. Susan H. Ropp spoke on behalf of the Women's Christian Temperance Union, which had given the bronze oasis as a gift to the town. Its intent, as well as design, was for people, horses, and dogs, and for that reason, it was important to remember where to drink. A souvenir was given to all in attendance. Sadly, an automobile accidentally demolished it on Valentine's Day 1942. (Dan Vaughn.)

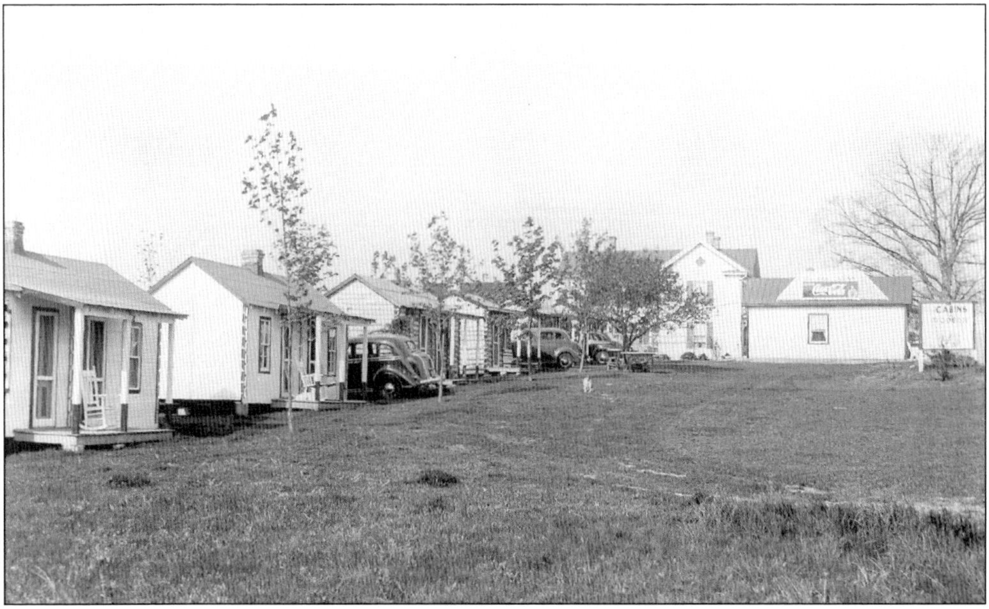

Tourist accommodations, such as proprietor J. A. Sours's Big Oak Cabins west of Luray, were popular from the 1930s to the 1960s. A desire to return to one's childhood has brought a resurgence of this type of overnight stay in rural areas such as Page. The allure of Luray Caverns, attracting approximately 500,000 visitors annually, has been an impetus. Big Oak's namesake, at far right, was felled in 2003 for commercial progress. (Dan Vaughn.)

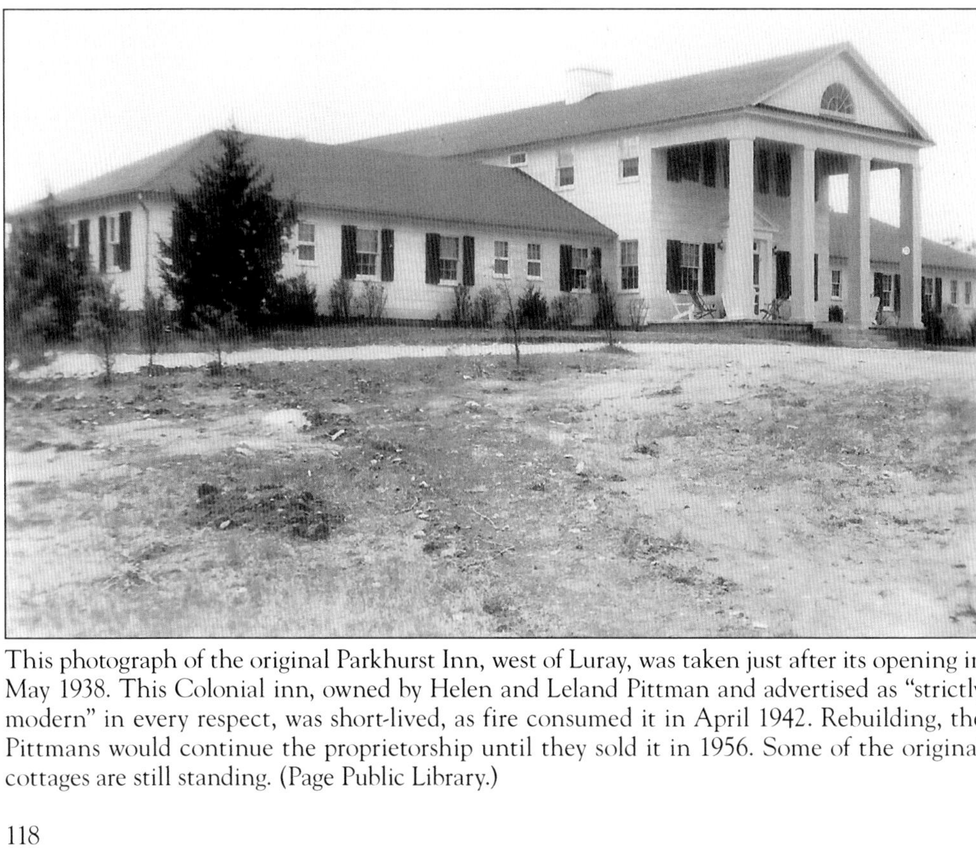

This photograph of the original Parkhurst Inn, west of Luray, was taken just after its opening in May 1938. This Colonial inn, owned by Helen and Leland Pittman and advertised as "strictly modern" in every respect, was short-lived, as fire consumed it in April 1942. Rebuilding, the Pittmans would continue the proprietorship until they sold it in 1956. Some of the original cottages are still standing. (Page Public Library.)

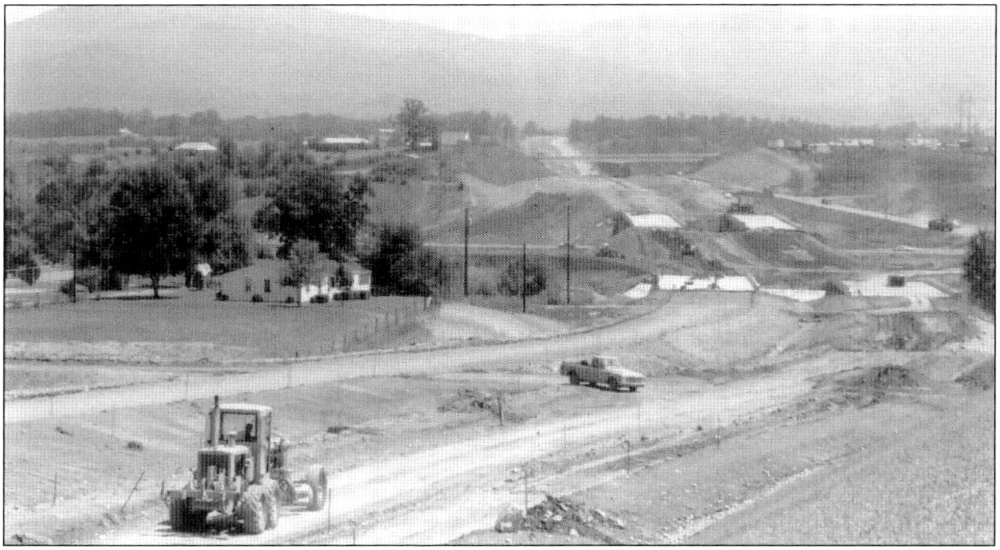

Noted civil engineer William M. Gillespie once stated, "The common roads of the United States are inferior to those of any other country." But when this photograph was taken around 1970, modern equipment could accomplish any road project. Looking east beyond the U.S. Route 340 underpass, the English Construction Company, of Altavista, Virginia, prepares for macadamizing a new parallel U.S. Route 211. Built in stages, the four-lane Luray bypass opened completely on December 23, 1971. (Steward Yowell.)

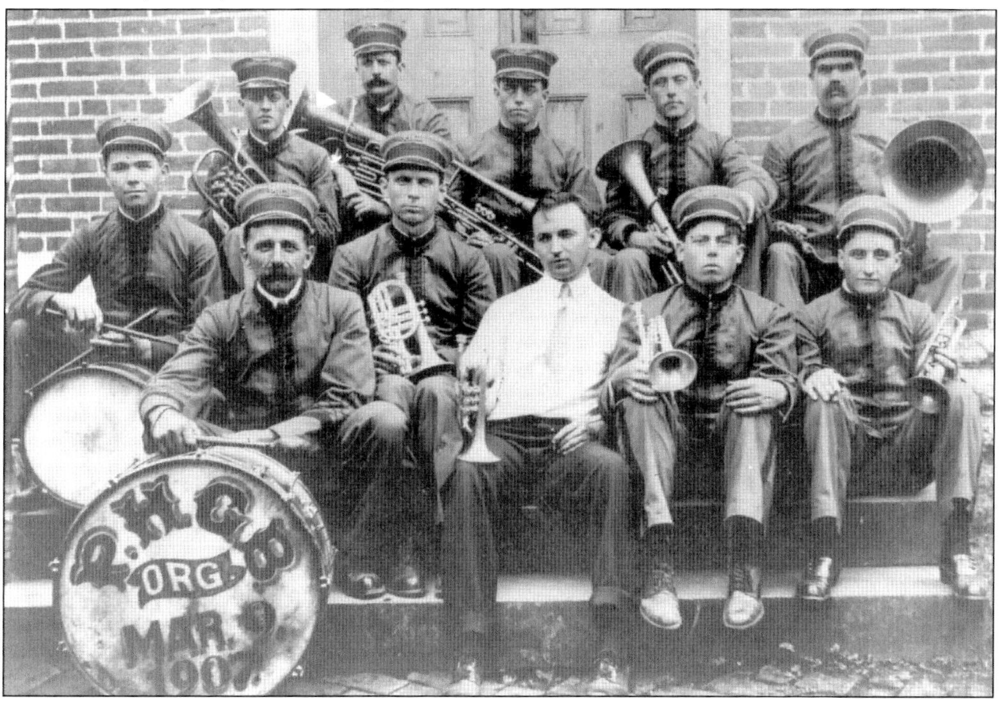

The Pumpkin Hill Cornet Band organized on March 9, 1907, in the Kimball area. Pictured here in 1909 from left to right are (first row) John S. Judd, Elmer Rickard, teacher Orville Aylor, Lester Griffith, and Poke Shenk; (second row) Ernest Alther, Floyd Shenk, Byron Shenk, Manuel Bradley, Cliff Shenk, and Will Alther. Rickard, a local Kimball photographer, took this image. (*PN&C*.)

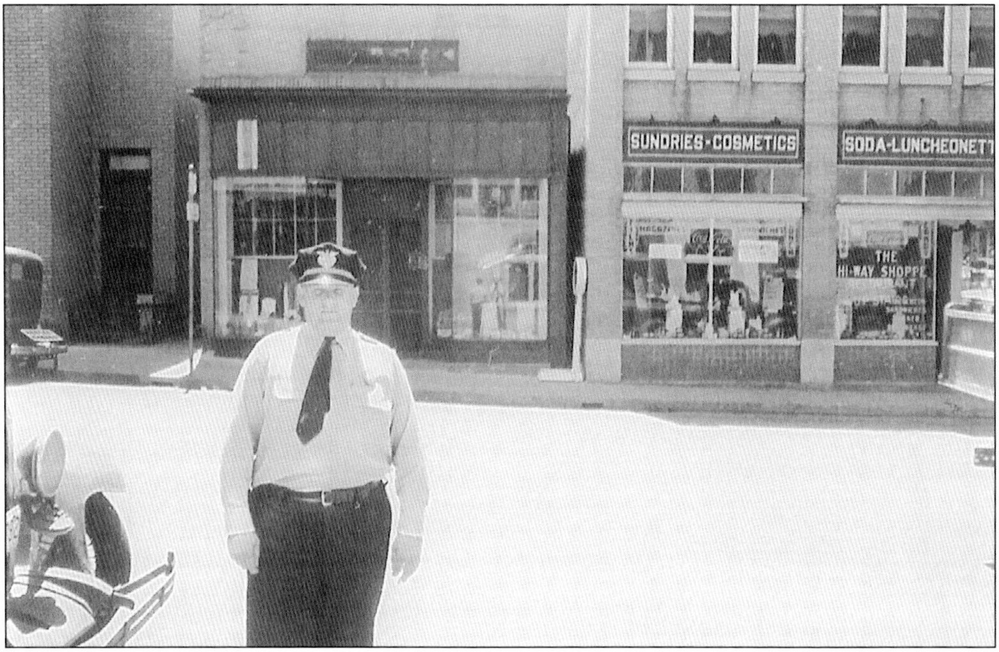

Luray police chief Haywood Leake paused for this 1938 photograph. Frank Garber's Hi-way Shoppe, at right, had opened in July 1934, with J. B. Batman's Store behind Leake. In 1935, the Page County Board of Supervisors voted to equip Luray police with, of all things, machine guns and tear gas. Recent displays of rowdiness had prompted the action. One could only wonder why this man would need a machine gun. (Lloyd Kibler.)

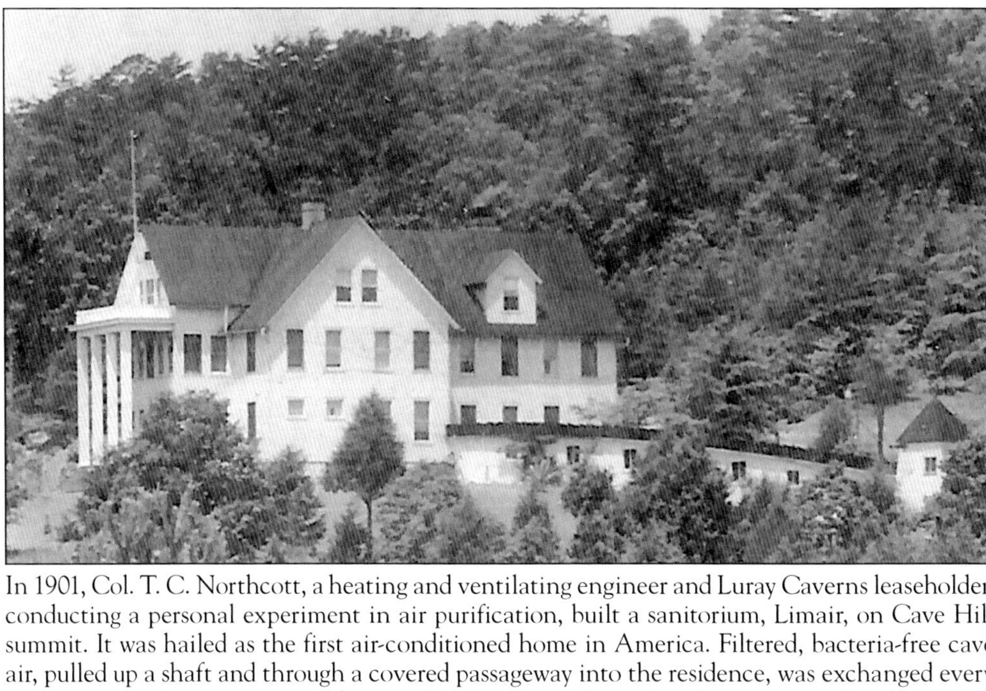

In 1901, Col. T. C. Northcott, a heating and ventilating engineer and Luray Caverns leaseholder, conducting a personal experiment in air purification, built a sanitorium, Limair, on Cave Hill summit. It was hailed as the first air-conditioned home in America. Filtered, bacteria-free cave air, pulled up a shaft and through a covered passageway into the residence, was exchanged every four minutes. The structure was destroyed by fire on April 29, 1940, being replaced by the present Limair II. (H. T. N. Graves.)

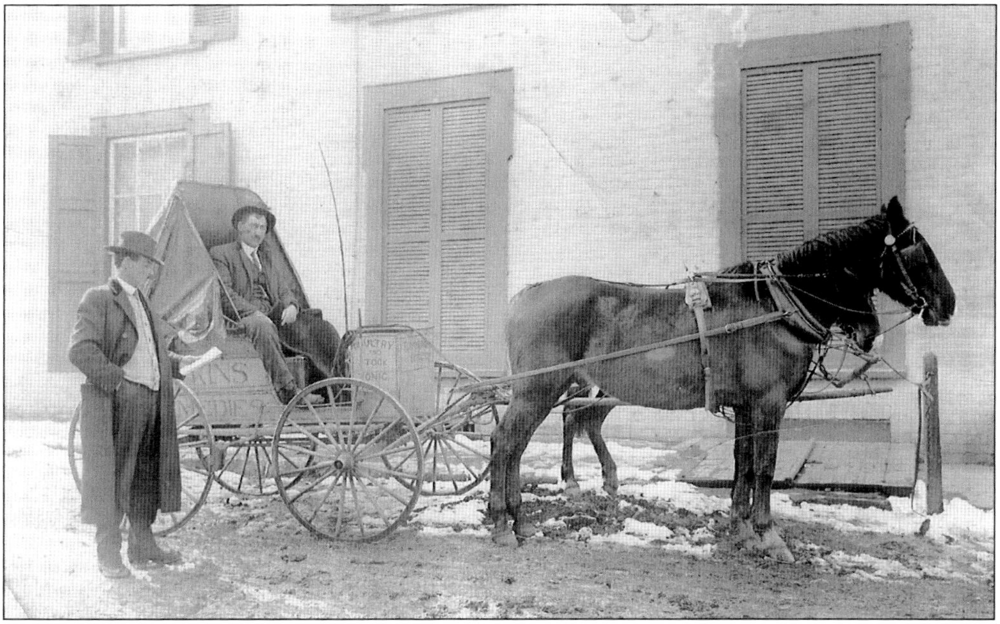

Dr. David Moyer, in buggy, pauses on Luray's South Bank Street in this vintage photograph around 1910. Watkins Remedies, the company originating in 1868, was represented by this local pharmacist as he traveled the town with its samples. A century later, the building, once home to William C. Alther General Merchandise, remains largely unchanged. (David Moyer.)

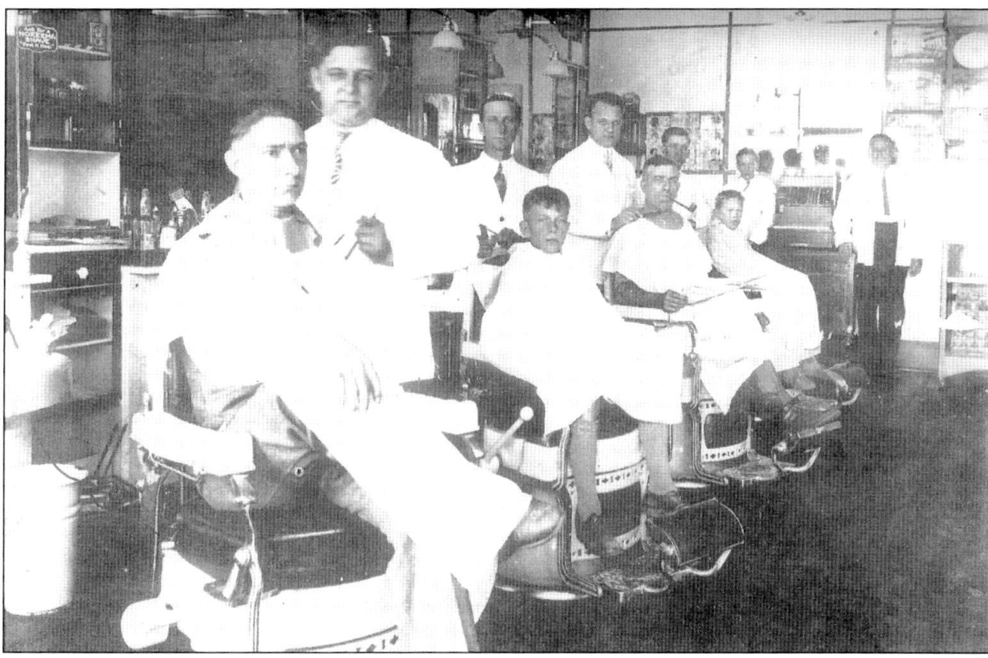

Orye's Barber Shop, on Shenandoah's Virginia Avenue, had a full house this day. Shown, with scissors idle, are, from left to right, U. S. Rinaca, Buck Orye, Howard Orye, unidentified, Bill Orye, V. P. LaParll, J. W. Thompson, unidentified, Arthur Cook, and Frank Orye. Before Christmas in 1937, they offered free haircuts to all children who couldn't afford them. (*Shenandoah: A History of Our Town and Its People*.)

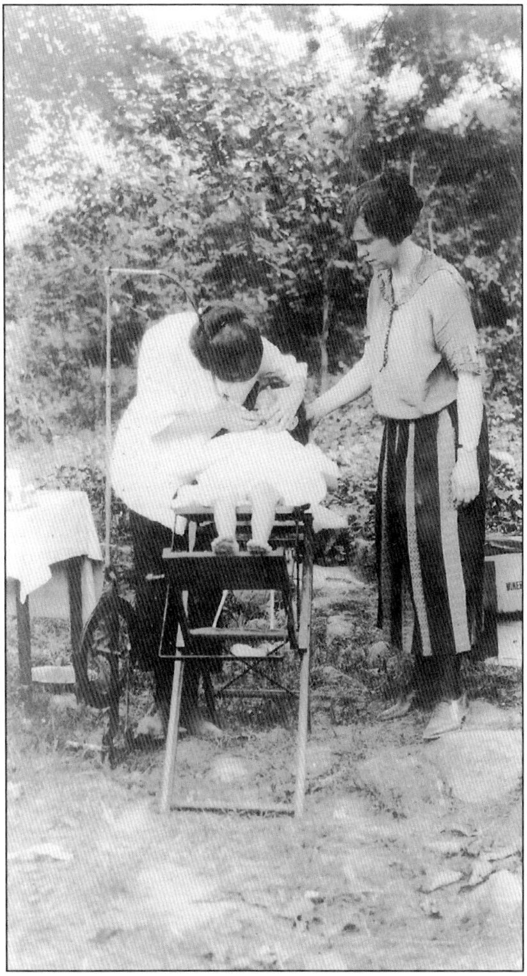

In September 1924, Dr. C. O. Heller, the dentist at left, along with nurse N. Vance, attended to the dental needs of this infant in Pine Grove. With the implementation of the Shepherd-Towner Act of 1921, they were sent out by the Virginia State Board of Health to hold clinics for preschoolers in an effort to curb children's mortality rates. (St. George's Episcopal.)

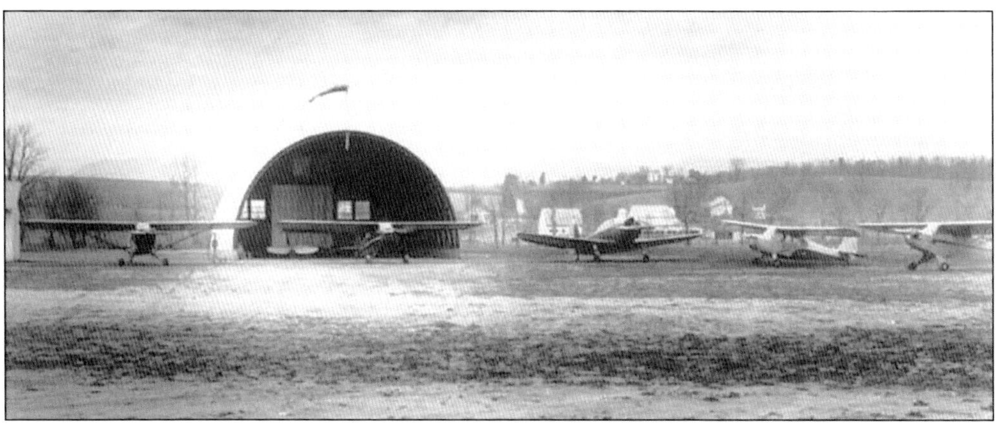

This U.S. military–initiated airport was built in 1946 on the James C. Kite farm south of Luray. Charles R. Wagner was co-owner along with, first, Leo Strickler Sr. and later Albert Black. Aviation Day was held on June 14, 1948, with free plane rides to high school students. A 1950 air show drew 3,000 attendees. Closing in the 1950s, the community was without an airport until the Luray Caverns facility opened in July 1971. (*PN&C.*)

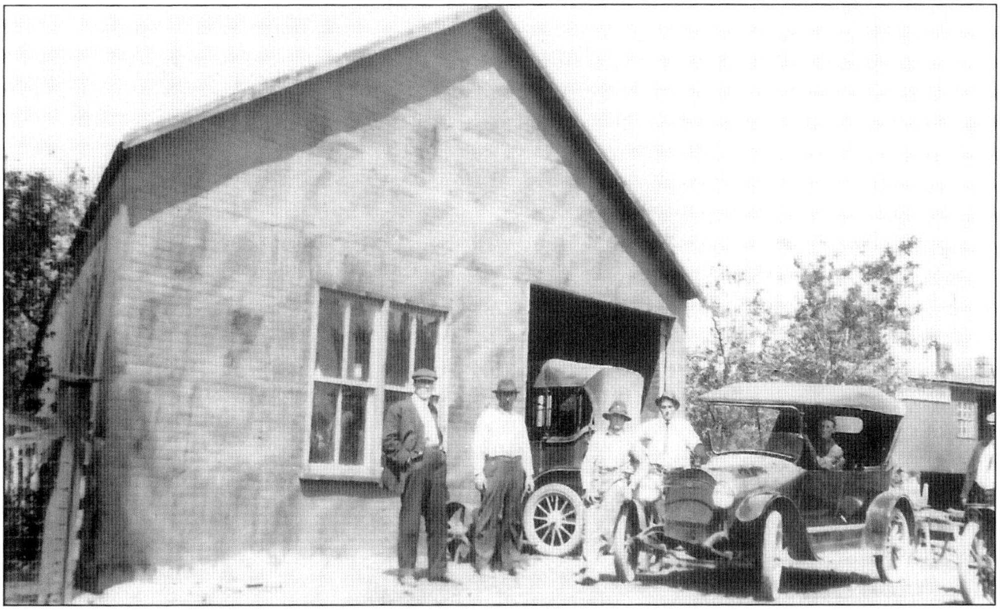

The Stanley Garage and Machine Shop, built in 1915 by Harry T. Shuler, was located at, and a forerunner to, present-day Stanley Auto. This picture, taken shortly thereafter, includes, from left to right, Virgil Petefish, "Barn" Weast, two unidentified, and Shuler in the 1915 Pullman. The H. L. Kibler Blacksmith Shop is at extreme right. (Dan Vaughn.)

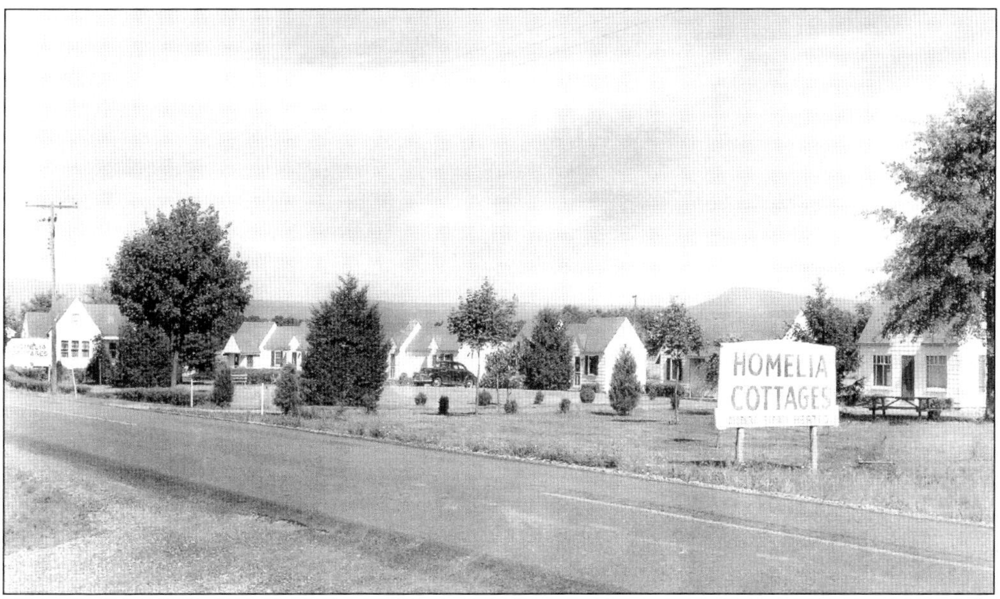

Homelia Cottages, with a purported meaning of "home-away-from-home," was located at the junction of Lee Highway and Kimball Road. The quaint tourist destination was run by Woodrow Moyer and named after his World War II association with a like business of the same name. Complete with a view of the Blue Ridge Mountains and Luray Caverns to its west, it operated from the mid-1940s to the 1960s. (Eddie Moyer.)

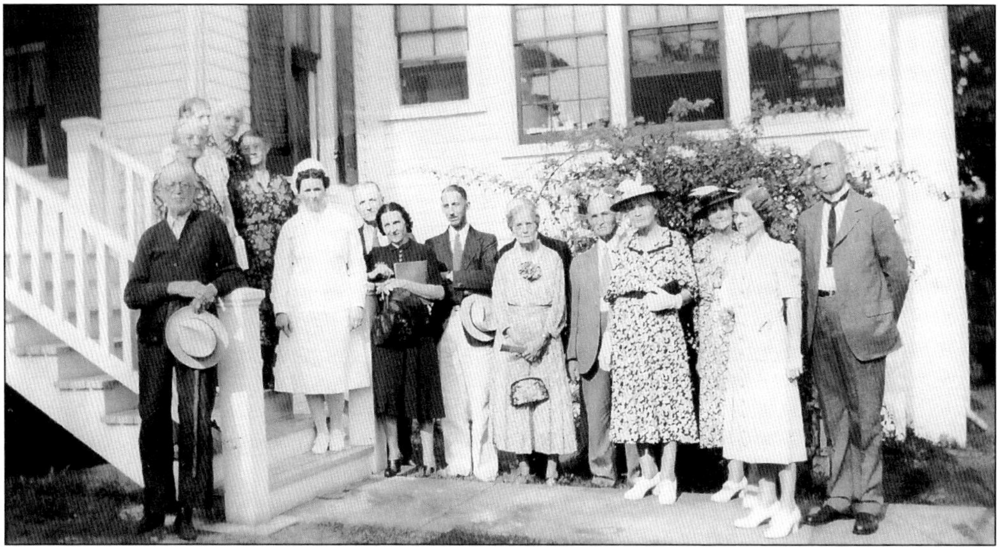

James Ambrose Beahm of Kimball, so moved with the loss of his mother, Mary Beahm, set aside $6,000 in his will for the purpose of a hospital. The Beahm Memorial Hospital Organization raised additional funds at a Page Theatre charity, and Rev. R. H. Pittman chose the 1885 M. J. Menefee residence on South Court Street in Luray as the site for the new hospital. Shown are the founding members and those instrumental in its 1928 initiation. (Lloyd Kibler.)

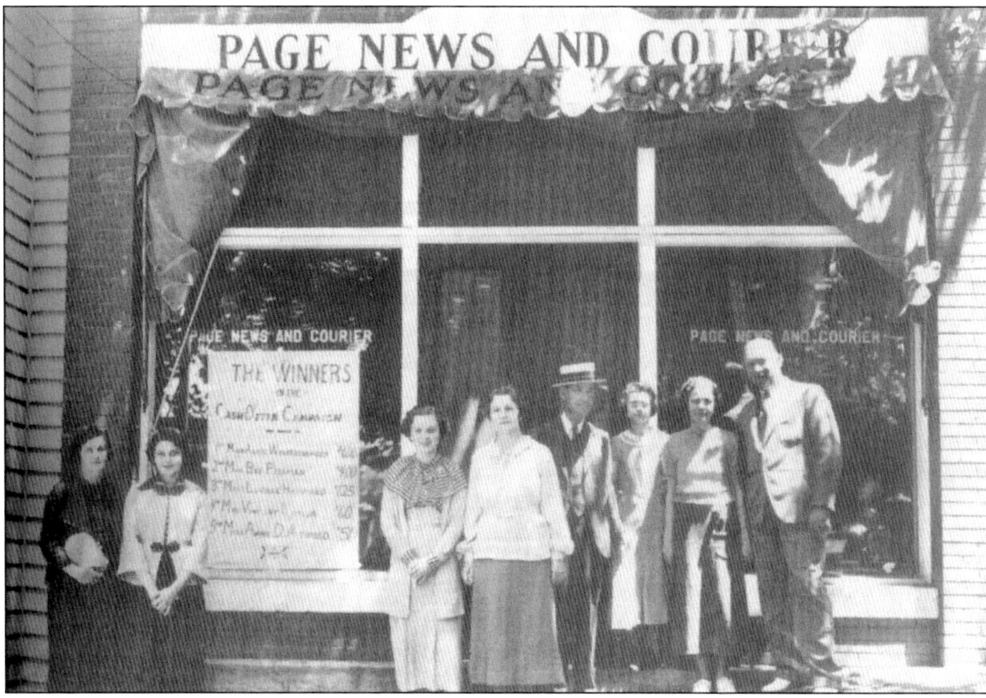

This 1935 *Page News and Courier* picture shows winners of a subscription promotion and staff members in front of their South Broad Street office in Luray. Winners included, from left to right, Alice Wolfersberger, Mary Barnes Pittman Hardin, Frances Hammond, and Anna Atwood. Farther right is editor Roy Broyles, Virginia Varner, Margaret Kibler, and A. M. Alexander, promoter of the campaign. (*PN&C*.)

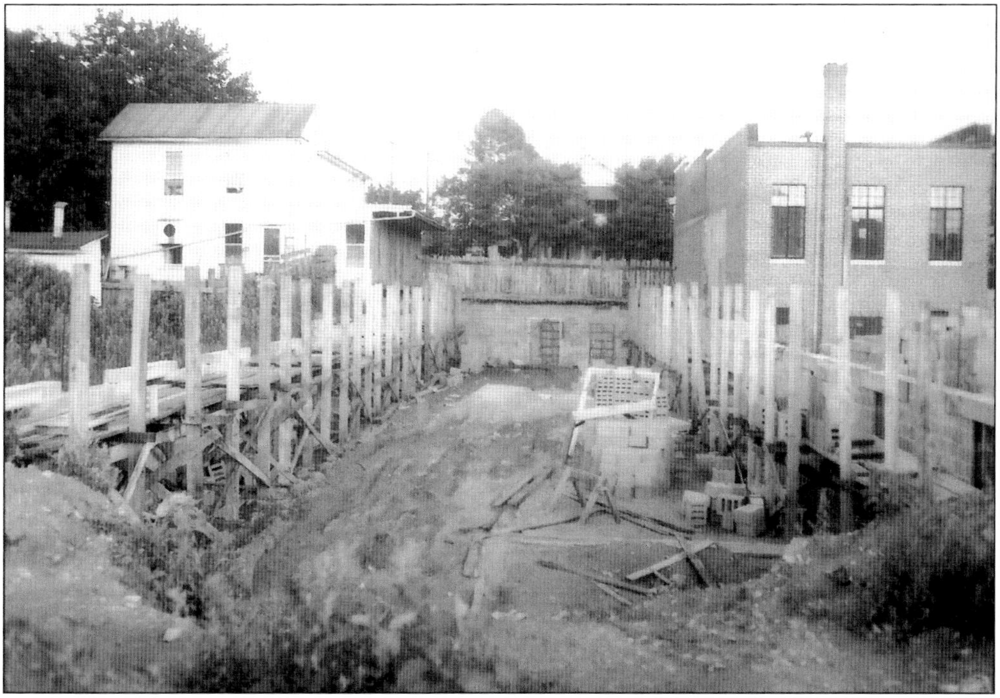

The Stanley Theatre, opening on December 1, 1949, with Karl Jenkins Sr. as owner, is shown still under construction. To promote his *Man in the Saddle* film, Hollywood cowboy hero Randolph Scott appeared in person at the theater in June 1952. Scott's mom was from Luray. An earlier theater had operated in Stanley in the old L. O. Housden Hardware Storeroom. (Dan Vaughn.)

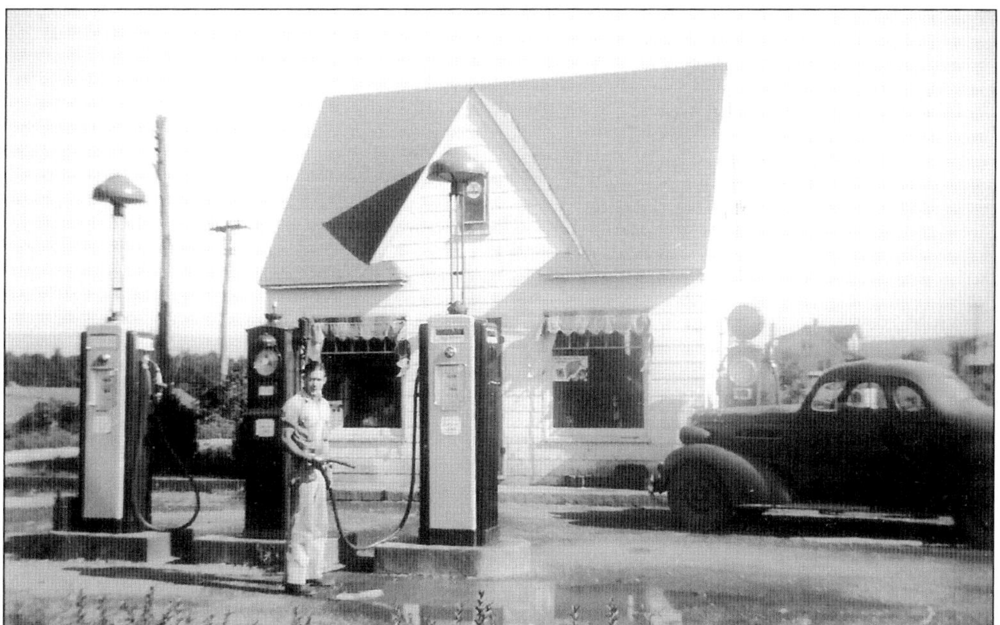

Shown is Jim Batman Jr. at the pumps of Moyer's Gas Station in Kimball. The humble structure stood on U.S. Route 211 near Kimball Road. Relocated in the late 1950s, it serves as a residence today. (Charlie Judd.)

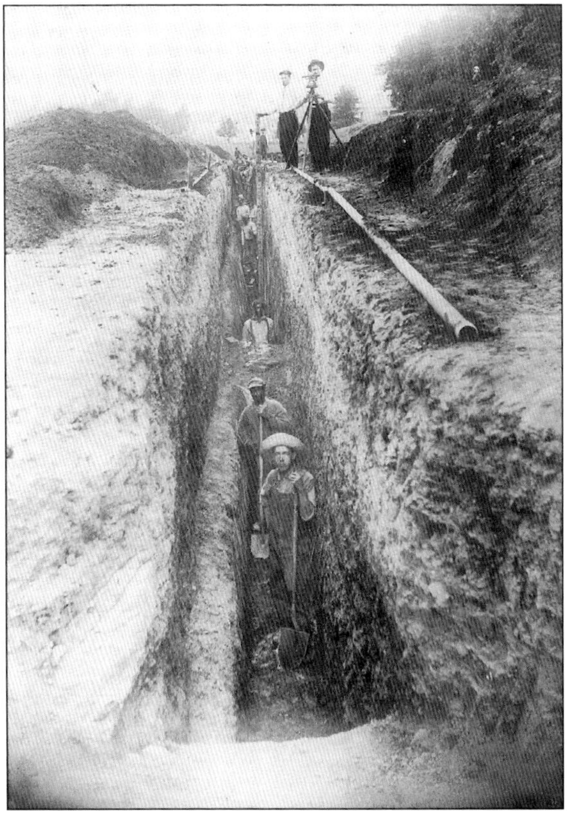

These men gladly pause for this photograph at 12 feet deep. The 1906 public works water project was headed by surveyor Frederick T. Amiss, standing at top right with transit. The Luray Land Corporation had hired Amiss to survey the building lots and streets for the newly proposed Luray Depot to be built the following year. (William and Frances Menefee.)

D. W. Jackson of Richmond was awarded the contract to macadamize Main Street in Luray, as seen in this 1937 WPA project. It was Scotsman John McAdam's principle of "layered" road construction that became standard the world over. Short-lived plank roads, constructed of wood poles and boards, were costly and labor intensive. The old Henry McKay house, its turret protruding from among the trees, is gone, but the need for the stoplight at this busy intersection is not. (Lloyd Kibler.)

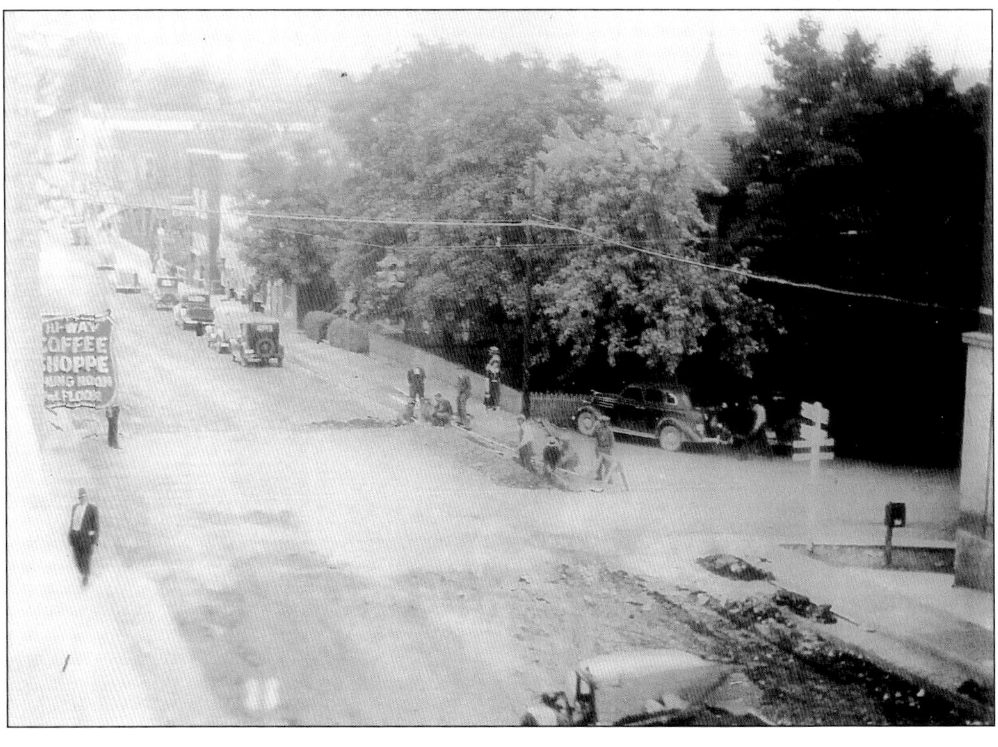

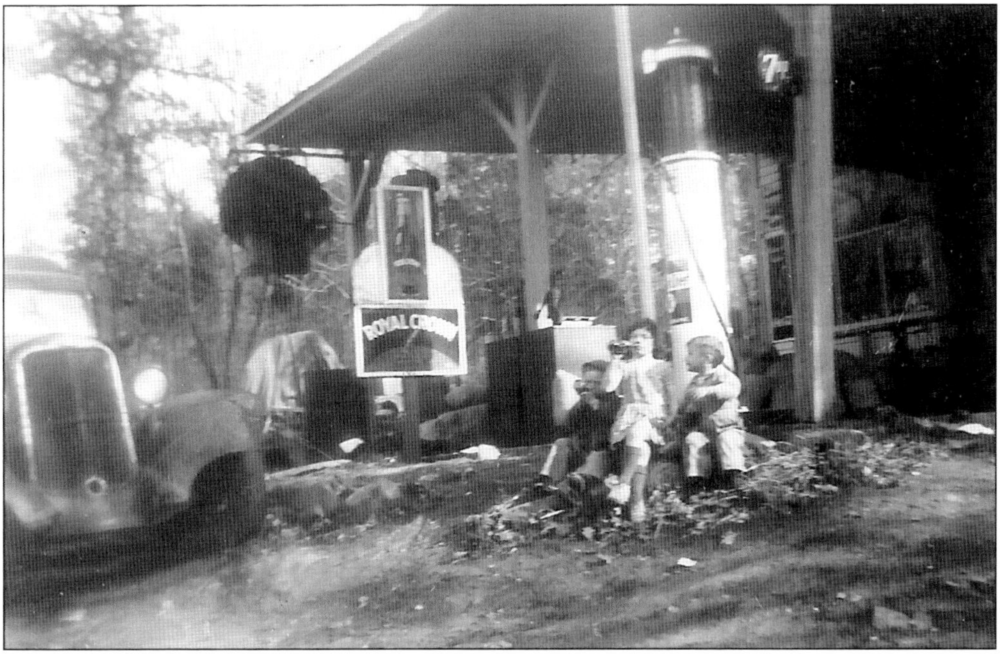

Keyser's Store was originally built in 1875 beside the N&WRR. The following year, the Compton, Virginia, Post Office originated inside and followed the store's relocation here in 1935. After nearly a century of operation in the Keyser family, the store closed in 1970. Here Josephine Knight (left), Jessie Knight (center), and Jimmy Keyser enjoy drinks outside the store in the 1930s. (Lorraine Keyser.)

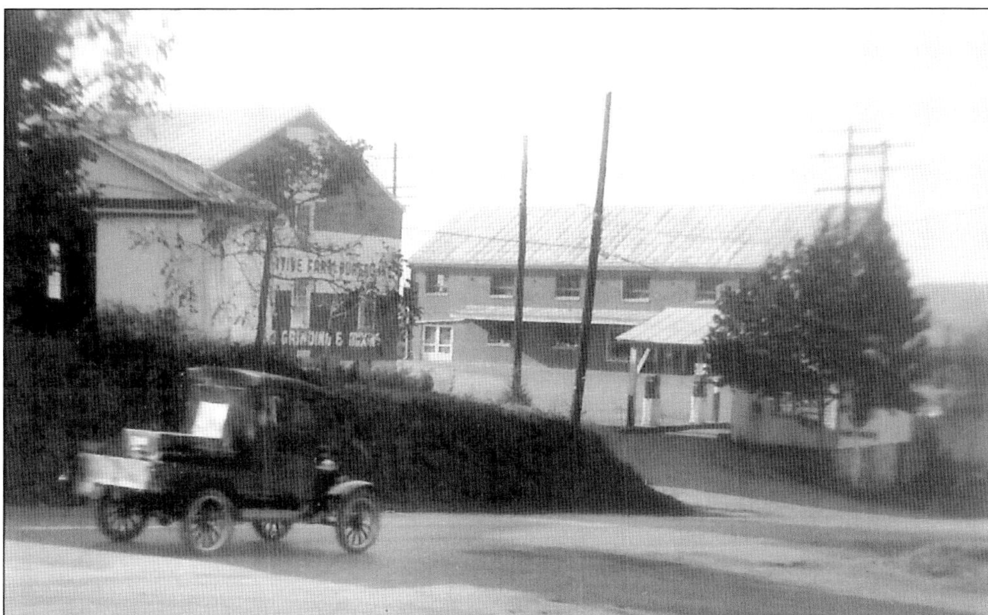

As this Model T Ford truck exits Luray heading south on Virginia Avenue in October 1957, the reader is once again left with a vintage view of "old" Page Cooperative Farm Bureau as in the author's first volume of historical images, titled *Luray and Page County*. (Audrey Taylor.)